daily awakenings

A devotional that will prepare you for life's battles and draw
you to the Father's heart. Stephen Hill has brilliantly woven together
teachings of powerful leaders of the past with his own message which
God has given him for our generation. You will be glad you spent time
each morning filling your soul with these life-giving messages.

JOHN BEVERE

Author and Speaker,
Colorado Springs, Colorado

Build encouragement and strength into your daily walk with
Jesus with this challenging book. Steve Hill will introduce you to a
wealth of spiritual truth from Christian men and women who have
known what it is to live for the Lord. Their profound insights testify
to the truth of Steve's own life-changing message.
Read *Daily Awakenings* and be changed!

COLIN DYE

Pastor, The Tabernacle
London, England

What a wonderful book! What a faithful companion it will be
for all who love Jesus. As I read, I was introduced not only to the wisdom
and passion of Stephen Hill, but also to a great cloud of witnesses—
spiritual leaders and revivalists who had been apprehended and
transformed by Christ's power. Stephen Hill has given us a volume
of sacred truths that will abide in God's service for many years.

FRANCIS FRANGIPANE

Senior Minister, River of Life Ministries
Cedar Rapids, Iowa

Stephen Hill's experience with revival and his personal testimony, his pointed, scriptural reflections, along with his words of encouragement and refreshing make *Daily Awakenings* a precious jewel for every Christian who is spiritually thirsty.

CLAUDIO FREIDZON

Pastor, King of Kings Church
Buenos Aires, Argentina

There are many daily devotionals from which to choose. Many are good; Stephen Hill's *Daily Awakenings* is *very* good! These selections will wake you up every morning with a healthy jolt. What a way to start the day!

BILL McCARTNEY

Founder and CEO, Promise Keepers
Denver, Colorado

Stephen Hill has given us some excellent fuel to feed our fire and passion for God. Allow these truths to transform you.

DAVID RAVENHILL

Author and Teacher
Lindale, Texas

Stephen Hill's story is one of the most remarkable in the unfolding of God's activity in twentieth-century America. His daily devotional breathes the fire that Steve has experienced in the remarkable outpouring of the Holy Spirit at the Brownsville Assembly of God in Pensacola, Florida, where millions of people have been touched by God.

PAT ROBERTSON

Host of "The 700 Club"
Chairman and CEO, The Christian Broadcasting Network, Inc.
Virginia Beach, Virginia

This wonderful devotional book was born in the fires of the Brownsville revival. *Daily Awakenings* will bless and stir the hearts of those who desire a closer walk with the Lord.

VINSON SYNAN

Dean of the School of Divinity, Regent University
Virginia Beach, Virginia

Daily Awakenings is morning soul food for hungry hearts. Written with a deep passion for God, these daily calls to holiness are penetrating, convicting and uplifting. An extraordinary devotional book.

DON WILKERSON

Executive Director, Teen Challenge International
Locust Grove, Virginia

Stephen Hill is an evangelist of the original brand, being saturated with a powerful anointing of the Holy Spirit and carrying the burden of the Lord for the lost. Although he castigates sin, one hears and feels the love of Jesus in every sentence Hill writes. *Daily Awakenings* has blessed me greatly and I highly recommend it.

REINHARD BONNKE

Founder, Christ for All Nations
Frankfurt, Germany

Anyone who spends even five minutes talking to Steve Hill will feel his fire and passion for God. That's exactly what I've experienced. The pages of *Daily Awakenings* are filled with this fire and passion.

DR. JERRY FALWELL

Pastor, Thomas Road Baptist Church
Lynchburg, Virginia

DAILY AWAKENINGS

daily
awakenings

A Devotional STEPHEN HILL

Regal

A Division of Gospel Light
Ventura, California, U.S.A.

Published by Regal Books
A Division of Gospel Light
Ventura, California, U.S.A.
Printed in U.S.A.

Published in association with the literary agency of Alive Communications, Inc., 1465 Kelly Johnson Blvd., Suite 320, Colorado Springs, CO 80920.

Cover Design by Kevin Keller
Interior Design by Rob Williams
Edited by Deena Davis

LIBRARY OF CONGRESS CATALOGING-IN-PUBLICATION DATA
(Applied for)

Third Printing – 2003

3 4 5 6 7 8 9 10 11 12 13 14 15 / 05 04 03

Rights for publishing this book in other languages are contracted by Gospel Literature International (GLINT). GLINT also provides technical help for the adaptation, translation and publishing of Bible study resources and books in scores of languages worldwide. For further information, contact GLINT, P.O. Box 4060, Ontario, CA 91761-1003, U.S.A. You may also send E-mail to Glintint@aol.com, or visit their website at www.glint.org.

Introduction

From the very beginning of my Christian life, I have loved morning devotionals. I believe we should give God the best time of the day, and for most of us that is the morning.

While we're waking up physically, it makes sense to also wake up spiritually and put on the whole armor of God. We need to get ready for the spiritual battles we will face during the rest of the day.

I agree with Robert Murray McCheyne, a Scottish minister from the early nineteenth century, who said that "a calm hour with God is worth a whole lifetime with men."

I'm thankful that those who trained me in the faith introduced me to the work of McCheyne and other great preachers and writers from centuries gone by. We are who we hang around, and we are what we read. That's part of why I like reading the work of seventeenth-century British believers like Jeremy Taylor, John Flavel and John Owen; as well as towering figures like Jonathan Edwards, who documented America's First Great Awakening during the eighteenth century; and Charles Spurgeon, a nineteenth-century pastor who spent 38 rich years preaching and teaching in London.

In the pages that follow, you'll be reading selections from these and other servants of God, who were well known for their holy lives, their unrelenting devotion to the Lord and their dedication to personal evangelism.

You'll also be reading selections that I've written from the lessons the Lord has taught me. I'm certainly not trying to equate myself with those who have gone before. Rather, I'm sharing with you areas where God has strengthened my life.

Some of the messages the Lord has given me over the years are about pleasant topics like joy, faith and peace. Others are about hard subjects like sin, selfishness and the need for repentance.

There is a mix of both kinds of readings because I believe our spiritual lives require a balanced diet. You may enjoy Twinkies or filet mignon more than you like brussels sprouts or a ripe banana, but if you want a healthy body, it's best to eat something from all the recommended food groups. Our spiritual lives are the same way. We can't survive if all we eat is spiritual sugar or milk.

When you come to a reading that seems a little bit harsher than the day before, or perhaps more difficult to understand, I would encourage you to chew on it as long as it takes to swallow it and allow the Holy Spirit to help you digest it. Personally, I love being challenged; that's how I've grown spiritually over the years.

Regardless of whether the words you read seem challenging or uplifting, I ask you to allow them to speak to your heart. Hopefully, these daily awakenings can be God's alarm clock, waking you up to the reality of God in your life, whether you read them early in the morning or late at night.

There's one other thing. At the bottom of each reading you will see a listing of four chapters from the Bible. These chapter suggestions are designed for those who would like to read more of God's Word. If you read the suggested chapters every day, by the end of the year you will have read through the Old Testament once, and through the New Testament and the Psalms twice. This Bible reading plan was developed by McCheyne for his Scottish congregation. He believed that both his personal spiritual growth and his fruitful preaching ministry were due to his strict daily program of Bible reading, prayer and meditation.

In the long run, the words I am writing will disappear. But God's Word will live forever. Perhaps this reading plan will help you store away more of God's truth deep in your heart, where it can be your inspiration and your guide every day.

Stephen L. Hill

Peace I Leave with You

I will hear what God the LORD will say; for He will speak peace to His people, to His godly ones; but let them not turn back to folly.
PSALM 85:8, NASB

Only true Christians have peace in this world. Often when we look at the Christian's life, it can seem that there is no trace of peace. But remember that while an ocean during a severe storm is lashed into huge waves and breakers, foaming up in violent tumult, not far below the surface the depths are as still and calm as a summer afternoon—not a ripple, a breath or a motion.

Though waves may be crashing on the surface of your life, you can have the inward peace of perfect faith in God. Amid the dreary noises of this world, amid its cares and tears, its hot contentions, ambitions and disappointments, you can have an inner calm like the serene ocean depths against which the influence of the wild winds and waves can never prevail!

Trust in the Lord and do not return to the trappings of the world in search of peace. The world can at best offer only a temporary substitute, which is why the Bible calls it *folly*.

Jesus said, "Peace I leave with you, my peace I give unto you: not as the world giveth, give I unto you. Let not your heart be troubled, neither let it be afraid" (John 14:27). Living in this peace requires daily surrender of our fears, doubts and self-sufficiency—anything that troubles our hearts—and daily reliance on His promises.

GENESIS 1; MATTHEW 1; EZRA 1; ACTS 1

The Christian in Prayer

Let us therefore come boldly unto the throne of grace, that we may obtain mercy, and find grace to help in time of need.

HEBREWS 4:16

Prayer is a natural result of close communion with God. How awesome to think that the Lord desires that we share our petitions, concerns, frustrations and joys with Him through prayer! The closer we draw to Him in prayer, the more clearly we see Him and the more intimately we know Him. Dr. F. W. Krummacher, a fiery German preacher in the 1800s, shared the following thought:

When you stand before His gate, knock loudly and boldly. Do not knock as a beggar knocks, but as one who belongs to the house. Not as a vagabond, who is afraid of the police, but as a friend and an intimate acquaintance. Not as one who is apprehensive of being troublesome, or of coming at an improper time, but as a guest who may rest assured of a hearty welcome.

Dear Christian friend, always remember that you can approach the Lord anytime, day or night, and find Him attentive to your needs. He will never leave you nor forsake you. Stay in communication with the Lord. Seek Him while He may be found, call upon Him while He is near.

Prayer is the breath that keeps our spirits alive.

GENESIS 2; MATTHEW 2; EZRA 2; ACTS 2

Keep Knocking

Ask, and it shall be given you; seek, and ye shall find; knock, and it shall be opened unto you: for every one that asketh receiveth; and he that seeketh findeth; and to him that knocketh it shall be opened.

MATTHEW 7:7,8

William Jay is perhaps best known for his classic work, *Mornings and Evenings with Jesus.* A well-loved orator of eighteenth-century England, Jay's thoughts on how to petition the Lord are timeless.

How are we to knock? *Persistently*—we cannot knock too loud. Prayer is nothing unless it be sincere and earnest. God will not regard the petition that we ourselves do not feel. Jacob said, "I will not let thee go, except thou bless me," and he prevailed. How? *With perseverance*—the Lord does not always immediately appear with the answer. "I waited patiently for the Lord," says David, "and at last He inclined His ear unto me and heard my cry."

How marvelous it would be to truly know the power of prayer. If we could actually witness with our eyes the effect of our prayers on our circumstances, there is no doubt we would spend more time on our knees.

I am certain the reason many prayers go unanswered is due to our lack of perseverance. John Flavel once said, "According to the weight of the burden that grieves you is the cry to God that comes from you." Let the Lord hear your cry. Don't stop knocking.

GENESIS 3; MATTHEW 3; EZRA 3; ACTS 3

Made Perfect in Suffering

Dear friends, do not be surprised at the painful trial you are suffering,
as though something strange were happening to you. But rejoice that
you participate in the sufferings of Christ, so that you may be
overjoyed when his glory is revealed.

1 PETER 4:12,13, NIV

Everyone will face some pain in this life. How we face it makes all the difference in how we get through it. Over 200 years ago, the English preacher John Fletcher gave a fresh perspective on how we can face such difficulties. It still applies to all who have placed their lives in the hands of Jesus.

Be an example to all of how to deny yourself and take up your cross daily. Let them see that you have no interest in any pleasure that doesn't bring you nearer to God. Disregard any pain as irrelevant which does bring you closer to Him. Show that you simply aim to please Him, whether by doing or suffering.

The best soldiers are sent on the most difficult and dangerous expeditions. If you are such a soldier of Jesus Christ, you will probably be called to drink deepest of His cup and carry the heaviest burdens. Consider the words of the Apostle Paul, "unto you it is given in the behalf of Christ, not only to believe on him, but also to suffer for his sake" (Philippians 1:29). God grants opposition or reproach as a fresh token of His love. Will you disown the Giver, or spurn His gift, by considering it to be a misfortune?

Remember, dear friend, God would not allow you to go through a difficult time if He didn't think you could handle it. According to His promise, it will turn out for the good.

GENESIS 4; MATTHEW 4; EZRA 4; ACTS 4

True Agony of Hell

And these shall go away into everlasting punishment:
but the righteous into life eternal.
MATTHEW 25:46

If you knew you were about to die an excruciating death, what kind of thoughts would be racing through your mind? Would you be consumed with pleading your case? Would you indulge yourself in a few last "good times"? Would you have to spend a great deal of time repenting and asking God to forgive you of your sins? Jesus, when faced with such a death, spent time with His Father. His mind was set on only one thing—to do His Father's will.

A great deal of the anguish Jesus experienced in the Garden of Gethsemane was due to His awareness that very soon, for the first time, He would experience separation from God the Father. At His crucifixion, the Bible doesn't record Jesus crying out at the horrific physical pain and torment He endured. However, as He experienced the agony of His Father turning away from the sight of our sins upon His son, Jesus cried out in a loud voice, "My God, my God, why have you forsaken me?" (Matthew 27:46, *NIV*).

Friend, sin separates—*that is the true agony of hell*—and Jesus knew it. No matter how difficult the trials or how painful the circumstances may be, remember that our Lord considered nothing to be more agonizing than even momentary separation from the Father.

Stay close to God. Don't let anything block your fellowship with Him. There is nothing more painful than to be separated from Jesus.

Wrath or Favor?

Therefore the Lord shall have no joy in their young men, neither shall have mercy on their fatherless and widows: for every one is an hypocrite and an evildoer, and every mouth speaketh folly. For all this his anger is not turned away, but his hand is stretched out still.

ISAIAH 9:17

Though many in this day pretend that God is simply loving and forgiving, men of old grasped the gravity of the truth about God's wrath. Jonathan Edwards (1703-1758) possessed an unparalleled ability to convey this truth to his listeners:

> The wrath of God is like great waters that are damned for the present. They increase more and more, and rise higher and higher, till an outlet is given. The higher the stream is stopped, the more rapid and mighty is its course when it is let loose. If God should only withdraw His hand from the floodgate, it would immediately fly open, and the fiery floods of the fierceness and wrath of God would rush forth with inconceivable fury. They would come upon you with omnipotent power. Even if your strength were ten thousand times greater than it is—even ten thousand times greater than the strength of the stoutest devil in hell—it would be nothing to withstand or endure it.

With such a clear understanding of God's wrath, His mercy becomes all the more precious. His wrath is as real toward the disobedient and stubborn as is His mercy toward the humble and contrite. If only we were more mindful of His wrath than His forgiveness, we might not need to make such frequent use of His forgiving nature.

GENESIS 6; MATTHEW 6; EZRA 6; ACTS 6

The Heart Jesus Loves

She has done what she could.
She has come beforehand to anoint My body for burial.
MARK 14:8, NKJV

Though he only lived to the age of 29, Scottish pastor Robert Murray McCheyne had developed a tremendous insight into the true heart of his Savior. This passage about today's text comes from one of his sermons.

> What this woman did, she did to Christ. Jesus had saved her soul, had saved her brother and sister, and she felt that she could not do too much for Him. She bought a very costly alabaster box of ointment. Breaking it open, she poured out the precious ointment on His blessed head that was so soon to be crowned with thorns, and on His blessed feet that were so soon to be pierced with nails.
>
> This is what *we* should do. If we have been saved by Christ, we should pour out our best affections on Him. It is well to love His disciples, His ministers, His poor, but it is best to love *Him*. We cannot now reach His blessed head nor His holy feet; but we can fall down at His footstool and there pour out our affections.
>
> It was not the ointment Jesus cared for—what does the King of Glory care for a little ointment? But it is the loving heart, poured upon His feet; it is the adoration, praise, love and prayers of a believer's broken heart that Christ cares for. The new heart is the alabaster box that Jesus loves.

That box cost Mary nearly all she had, yet it was nothing compared to the worth of one act of worship. After all, what value are all the distractions in the world compared to such a heart? Like Mary, lay down all you have, for the heart Jesus loves.

GENESIS 7; MATTHEW 7; EZRA 7; ACTS 7

Every man's work shall be made manifest:
for the day shall declare it, because it shall be revealed by fire;
and the fire shall try every man's work of what sort it is.
1 CORINTHIANS 3:13

A man who prided himself on his morality and expected to be saved by it was constantly saying, "I'm doing pretty well on the whole. I sometimes get mad and swear, but then I *am* perfectly honest. I watch some questionable movies and have a minor lust problem, but I give a good deal to the poor, and I've never been drunk in my life."

He hired a neighbor to build a fence around his pasture. When the neighbor came in from his work, the man said, "Well, Jim, is the fence built, and is it tight and strong?"

"I cannot say it is *all* tight and strong," replied Jim, "But it's a good average fence. If some parts are a little weak, other parts are extra strong. There may be a little gap here and there, but I made up for it by doubling the rails on each side. I daresay the cattle will find it a good fence on the whole."

"What?" cried the man, not seeing the point. "Do you mean to tell me that you built my fence with weak places and gaps in it? You might as well have built no fence at all! If there is even one opening or weak place, the cattle will be sure to find it and go through. Don't you know that a fence must be perfect or it is worthless?"

"I used to think so," Jim said. "But I hear you talk so much about averaging out matters with the Lord, it seemed to me we might try it with the cattle. If an average fence will not do for them, I am afraid an average character will not do on the Day of Judgment."

GENESIS 8; MATTHEW 8; EZRA 8; ACTS 8

Relationship Makes All the Difference

Who may ascend the hill of the Lord? Who may stand in his holy place?
He who has clean hands and a pure heart, who does not lift up his soul to
an idol or swear by what is false. He will receive blessing from the Lord
and vindication from God his Savior.

PSALM 24:3-5, NIV

This scripture is so clear. God is not a "Santa Claus," waiting to grant our every whim and wish. He is holy. Yet He is not distant to those given the power to become sons through the sacrifice of His only Son.

> In making a request of God, the first thing we have to be sure of is this: Is our relationship right? Once we are convinced by the *witness of the Spirit* that we are blood-related to the Father and not in conflict with others, we can come with boldness to the throne of grace. Soiled hearts that operate soiled hands cannot plunder the resources of God, for God's command is "Be ye clean that bear the vessels of the Lord." Assured that we are blood-related to God, and confident that we are joint-heirs with Christ of the fabulous riches of God, what manner of persons we ought to be! Is there any excuse at all for our present poverty? With the promise of the mighty Holy Ghost to empower us, is there any self-defense when we stagger under the load and fail to "put to flight the armies of the enemy"? Has God failed? Is God unwilling to bless? No! Ten thousand times no![1]

Leonard Ravenhill's words further clarify the precious relationship between the Father and His children. Salvation is about relationship. That relationship makes all the difference between victory and defeat, blessings and wrath.

1. Leonard Ravenhill, *Relationship Makes the Difference* (Minneapolis: Minn.: Bethany House Publishers, 1962), p. 32.

GENESIS 9—10; MATTHEW 9; EZRA 9; ACTS 9

Heavenly Minded

For our citizenship is in heaven,
from which also we eagerly wait for a Savior, the Lord Jesus Christ.
PHILIPPIANS 3:20, NASB

Early one morning, the Lord spoke this reminder to my heart: "Live unsettled. Don't sink too deep into the soil of this earth. Keep your head up and your feet moving. Stay alert. Be sober. I am coming. Loose yourself of any ties that bind. If you don't loose yourself, I'll help loose you. Prepare the way in your own heart and then help prepare the way in others. I want no obstacles. I will return for a 'pilgrim' people."

To live "heavenly minded" doesn't mean to act as if the things of this world don't exist. Rather, as the anointed theologian Phillip Doddridge (1702-1751) conveyed, it means to live with heaven—and this world—in proper perspective.

Since heaven is our country, let us be careful to live like those who belong to such a country. Let us behave like citizens of heaven, remembering that while we are in this world, we travel in a strange land and are at a distance from our home. Therefore, let's not be too affected with anything in this land. Let us not be overly preoccupied with the entertainment or be too dejected with the disappointments during our pilgrimage on this earth. But let us be in constant remembrance of our happy dwelling in that glorious country. Let all the actions of our life have a tendency toward it. Let us advance along with the greatest vigor and cheerfulness as we endeavor to form an acquaintance with it.

No Time to Wash Up!

Hallelujah! For the Lord our God, the Almighty, reigns. Let us rejoice and be glad and give the glory to Him, for the marriage of the Lamb has come and His bride has made herself ready. And it was given to her to clothe herself in fine linen, bright and clean; for the fine linen is the righteous acts of the saints.
REVELATION 19:6-8, NASB

Is your wedding garment stained and dirty? Are you doing things Jesus would never do? Perhaps you have just left a wonderful service where you praised God and felt His presence in an awesome way. But then you got home, turned on the television and within minutes there was filth all over your garment. The Lord looks at that and says, "I cleansed you, I washed you in My blood, you were whiter than snow...now look at you!" Listen, my friend, He is coming for a spotless bride!

In the days of Jesus, the groom often came in the dark of night to retrieve his bride. She had to be as ready at midnight as she would have been at noonday.

In the darkness of sin, you can hardly see the gown, not to mention the stains. Will you be ready at midnight? You won't have time to say, "Wait, Jesus, let me go to the dry cleaner's. Forgive me for that pornography, the lust and my sudden fits of anger, I...I thought you understood my little problem."

No, friend, there won't be time. The wedding gown represents your righteousness! If you're not holy—if you're not living for Jesus—then it is *filth*.

The bridegroom's appearance will be sudden and there will be no time to wash up, so be ready!

GENESIS 12; MATTHEW 11; NEHEMIAH 1; ACTS 11

No More Excuses

Then I acknowledged my sin to you and did not cover up my iniquity.
I said, "I will confess my transgressions to the Lord"—
and you forgave the guilt of my sin.
PSALM 32:5, NIV

Someone once said, "Any man who has himself for an attorney has a fool for a client." The great evangelist Charles Finney (1792-1875) clarifies this great mystery.

> Now it is understood that when a man pleads guilty to something, he must refrain from making excuses and appeal only to mercy. If I defend myself fully, knowing I am innocent, I surely have no need for a confession. But if I am conscious of having done wrong, and freely confess my wrong, I appeal to mercy. Confession is the direct opposite of self-justification or defense. So it is in parental discipline. If your child is defensive, and sternly justifies himself, he makes no appeal to mercy. But the moment he throws his arms around you with tears, and says, "I am all wrong," he ceases to make excuses and trusts himself to mercy.
>
> This is also how it is in the government of God. To trust in mercy you must finally give up all reliance upon being your own defense. You can make no more excuses.

Mercy by definition is undeserved forgiveness. Every sin we commit requires God's forgiveness. Any attempt to defend ourselves is in vain and mocks mercy. Let us all strive, at the first inclination of conviction, to fall face first at the feet of our Savior, confess our sin and plead His great mercy.

GENESIS 13; MATTHEW 12; NEHEMIAH 2; ACTS 12

Breaking Up with the Devil

And the devil said unto him, All this power will I give thee, and the glory of them: for that is delivered unto me; and to whomsoever I will I give it.

LUKE 4:6

This scripture speaks of the devil's enticements. Jesus rebuked him—threw him out of His life—leaving us an example to follow. If you are a born-again, on-fire-for-God Christian, then you also have a "jilted lover" (the devil), who still doesn't want to admit defeat even after all this time. So, what do you do?

You must want to break up with the devil—that is the bottom line. You must be sick and tired of the relationship. When Satan gets what he wants—your soul—he'll drop you into hell with all his other deceived lovers. Remember: Satan is like a pig farmer. A pig farmer always fattens up the pig, filling his trough with carnal delights in preparation for the slaughter. Satan will promise you everything and leave you with nothing.

Destroy any evidence of your relationship. Get rid of the "articles of affection"...tear up his notes...give him back his varsity jacket...give him back his promise ring. Burn his music, get rid of any videos that grieve the Holy Spirit, mutilate the devil's books. Destroy the articles of affection!

Remember: He will flee, but he'll be back. You must continue to resist. He'll remind you of the good times, but never remind you of the depression, suicidal thoughts, fits of anger, rage and hopelessness. Friend, don't fall for his lies. Break up with the devil and never look back!

GENESIS 14; MATTHEW 13; NEHEMIAH 3; ACTS 13

Let the World Fade Away

He must become greater; I must become less.
JOHN 3:30, NIV

John Flavel, who ministered in England in the 1600s, used a simple illustration to describe growth in our Christian lives. He shared this observation:

> When the corn is near ripe, it bows the head and stoops lower than when it was green. When the people of God are near ripe for heaven, they grow more humble and self-denying than in the earliest days of their salvation. The longer a saint grows in this world, the better he is still acquainted with his own heart and his obligations to God, both of which are very humbling things. Paul had one foot in heaven when he referred to himself as the least of saints. He was recognizing the exceeding abundant grace of heaven when he said, "Christ Jesus came into the world to save sinners; of whom I am chief" (1 Timothy 1:15).

Each day is an opportunity for us to draw closer to Jesus than the day before. May we live in constant obedience to Him, so that He can make us more into His image. We want to be ready, spotless and pure, when the time comes to stand before Him in heaven. Make it your prayer today to ask the Lord to shine His light in you and through you. Let it get brighter each day, and let the world grow more dim.

"Up with It!"

And when they led Him away, they laid hold of one Simon of Cyrene, coming in from the country, and placed on him the cross to carry behind Jesus.

LUKE 23:26, NASB

This is one of the most beautiful scriptures in the Bible. Up to this point, Jesus had been whipped (Matthew 27:26); beaten with fists (Matthew 26:67,68); beaten with a reed (Matthew 27:30); spat upon (Mark 15:19); mocked (Luke 22:63-65); and crowned with thorns (Matthew 27:29); and this was all before the actual crucifixion. I've always found such comfort in knowing that a man helped lift the heavy load from my Savior. What an opportunity for Simon. As Charles H. Spurgeon points out, the opportunity continues for each one of us as well.

What an honorable position was that of Simon, the Cyrenian, to be a cross-bearer to Jesus Christ! We could almost weep that we were not there that we might have had the honor of carrying Christ's cross for Him. But we need not weep, for we shall have His cross to carry if we are His people. There are no crown-wearers in Heaven who were not cross-bearers here below. There shall be none among the throng of the glorified who had not their cross on earth. Have you a cross, believer? Shoulder it manfully! Up with it! Go along your journey with unshrinking footsteps and a rejoicing heart, knowing that since it is Christ's cross it must be an honor to carry it; and that while you are bearing it you are in blessed company, for you are *following Him.*

Simon stopped everything to carry the Cross. Be willing, today, to shoulder whatever burden the Lord places on you.

GENESIS 16; MATTHEW 15; NEHEMIAH 5; ACTS 15

With the Holy Spirit

I am the vine, ye are the branches: He that abideth in me, and I in him,
the same bringeth forth much fruit: for without me ye can do nothing.
JOHN 15:5

There is such a danger in trying to make it on our own. When we move forward without the guidance of God, we are doomed to failure. The English preacher William Plumer (1802-1880) stated this truth well.

Our great error is in trying to do without the aid of the Holy Spirit. He is our guide; without Him we err always. He is our light; without Him we are in darkness. He is our strength; without Him we are as weak as water. He is our sanctifier; without Him we are wholly polluted. He applies to us the word of God for comfort, and for warning, and for cleansing, and for complete salvation. As He garnishes the heavens, so He beautifies the soul and adorns it with the richest graces. To all who receive Him, He is a fountain of joy, life, peace and purity.

We must remain attached to the vine; the life-giving flow of the Holy Spirit must be continually flowing through our lives. Then, and only then, will the promise come true: "He that abideth in me, and I in him, the same bringeth forth much fruit."

The problem with most Christians is self-reliance. They try to do things on their own. We must heed the words of Jesus, "I am the vine, ye are the branches: He that abideth in me, and I in him, the same bringeth forth much fruit: for without me ye can do nothing" (John 15:5).

GENESIS 17; MATTHEW 16; NEHEMIAH 6; ACTS 16

Choose Your Friends

A righteous man is cautious in friendship,
but the way of the wicked leads them astray.
PROVERBS 12:26, NIV

William Gurnall (1617-1679), an English pastor, knew the value of maintaining godly friendships. Although his words of advice are over 300 years old, they still ring true and sound.

Flee from ungodly company, as it is most harmful to the power of holiness in your life. Be as careful for your soul as you would be for your physical body. You wouldn't at all consider it wise to drink from the same cup, or share the same plate, with one who has a highly infectious disease. Isn't sin as catching as the plague itself?

Your walk with Jesus is just that—your *personal* walk with Jesus. It doesn't depend on circumstances or what others around you are doing. Jesus has entered your life to be your Savior, your Lord, and your best friend.

As Savior, Jesus breaks the power of sin and provides the strength to reject it, but if you choose to remain friends with the world, you make yourself vulnerable to failure. To give Jesus full control as Lord, any ungodly influences must be evicted from your life. As your best friend, Jesus has a purpose and a plan for your life. Listening to the voices of ungodly friends around you can completely drown out the sweet whispers of heaven.

Experience all that the Lord has in store for you by choosing your friends wisely.

GENESIS 18; MATTHEW 17; NEHEMIAH 7; ACTS 17

Another Broken Treaty

And Jesus said unto him, No man, having put his hand to the plough,
and looking back, is fit for the kingdom of God.
LUKE 9:62

Did you know that in the last 3,100 years of recorded history there have only been 286 years where no war was being fought? Over 8,000 treaties signed to end wars were broken, and the wars raged on again.

There is a spiritual parallel here that is beneficial for us to understand. Many of us have signed spiritual treaties with the Lord—a vow to God. Are you keeping this treaty with the Lord?

The greatest difficulty in conversion is the initial signing of the treaty with God. The greatest difficulty after conversion is keeping the treaty with God. Friend, God is going to keep His part of the treaty. Are you?

Maintain your relationship with God. Don't slip out of fellowship with Him. Trust in His promises. Stay in harmony with the Lord. Go daily to the Cross. Go back to the place and time you accepted Jesus into your heart as the peacemaker between you and God. Remember, you dedicated your life to the Lord. No matter what comes your way, regardless of the trials and difficulties, you will keep your part of the treaty. You have put your hand to the plow; you've signed the dotted line. There is no turning back.

GENESIS 19; MATTHEW 18; NEHEMIAH 8; ACTS 18

January 19

Your First Thought

O God, thou art my God;
early will I seek thee: my soul thirsteth for thee,
my flesh longeth for thee in a dry and thirsty land, where no water is.
PSALM 63:1

Any habit takes time to establish. As Stephen Charnock so eloquently expressed, there is perhaps no habit more necessary than fixing our minds on God from the moment we arise, and continually throughout the day.

Accustom yourself to a serious meditation every morning. Fresh airing our souls in heaven will engender in us a purer spirit and nobler thoughts. Though other necessary thoughts about our calling will and must come in, yet when we have dispatched them, let us attend to our morning theme as our chief companion. As a man that is going with another about some considerable business, though he meets with several friends on the way, and salutes some, and with others with whom he has some affairs he spends some time, yet he quickly returns to his companion, and both together go to their intended stage.

Our minds are active and will be doing something, though to little purpose; and if they be not fixed upon some noble object, they will, like madmen and fools, be mightily pleased in playing with straws. The thoughts of God were the first visitors David had in the morning. God and his heart met together as soon as he awoke, and kept company all the day after.

Purpose in your heart to devote the time necessary to awaken as David did. He was known as a man after God's own heart. As the day unfolds you will see the difference when your mind is fixed on God.

GENESIS 20; MATTHEW 19; NEHEMIAH 9; ACTS 19

The Gain of Dying

For to me to live is Christ, and to die is gain.
PHILIPPIANS 1:21

The thought of death deeply terrifies some people. To the one who doesn't know Jesus personally, it is the horrific passage to eternal suffering. But to the apostle Paul, death was appealing. He knew that to be absent from the body meant that he would be forever in heaven with Jesus—his best friend, his Savior and the lover of his soul. John Bunyan (1628-1688), author of *Pilgrim's Progress,* wrote:

> Let death come when it will, it can do the Christian no harm, for it will be but a passage out of a prison into a palace; out of a sea of troubles into a haven of rest; out of a crowd of enemies to an innumerable company of true, loving and faithful friends; out of shame, reproach, and contempt into exceeding great and eternal glory.

There is an inexplicable peace that calms the heart of the one who truly knows Jesus. For that Christian, death is merely the threshold of the door to eternity with Him.

John the Beloved wrote, "There is no fear in love; but perfect love casteth out fear: because fear hath torment. He that feareth is not made perfect in love" (1 John 4:18). Every fear, even the fear of dying, was dealt with on the Cross by our Savior, Jesus Christ. From this point on, join with the apostle Paul in saying, "For to me to live is Christ, and to die is gain."

GENESIS 21; MATTHEW 20; NEHEMIAH 10; ACTS 20

Your Prayers Count

And fixing his gaze upon him and being much alarmed, he said, "What is it, Lord?" And he said to him, "Your prayers and alms have ascended as a memorial before God."

ACTS 10:4, NASB

The graveyards of America are full of grandmas and grandpas who plowed the spiritual soil of their loved one's lives. Often, way into the night, heaven was hearing their cries of intercession.

One of my books, *White Cane Religion*, is dedicated to these soldiers. You see, I know that at the conclusion of each one of my simple evangelistic messages, every soul that was touched was due to the labor of someone else. Every hungry heart that slips out of the pew and races toward the altar—every man, woman and child who feels the pull of God's Spirit upon their hearts—every hardened sinner and broken backslider who falls in repentance at the feet of Jesus is a direct result of someone's intercessory prayers!

My own mama agonized for years over what others deemed a hopeless miserable soul. I was a rebellious drug addict, destined for eternity without God. But her unrelenting prayers, regardless of the circumstances, never went unheeded. Her pleas of, "Jesus, save my boy!" were answered on October 28, 1975, when I was miraculously saved from the edge of death.

Your intercessory prayers count in heaven. Don't stop crying out to God for your lost loved ones. No matter how hopeless it looks, God hears. Don't give up the battle!

Busybodies

And why do you look at the speck that is in your brother's eye,
but do not notice the log that is in your own eye?
LUKE 6:41, NASB

If we were continually checking our motives to make sure we were in line with God, we would have little time to look upon the shortcomings of others. It was Ira Sankey, evangelist D. L. Moody's song leader, who made the pointed statement: "It doesn't take half a man to criticize."

There are some whose restless, insinuating, searching humor will never suffer them to be quiet unless they dive into the concerns of all those about them. They are always outward bound but never homeward. They are perpetually looking about them but never within them. They can hardly relish or digest what they eat at their own table unless they know what and how much is served up to another man's. They cannot sleep quietly themselves unless they know when their neighbor rises and goes to bed. They must know who visits him and who is visited by him; what company he keeps; what revenues he has and what he spends; how much he owes and how much is owed to him.

These words, penned by Dr. Robert South over 250 years ago, remarkably describe many of us today. It would be wise for us to heed the counsel found in today's scripture text. Let us put more effort into the removal of what blocks our vision in order to see clearly how to genuinely help others.

GENESIS 23; MATTHEW 22; NEHEMIAH 12; ACTS 22

The Discipline of Adversity

Our fathers disciplined us for a little while as they thought best; but God disciplines us for our good, that we may share in his holiness. No discipline seems pleasant at the time, but painful. Later on, however, it produces a harvest of righteousness and peace for those who have been trained by it.

HEBREWS 12:10,11, NIV

Any earthly father who withholds correction from his children does them a sad disservice. Children cannot grow into healthy, responsible adults without loving instruction and discipline. Sound guidance teaches them right from wrong and protects them from making destructive decisions out of ignorance. Bishop Hopkins, nearly 250 years ago, gave an excellent analogy of this principle.

As weeds grow fastest in a richly fertilized soil, so our corruption grows and thrives—ready to overrun our soul—when our outward condition is most prosperous and successful. Therefore, God's love and care for us causes Him to sometimes use severe discipline to nip and cut us short in our temporal enjoyments. He sees that otherwise we would soon turn into a fertile plot for our own lusts.

In the same manner, we can rest assured that as God's children we will pass through seasons of His discipline. He loves us too much to abandon us to "raise ourselves." He recognizes that when we are left alone under the influence of our sinful nature, we will bring about our own ruin.

Father, bring our hearts to a place where we can welcome Your discipline and recognize it as a sign of Your loving care.

GENESIS 24; MATTHEW 23; NEHEMIAH 13; ACTS 23

God's Masterpiece

Even every one that is called by my name: for I have created him for my glory, I have formed him; yea, I have made him.
ISAIAH 43:7

Oh, the wonder of creation! From the infinite majesty of the universe to the intricate wing of the butterfly, we see the signature of the Almighty.

Though man excels in many extraordinary talents, God is the only one who can create. Man in all his glory can still do nothing more than re-create what has been created. Architects can build, scientists can combine, painters can depict life on canvas, but they work with materials already in existence. Isn't it interesting that man can make a planetary space probe, but he's yet to create a colorful, fluttering, monarch butterfly?

I'll never forget one time when I went snorkeling. I was in the most pristine, crystal clear, blue-green waters I had ever seen. Suddenly, a school of fluorescent blue fish, each no more than six inches long, surrounded me. They sparkled like a sea of gems in the sunlight. They allowed me to join their school and swim along in their world. As we twisted and turned through the coral, my thoughts raced to the majesty and creativity of God. The emotion of the moment became overwhelming, and I began to praise Jesus for His marvelous works.

Make it a point today to notice the creation around you. Always remember that we are at the very top of His creation. Praise Him—for you are His masterpiece!

GENESIS 25; MATTHEW 24; ESTHER 1; ACTS 24

All You Can Drink

But whoever drinks of the water that I shall give him shall never thirst;
but the water that I shall give him shall become in him a well
of water springing up to eternal life.
JOHN 4:14, NASB

Robert Murray McCheyne was well aware of heaven's precious fountain. He drank from it continually.

The Holy Spirit is an imperishable stream, not like those rivers which flow through barren sands till they sink into the earth and disappear. No, the stream of grace that flows from Jesus Christ flows into many a barren heart; but it is never lost there. It appears again—it flows *from* that heart in rivers of living water. When a soul believes on Jesus, drinks in His Spirit, it becomes as if the Spirit were lost in that soul. The stream flows into such a barren heart and can appear gone; but it is never lost.

If you come to Jesus and drink, you shall become a fountain of grace to your family. Through your heart, your words, and through your prayers the stream of grace will flow into other hearts. Those you love best in all the world may in this way receive grace.

Friend, Jesus is ready and waiting to pour His loving presence upon you. Allow Him to saturate you today as you drink deeply of His strength, His joy, His mercy and peace. It will seep down into the dry, forgotten areas of your heart and bring life. He then can use you as a vessel to bring His love to those who are parched and dying of thirst.

GENESIS 26; MATTHEW 25; ESTHER 2; ACTS 25

You Can Trust Him

Those who know your name will trust in you,
for you, Lord, have never forsaken those who seek you.
PSALM 9:10, NIV

"Trust"—a simple word, but it is sometimes most difficult to do. There aren't many things in life more disappointing than broken promises. It can be devastating when those we once trusted fail to live up to their vows and pledges. Charles Spurgeon had an interesting insight on trust.

All of us have a measure of faith we use in life's everyday circumstances. The farmer buries good seed in the earth, expecting it to be multiplied. He has faith in the principle that seedtime leads to harvest, and he is rewarded for his faith. The merchant places his money in a banker's care, trusting in the honesty of that bank. He entrusts his capital to another's hands, feeling far more secure than if he had solid gold locked up in an iron safe. The goldsmith puts precious metal into the fire, where the flame seems eager to consume it, but upon removing it again from the furnace he finds that the heat has purified it.

You cannot turn anywhere in life without seeing faith in action. Now, just as we trust in daily life, so are we to trust in God as He reveals Himself in Christ Jesus.

Throughout the day remember that you are putting your faith in the ultimate promise keeper. He is not like unfaithful men. His Word is true. He has never forsaken those who seek Him.

GENESIS 27; MATTHEW 26; ESTHER 3; ACTS 26

Boldness in God

Ye are of God, little children, and have overcome them: because greater is
he that is in you, than he that is in the world.

1 JOHN 4:4

Known as the "Reformer of Scotland," John Knox was highly respected for his powerful sermons. Though small in stature, he preached with fiery boldness, well aware of the heart of God and the destructive nature of the enemy. He incessantly confronted sin and hypocrisy—living much of his life under the threat of death, as a result. Yet to his eternal credit, at his funeral someone said of him, "There lies one who never feared the face of man." Knox once wrote:

> Satan, I confess, rages. But more powerful is He that promised to be with us in all tasks we undertake at His commandment, for the glory of His name, and for the maintenance of true Christianity. And, therefore, the less we fear any contrary power; in the boldness of our God, we altogether despise them, be they kings, emperors, men, angels or devils. For they will never be able to prevail against the simple truth of God which we openly profess. Though by the permission of God they may appear to prevail against our bodies; still our cause shall triumph in despite of Satan.

The fact that there were souls hanging in the balance of an eternity in hell drove Knox to preach with all he had. Such boldness in God comes from realizing the power that dwells within every believer. Within you resides the unlimited power of God. Be bold, and reach out today to someone who needs His freeing touch!

GENESIS 28; MATTHEW 27; ESTHER 4; ACTS 27

January 28

It's Almost Over

*Behold, I am coming quickly, and My reward is with Me, to render to
every man according to what he has done.*
REVELATION 22:12, NASB

To the Christian, heaven is our hope, and spending eternity with
the Lord is our ultimate desire. John Wesley (1703-1791) offered this
encouragement to those who are watching for the skies to part and listening for the trumpet to sound.

> The time of our eternal redemption is drawing near. Let us hold
> out a little longer, and all tears will be wiped from our eyes, and
> we will never again sigh or feel sorrow. And how soon will we
> forget all we endured in this earthly body of ours. We will be
> clothed in glory, which is from above. We are, for now, only on
> our journey toward home. We must expect to struggle with
> many difficulties, but it won't be long before we come to our
> journey's end; and that will make amends for it all. We will then
> be in a quiet and safe harbor, out of the reach of all storms and
> dangers.

Friend, if you are a blood-washed believer and your heart is in fellowship with Jesus, then you have something to look forward to. The
day will come when His glory will at last be revealed and our eyes will
see Him. Those who remained faithful to Him while on this earth will
finally be welcomed home. This journey called life is almost over. Soon
we will see Him face-to-face. Make it your goal today to encourage others in that great hope!

GENESIS 29; MATTHEW 28; ESTHER 5; ACTS 28

Trust in the Lord

Trust in the LORD with all thine heart; and lean not unto thine own under-
standing. In all thy ways acknowledge him, and he shall direct thy paths.
PROVERBS 3:5,6

This is one of my favorite scriptures in the Bible. It is one that I hid in my heart during the first few months of my Christian life. It has been like a wonderful, bright lantern during those dark and dreary nights of uneasiness and hardship. It has been used of God to calm the tempest and settle the raging sea. It has been an anchor in the midst of the storm.

Why? Because it reminds me of my limitations and God's limitless provision. To rely on self is to rely on nothing at all. J. B. Stoney's description says it well:

> The moment a difficulty occurs, the heart turns to its resource as a bird in trouble turns to its wings to carry it away. If you lean on your own understanding, when a difficulty occurs you begin to think how you can get out of it. Unfortunately, you are as one frantically pumping an empty well for water with which to extinguish a fire, but after all your toil you never succeed. You are anxious and devising, and with all your toil you're still unable to produce the thing required.

Yes, this conditional promise of God is indeed a friend in the midst of our enemies, hope in the midst of a seemingly hopeless situation. It reminds us to put *all* of our trust in Him, for all else is futility.

Take these words of wisdom with you throughout your day, throughout your life. Delight yourself in His faithfulness!

GENESIS 30; MARK 1; ESTHER 6; ROMANS 1

Blessed Assurance

And the work of righteousness shall be peace; and the effect of
righteousness quietness and assurance for ever.
ISAIAH 32:17

Thomas Watson (1620-1686) ministered at St. Stephen's, Walbrook, in London for 16 years. Within this small sample of his writing, this Puritan preacher shares a glimpse of the joy of heaven.

How sweet it is. This is the manna in the golden pot, the nectar of paradise that cheers the heart. How comfortable is God's smile! The sun is more refreshing when it shines out than when it is hidden in a cloud; it is a preview and a foretaste of glory. It puts a man in heaven before his time; none can know how delicious and ravishing it is unless they have felt it; as none can know how sweet honey is but those who have tasted it.

What a beautiful promise we have from the Lord. The Bible says it like this, "Thou wilt make known to me the path of life; in Thy presence is fulness of joy; in Thy right hand there are pleasures forever" (Psalm 16:11, *NASB*).

Those who live righteously here on earth will reap the joyful rewards of heaven for eternity. However, let us keep in mind that there are many who haven't yet tasted the sweet honey of heaven. We can describe it to them all day long, but until they taste of it themselves, they can never understand it to the fullest.

May you live in the fullness of His joy. Quietness and blessed assurance will be yours—both now and forever.

GENESIS 31; MARK 2; ESTHER 7; ROMANS 2

I Want to See Jesus

For the gate is small, and the way is narrow that leads to life,
and few are those who find it.
MATTHEW 7:14, NASB

George Whitefield was mightily used of God in the 1700s to kindle revival in America. He chose to walk the narrow way and received no small amount of trouble for it. Here, he shares from his own experience on the subject of seeing Jesus.

We cannot expect to see Christ in glory unless we are willing to run alone, being counted as one of those despised few who take the kingdom of God by violence. Many choose the broad road, but it is the straight and narrow path that leads to life. When we stay focused on Jesus with the cross before us, and when we are considered fools for His sake and still rejoice, we will see Jesus with eager joy when He appears in glory.

Consider Zacchaeus as he scurried up the sycamore tree. Perhaps that was difficult for him to do, but he knew he had to climb it. No doubt he heard people laugh at him as he ran along! But Zacchaeus didn't care; his curiosity was strong: He wanted to see Jesus. Similarly, those who would see Christ must undergo difficulties and hardships, besides contempt.

Those who have a fervent desire to see Jesus in heaven will be ridiculed on earth, but they will go on from strength to strength, breaking through every difficulty lying in their way, and caring not what men think.

Press on, friend! As Whitefield described, the road is narrow and difficult, but you are divinely empowered to succeed!

Tears in a Bottle

*My tears have been my food day and night, while they say to me all day
long, "Where is your God?" Thou hast taken account of my wanderings;
put my tears in Thy bottle; are they not in Thy book?*

PSALMS 42:3; 56:8, NASB

Does God really understand our pain or sorrow when we cry? Can
He sincerely empathize with our suffering?

Just as we sense sorrow and have our "nights of weeping," so does
Jesus. He experienced every tear of joy and every tear of sorrow: "For we
do not have a high priest who cannot sympathize with our weakness-
es" (Hebrews 4:15, *NASB*). Our High Priest strolls the corridors of our
homes, leans over and gently places a bottle under our eyes. *Weep, my
beloved,* He assures us, *I'll catch every drop. I will remember your suffering. I
am recording your pain.*

Of all things for God to collect, you ask, why would He store up
tears? Could it be to show how precious they are in His sight and to
suggest that they are preserved for a future use? The tears His children
shed and give to Him to keep cannot be tears of rebellious or insincere
weeping. True godly tears will be given back one day to those who shed
them, converted into refreshment by the same power which of old
turned water into wine.

Perhaps you can relate to what I'm saying. You need refreshment
from the Lord like never before. My friend, He is with you. "Weeping
may endure for a night, but joy cometh in the morning" (Psalm 30:5).
Let the tears well up and flow freely. God is patiently waiting to collect
every drop.

GENESIS 33; MARK 4; ESTHER 9—10; ROMANS 4

Perpetual Surrender

*And do not present your members as instruments of unrighteousness to
sin, but present yourselves to God as being alive from the dead, and your
members as instruments of righteousness to God.*

ROMANS 6:13, NKJV

Devotion is not the trivial expression our modern society has
endeavored to make it. God takes devotion very seriously. In God's language, a devoted thing is that which is set apart to the Lord—not to be
taken back at will. As Phillip Doddridge explains, it is easy to see that
once our lives are devoted to God, they are no longer ours, and our
claim on them must be relinquished. We are no longer our own; we
have been bought with a price.

> All you are—all you have and all you can do, your time, your
> possessions, your influence over others—will be devoted to
> Him, that in the future it may be employed entirely for Him
> and to His glory. You will desire to keep back nothing from
> Him; but will realize that you are most entirely His. Resign
> also all that you have to the disposal of His wise and gracious.
> providence. Not only realizing His power, but consenting to
> His undoubted right to do what He pleases with you, and all
> that He has given you; and declaring a hearty approval of all
> that He has done, and all that He may do. Further, let me
> remind you that this surrender must be perpetual. You must
> give yourself up to God in such a manner as never more to
> pretend to be your own.

Remember, to be devoted is to be set apart to the Lord. Because
the flesh wars against the Spirit, this must be a perpetual act of surrender, a frequent offering, which will become a delightful discipline.

GENESIS 34; MARK 5; JOB 1; ROMANS 5

Far from the Rocks

Abstain from all appearance of evil. And the very God of peace sanctify you wholly; and I pray God your whole spirit and soul and body be preserved blameless unto the coming of our Lord Jesus Christ.
1 THESSALONIANS 5:22,23

Nothing compares to the wonderful counsel we find in the Word of God! His Word is like a compass guiding us through treacherous waters. Andrew Murray tells this story.

> A captain of a ship, sailing between two harbors on a rocky coast, was once asked by an anxious passenger if the coast was very dangerous. The answer was, "Very."
> "And are you not afraid?" the passenger asked.
> "No," replied the captain. "Our way is perfectly safe; you can be at ease."
> "But how, if the rocks are so dangerous?"
> "Oh, very simply! I put out to sea, and keep far from the rocks."
> Oh, Christian! Here is your only safe passage: launch out into the deep of full obedience to the will of God; keep far from all sin, and you shall be kept from willful sinning.

What more can be said? Abstain from *all* appearance of evil. Go full-steam ahead in obedience to God and you will arrive safely in heaven's harbor.

GENESIS 35—36; MARK 6; JOB 2; ROMANS 6

Room with a View

I beseech you therefore, brethren, by the mercies of God,
that ye present your bodies a living sacrifice, holy, acceptable unto God,
which is your reasonable service.
ROMANS 12:1

The only problem with being a "living sacrifice" is the living part; that is, we can crawl on and off the altar at will. Leonard Ravenhill often said to me, "The only reason you have to get back on the altar today is if you got off yesterday. We should quit singing, 'There's room at the Cross for you,' and begin singing, 'There's room *on* the Cross for you.'" Religion is hanging around the Cross; Christianity is getting on the Cross.

From the Cross we gain a whole new perspective. Suspended between heaven and earth, eternity becomes clearer. Nailed down, unable to move, sapped of all physical strength and stamina, stripped of all selfish desires and ambitions, we are defenseless. That is where the true man or woman of God learns about trust.

Suddenly, you begin to see lost humanity through the eyes of Christ. You see the lost, starving sheep without a shepherd—without hope and destined for destruction. True compassion comes from a deep understanding of the entire picture, not out of works of the flesh.

Stay on the Cross, my friend. The longer you hang there, the better your view will become. As the flesh dies, the spirit will begin to emerge. Soon you will see that to know Him, walk with Him and commune with Him is our whole duty and His greatest desire.

Rewards of Doing Good

He must turn from evil and do good; he must seek peace and pursue it.
For the eyes of the Lord are on the righteous and His ears are attentive to
their prayer, but the face of the Lord is against those who do evil.
1 PETER 3:11,12, NIV

In the Gospels, we read of Jesus going throughout the land doing good. He loved people and His tender kindness drew people to Him. Even those whom society deemed undesirable, such as prostitutes and tax collectors, were found in His company. No doubt they could sense this was a man who truly cared for them, when people who truly cared were a rare thing. John Bunyan gave an example of good works in his writing.

The Shepherds led the Pilgrims to Mount Charity. There, they showed them a man who had a bundle of cloth lying before him, out of which he cut coats and garments for the poor, yet his bundle of cloth never diminished. Then said they, "How could this be?"

"This is," said the Shepherds, "to show you that he who has a heart to give of his labor to the poor shall never himself be in want. He that waters shall be watered himself. The cake that the widow gave to the prophet did not cause her to have less in her barrel."

If we truly desire to be a reflection of Jesus, then we will love people as He did. Kindness and mercy will be our trademark if His love truly rules in our hearts. We will give of ourselves as He did, knowing we will never be in want, as that is the way of His kingdom.

GENESIS 38; MARK 8; JOB 4; ROMANS 8

But let the righteous be glad; let them rejoice before God:
yea, let them exceedingly rejoice.

PSALM 68:3

Thomas Watson recognized the importance of being a positive testimony for Christ. Believers who were happy and light-hearted were far more apt to influence unbelievers toward the Lord than those who were sober to the point of being morbid. The Christian who is burdened by life's trials, to the point of having all joy squelched is doing his testimony more harm than good.

Being cheerful brings honor to Christianity, it proclaims to the world that we serve a good Master. It is a friend to grace; and it puts the heart in tune to praise God. Downhearted Christians, like the spies in Numbers 13:33, bring an evil report on the good land; others suspect there is something unpleasant in serving the Lord. The observer is often left to assume that those who profess to Christianity hang their harps upon the willows and walk so dejectedly. Be serious, yet cheerful. Rejoice in the Lord always.

There is a deep joy that only comes from living in communion with the Lord. When the fruit of His spirit is alive in us, the spiritually hungry will be drawn to taste and see that the Lord is good. When the light of the Lord's joy shines from our hearts, it illuminates this dreary world, and those living in the darkness will be drawn to that light. If you call yourself a Christian, a follower of Jesus Christ, then you are His ambassador, His representative. Let His joy radiate from you.

Also I heard the voice of the Lord, saying, Whom shall I send, and who
will go for us? Then said I, Here am I; send me.
ISAIAH 6:8

Charles Finney knew that the Lord had His gaze set on the harvest field. Lost souls needed to hear the gospel, and someone must go tell them. Who would go? Finney answered the call and challenges us to do the same.

> You profess to have the Spirit of Christ; but when you see the multitudes as He saw them, perishing for lack of gospel light, do you cry out in mighty prayer with compassion for their souls?
>
> Many do not pray for God to send out laborers because they are afraid He will send them. I remember when Christianity was repulsive to me because I feared that if I were converted, God would send me to preach. But after thinking about it, I realized that God has a right to do with me as He pleases, and I have no right to resist. If I do resist, He will put me in hell. If God wants me to be a minister of His gospel and I rebel, He surely ought to put me in hell, and doubtless will.
>
> But there are many who never give themselves to prayer for the conversion of the world because God may send them. You would blush to pray—"Lord, send laborers, but don't send me." If the reason you don't want to go is that you have no heart for it, you may write yourself down as hypocrite, and make no mistake in so doing.

It's time for us to truly hear the heart cry of the Lord and with Isaiah shout, "Send me, Lord...send me!" Do you know someone who needs to hear the gospel from your lips?

A Word from Heaven

And there were in the same country shepherds abiding in the field, keeping watch over their flock by night. And the angel said unto them, Fear not: for, behold, I bring you good tidings of great joy, which shall be to all people.

LUKE 2:8,10

I wonder what these shepherds had been discussing just prior to that "heavenly interruption." Perhaps they had just finished counting the sheep and were discussing one that was missing. Or, one of them could have been commenting that the shepherd's pie he'd eaten for supper had given him indigestion. Of course, the new tax census Caesar Augustus ordered may have dominated their conversation.

You see, man spends much of his brief earthly sojourn choking on the smog of senseless speculations when what he needs to take in is a fresh word from heaven's throne. Being consumed with current events can lead us to be so engrossed in earthly things that when God does come on the scene with a fresh word, we often get frightened or angry. Be it a word of instruction, a prophetic word or a rebuking word—our *reaction* is pretty predictable. We are often startled and afraid, as were the shepherds, or we may become religious and offended like those of the synagogue in Nazareth (see Luke 4:28). Some even shake with conviction as Felix did after hearing the words of Paul (see Acts 24:25).

The shepherds stopped their chitchat long enough to hear a fresh word from heaven and it changed their lives forever. Do you find yourself buried in the deluge of worldly words? Shake them off and seek the fresh breath of heaven for your life and the lives of others. Remember, we live in a world that desperately needs to hear these heavenly words: "Fear not: for behold, I bring you good tidings of great joy!"

GENESIS 41; MARK 11; JOB 7; ROMANS 11

No More Murmuring

Do all things without murmurings and disputings: that ye may be blameless
and harmless, the sons of God, without rebuke, in the midst of a crooked
and perverse nation, among whom ye shine as lights in the world.
PHILIPPIANS 2:14,15

Ever heard the expression "You want to have your cake and eat it
too"? One of my favorite Puritan writers, John Flavel, demonstrates
how that selfish mentality affects the Christian.

> What if by removing outward comforts, God preserves your
> soul from the ruining power of temptation? There is surely
> little reason to let your heart sink from such sad thoughts.
> Don't earthly enjoyments make men shrink and warp in
> times of trial? If this is God's design, how ungrateful to mur-
> mur against Him for it! Sailors in a storm can throw the most
> valuable goods overboard to preserve their lives. Soldiers in a
> besieged city often destroy the finest buildings, thus elimi-
> nating walls in which the enemy may take shelter. No one
> doubts that this is wise. Those who have diseased limbs will-
> ingly agree to have them amputated, and not only thank, but
> pay the surgeon. Must God be murmured against for casting
> over that which would sink you in a storm; for pulling down
> that which would assist your enemy in the siege of temptation;
> for cutting off what would endanger your everlasting life?

Friend, these words, if taken seriously, will change our lives. When
God asks you to do something, or when He chooses to sever something from your life...rejoice! He loves you and knows what's best.

He Sees

The eyes of the Lord are in every place,
beholding the evil and the good.
PROVERBS 15:3

Today's text is one that every Christian should keep in constant remembrance. Rev. Alexander Dickson expounds on the eyes of the Lord.

> The all-seeing eyes of Jesus are always upon us. His eyes notice all our shortcomings and sinful wanderings; they scan not merely our outward conduct, but all our secret purposes...they are truly heart searching eyes.
>
> Before our thoughts are expressed by the tongue or born in the brain, they are known to Jesus. He is acquainted with them afar off: and if they are holy like Himself, He takes pleasure in them. But if they are unholy, He turns away in abhorrence from them and from us also.
>
> In His book of remembrance, all our works and words and thoughts are written, and by this record we will be judged in the last day, when the throne shall be set and the books shall be opened.

There are always at least three witnesses to everything we do—the Father, Son and Holy Spirit. Nothing goes unnoticed. Nothing is done in "private." At home, on vacation, in the daylight or at night, Jesus sees us.

Today, if there is anything in your heart or thoughts that is unholy, that would make the Lord turn away from you in abhorrence, get rid of it! Repent and ask Jesus to wash you clean.

GENESIS 43; MARK 13; JOB 9; ROMANS 13

The Furnace of Adversity

If thou faint in the day of adversity, thy strength is small.
PROVERBS 24:10

Quoting from one of Thomas à Kempis's works, the Rev. John Fletcher brings illumination to today's scripture.

"Temptations," says à Kempis, "are often very profitable to men...for in them a man is humbled, purified, and instructed. All the saints have passed through and profited by many tribulations; and they that couldn't bear temptations became reprobates and fell away."

If you come to serve the Lord in the perfect beauty of holiness, prepare your soul for temptation. Set your heart firm, and constantly endure; don't rush through the time of trouble. As gold is tried and purified in the fire, so are men tried in the furnace of adversity. Scripture reads, "Blessed is the man that endures temptation; for when he is tried [if he stands the fiery trial] he will receive the crown of life which the Lord has promised to them that love Him." Patiently endure, then, when God allows you to experience heaviness and temptations. The trial of your faith, which is much more precious than that of gold which perishes, though it be tried in the fire, will be found unto praise and honor and glory at the appearing of Jesus Christ.

Regardless of the trials you may be facing today, remember that the Lord is in control. Draw close to His side and He will guide you through.

GENESIS 44; MARK 14; JOB 10; ROMANS 14

True Compassion

For God so loved the world, that he gave his only begotten Son, that whosoever believeth in him should not perish, but have everlasting life.
JOHN 3:16

Once, as Jesus drew near the city of Jerusalem, He began to weep, saying, "If you had known, even you, especially in this your day, the things that make for your peace! But now they are hidden from your eyes" (Luke 19:42, *NKJV*). What motivated the Son of God to mourn over Jerusalem? Not mere human compassion. Whenever we hear the word "compassion," most of us consider the present plight of man and human suffering. Although these needs are for the most part legitimate, there is more to weep over—much, much more.

Jesus saw far beyond the present troubles. Our present conditions have to do with the temporal, not the eternal. Although one flows into the other, the latter carries inexpressible importance. After all, what does it profit a man if he gains the whole world and loses his own soul? What sense does it make for him to fill his belly when his heart is empty? What good is it if a man is given another pair of shoes to walk on this earth, when in a flash he'll stand naked and barefoot at the Judgment Seat?

True compassion has eternity in focus. Jesus saw everything through the eyes of eternity. His compassion was intermingled with eternal tears, and when the Lord wept, He always took action. Just as Jesus fixed His eyes on eternity, so should we in our pilgrimage. Every person we meet, every cup of water we give, every grain of wheat we distribute should be directly connected to a desire to see that person's soul find eternal life.

The Devil at the Door

The thief comes only to steal, and kill, and destroy; I came that they might
have life, and might have it abundantly.
JOHN 10:10, NASB

Since his fall from heaven, one of Satan's most successful ploys
has been to cause us to forget that he's out there. William Gurnall
understood that it is imperative to know your enemy and be aware of
his tactics.

Remember that the devil is always awake. Who could dare to
go to bed and fall asleep, knowing that there is an enemy outside, climbing over fences and possibly surrounding the
house? Jesus takes it for granted that if "the good man of the
house" had known when the thief would come, he would have
watched. Hearing the warning, "The devil is at your door!"
should be enough to keep you out of the comfortable bed of
laziness, apathy and negligence!

Never allow yourself to grow casual toward the fact that the devil
is out to destroy you. He's going down and he wants to pull as many
people down with him as he can. He knows that sin will separate us
from God. Scripture calls him our enemy, the one who prowls around
like a roaring lion looking for someone to devour (see 1 Peter 5:8).

These warnings are unpleasant and unsettling, but be encouraged—we don't have to fight him by ourselves. Christ overcame him on
Calvary, completely sealing his fate. We are clearly told that if we submit ourselves to God, we can resist the devil and he will flee. The
Christian who is living in holy obedience to the Lord has nothing to
fear. The devil might be at the door, but he'll answer to the Lord.

GENESIS 46; MARK 16; JOB 12; ROMANS 16

What Is Prayer?

My voice shalt thou hear in the morning, O LORD; in the morning will
I direct my prayer unto thee, and will look up.
PSALM 5:3

Jeremy Taylor, the seventeenth-century Anglican bishop, paints for us an elaborate picture of prayer:

> Prayer is the peace of our spirit, the stillness of our thoughts, the evenness of recollection, the seat of meditation, the rest of our cares, and the calm of our tempest. Prayer is the issue of a quiet mind, of untroubled thoughts.
>
> Prayer can obtain everything. It can open the windows of heaven and shut the gates of hell. It can put a holy constraint upon God and detain an angel till he leave a blessing. It can open the treasures of rain and soften the iron ribs of rocks till they melt into tears and a flowing river. Prayer can arrest the sun in the midst of its course and send the swift-winged winds upon our errand. All those strange things, secret decrees and unrevealed transactions which are of heaven, shall combine in ministry and advantages for the praying man.

Prayer is not an option. It is not merely a safety net. Prayer is to be a lifestyle—one which incorporates constant communication with the Lover of your soul. The true test of a man's soul is when he's alone with God and it is certain that no man is greater than his prayers.

Oh, to Be Like Thee!

And he said to them all, If any man will come after me, let him deny himself, and take up his cross daily, and follow me.

LUKE 9:23

It is a noble thing to want to be like Jesus; it is quite another thing to follow His disciplined example in order to indeed *be* like Jesus. Leonard Ravenhill frequently reminded me of the vast difference between the two.

> When we sing in a sunlit church, "Oh, to be like Thee; Oh, to be like Thee," we get weepy and feel an emotional lift. But permit this simple challenge: Do we really mean "Oh, to be like Thee"—like the Christ of God, who was a man of discipline? Do we really mean "Oh, to be like Thee"—fasting alone in the desert? Do we mean "Oh, to be like Thee"—so that without our wilting under it, the world can say of us as of Him, "He hath a devil"? Do we mean "Oh, to be like Thee"—to touch the depths of prayer that make us cry "All Thy billows are gone over me"? Do we mean "Oh, to be like Thee"—to become habituates of the fastness of the prayer chamber? Do we mean "Oh, to be like Thee"—in a will like His, for He said, "I always do the will of my Father"? Is not that discipline?[1]

Do you still want to be like Jesus? Do you want an agonizing Gethsemane experience? Do you want a Judas in your life? Do you want a friend, who spent over three years by your side, to curse and say he never knew you?

Jesus has shown us the way. We must daily die to self, pick up our cross (disciplines), and follow in His footsteps.

1. Leonard Ravenhill, *Meat for Men* (Minneapolis, Minn.: Bethany House Publishers, 1989), p. 32.

GENESIS 48; LUKE 1:39-80; JOB 14; 1 CORINTHIANS 2

Give thanks in all circumstances, for this is God's will for you in Christ Jesus.
1 THESSALONIANS 5:18, NIV

Gratitude is simply appreciation for favors received. In each of our lives, God has freely poured forth favors from His hand. The fact that we are breathing is at least one proof that the Lord has done much for us. But how do we respond to those blessings? These words from William Jay should help us put things into perspective:

> The proud are never thankful. Heap whatever favors upon them, and what reward do you get? They think they deserve it! You are only doing your duty—you are doing justly, rather than loving mercy. But when we are humble, in the same proportion we should be grateful. When we realize that we are not worthy of the smallest of all God's mercies, how thankful we would be for the bread we eat, and the water that we drink!

Sometimes life's difficulties can block our view of all that God has done for us. Becoming preoccupied with all that we *don't* have can blind us to all that we *do* have. How sweet our peace when we realize that without the Lord we are nothing and can do nothing. In Him we live and breathe and have our being. He created us, loves us, knows us intimately and is constantly pouring out His mercy on us. How pleasing it must be to Him when we take the time to look up and say, "Thank you."

GENESIS 49; LUKE 2; JOB 15; 1 CORINTHIANS 3

Not a Cardboard Crown

And he said unto them, Go ye into all the world,
and preach the gospel to every creature.
MARK 16:15

I am under obligation to my Savior. My Redeemer's last command was for us to go into all the world and preach the gospel to every creature. He did not use the last moments before His ascension to speak to the disciples about their own personal welfare. His parting message was not in regard to houses or health. Rather, it was about heaven or hell. His concern was for the lost.

I am under obligation to my neighbor. Paul said, "Knowing therefore the terror of the Lord, we persuade men" (2 Corinthians 5:11). Paul understood that this world is like a burning house. We, as Christians, have escaped the fire and can hear the agonizing screams of those still trapped in the inferno. What kind of man, upon seeing his neighbor's house ablaze and hearing the cries of the doomed children, would slouch back in his easy chair with no intention of helping?

I am under obligation to myself. Paul spoke of the Coronation Day when he said, "There is laid up for me a crown of righteousness" (2 Timothy 4:8). Personally, I want a magnificent crown such as would even make the angels gasp in awe. Why? Not vanity, I assure you. You see, that crown will represent my life's work for Jesus. Of course, all that I've done won't come close to His tremendous sacrifice for me. However, it will be the only thing of any value that I will have to lay at His feet on that day as I bow and cry, "Holy, and worthy are You, Jesus!"

Burn Steadily

You are the light of the world. A city on a hill cannot be hidden.
MATTHEW 5:14, NASB

How brightly we may burn once we fully realize we are nothing without Jesus! As the British clergyman F. B. Meyer shows us, even a smoldering wick has the potential to be ignited and used of God.

> What a sermon there is in a wick! Sit beside it and ask how it dares hope to be able to supply light for hours and hours to come. "Will you not soon burn to an end, you wick of lamp?" "No; I do not fear it, since the light does not burn me, though it burns on me. I only bear to it the oil which saturates my texture. I am but the ladder up which it climbs. It is not I, but the oil that is in me, that furnishes the light."
>
> Yes, that is it...we do not give light to the world, we only receive the oil from the Holy Spirit and the spark of His fire; and if we burn steadily through the long, dark hours it is because we have learned to translate into living beauty those supplies of grace which we receive in fellowship with Jesus. But how necessary it is that nothing interrupt the flow of oil; that there be no uncleanliness permitted to clog and obstruct the narrow bore of the golden spout of faith.
>
> It cannot be too often repeated, that it is not *what* we do for Him, but what *He does through* us, which really blesses men.

Do you feel dry? Are you but a smoldering wick in a world of darkness? Pray for the oil of the Holy Spirit to saturate your life. Let the fire of God burn brightly.

EXODUS 1; LUKE 4; JOB 18; 1 CORINTHIANS 5

Give Up All That Hinders

Wherefore seeing we also are compassed about with so great a cloud of witnesses, let us lay aside every weight, and the sin which doth so easily beset us, and let us run with patience the race that is set before us.

HEBREWS 12:1

As we run life's race, we must stay focused on the prize, which is eternity with Jesus. This world will compete for our time, attention and allegiance. For this reason, Robert Murray McCheyne frequently encouraged his flock to stay sharp and undaunted.

The duty here commanded is *diligence*—diligence in living so that when Christ appears He may find you in peace, without spot and blameless. Get your heart so engrossed with Jesus; make Him your main concern in all you do. Give up all that hinders.

The man who is diligent in worldly things gives up anything that would thwart his success. The man who is thoroughly intent on taking a journey rises out of bed early in the morning. The man who is running for his life throws off any cumbersome weight. Likewise, if you are diligent in seeking Christ, and your personal goals prevent or hinder you, know that they will be your ruin. Give them up. If any relationships are detrimental to you, by destroying your seriousness, or hampering your prayer, and wasting precious time, then break them off. Remove any idol that forms an obstruction between you and Christ.

What goal pushes you onward? Is it Jesus? Is it to do His will, to be found faithful, to see Him face-to-face? Let us not lose sight of the finish line. Don't let anything slow you down.

EXODUS 2; LUKE 5; JOB 19; 1 CORINTHIANS 6

Get Your House in Order

By faith Noah, being warned of God of things not seen as yet, moved with fear, prepared an ark to the saving of his house; by the which he condemned the world, and became heir of the righteousness which is by faith.

HEBREWS 11:7

We are living in days of chaos and disorder. Order, as referred to here, suggests a harmonious arrangement in proper condition. Paul described the days in which we now live in his second letter to Timothy. Men and women are lovers of themselves, covetous, boasters, unthankful, unholy. Many are without natural affection, lovers of pleasures more than lovers of God; having a form of godliness, but denying the power thereof (see 2 Timothy 3:1-5). As in the days of Noah, our houses (lives), are not in order.

There is an event on the horizon that will change the order of every man, woman and child. God said to Noah, "The end of all flesh is come before me; for the earth is filled with violence through them; and, behold, I will destroy them with the earth" (Genesis 6:13). Why? Because, "God saw that the wickedness of man was great in the earth, and that every imagination of the thoughts of his heart was only evil continually. And it repented the LORD that he had made man on the earth, and it grieved him at his heart" (verses 5, 6).

God's Word clearly warns us, "Get your house in order!" Once again, mankind is at the place where he has become an abomination in God's eyes. In His great mercy, God gives us fair warning—space to repent. It is time for godly men and women to rise up like Noah, who was moved with fear at the warning from God of things to come. Noah had his house in order; he obeyed the Lord and escaped the judgment that came. Would you be like Noah? In this day of chaos, is your house in order?

EXODUS 3; LUKE 6; JOB 20; 1 CORINTHIANS 7

Live Eternity~Conscious

Before the mountains were born, or Thou didst give birth to the earth and the world, even from everlasting to everlasting, Thou art God.
PSALM 90:2, NASB

Have you ever tried to imagine eternity? Of course, our finite minds tend to understand things better when we are able to compare the concept to something we already know. For instance, it would be difficult to describe how chocolate tastes to someone who has never tasted it. Similarly, eternity is not a concept easily grasped by humans, whose days are numbered. However, Samuel Davies, a Presbyterian evangelist during the 1700s, relates a beautiful comparison in this passage.

Eternity! We are alarmed at the sound! Lost in the prospect! Eternity with respect to God is a duration without beginning, as well as without end. It is a duration that excludes all number and computation. Days, months, years and ages are lost in it, like drops in the ocean. Millions of millions of years, as many years as there are sands on the seashore or particles of dust in the globe on the earth, all these are nothing to eternity. They do not bear the least imaginable proportion to it, for these will come to an end, as certain as day, but eternity will never, never come to an end. It is a line without an end; it is an ocean without a shore.

As many times a day as you can remember to do so, ask yourself this question: How will my words and deeds today affect eternity?

Will Work for Food

If anyone will not work, neither shall he eat.
2 THESSALONIANS 3:10, NKJV

A man in dirty jeans stands at an intersection with a hopeless expression on his face, holding a tattered, hand-lettered sign that reads, "Will work for food." It's becoming a common sight. What most unsuspecting motorists don't know is that many of these, though not all, are con artists making a good living capitalizing on the sympathies of others. A friend of mine once walked up to one of these panhandlers and offered him five dollars to read the Bible for one hour. The man flatly turned him down, knowing he could make more *not* doing anything for that hour. We've all heard the phrase, "Beggars can't be choosers." A truly hungry man is a grateful man, however his need is met.

Unfortunately, many Christians do the same thing. They sit in church pews figuratively holding a sign that says, "I'll do anything for you, Lord." The truth is they really only want a spiritual handout. Their sign should read, "I'll do anything as long as it's what I want to do."

Friend, don't be like that. There is nothing like a hard day's work in the vineyard of the Lord to help you appreciate a good, hot spiritual meal from God. Just as a farmer works by the sweat of his brow from sunup to sundown, we should be involved in active intercession and soul winning. There is nothing like sitting in a church service with a newly converted soul by your side. You've been working in the Lord's fields and the harvest beside you speaks loudly of your labor.

Something Old, Something New

Forget the former things; do not dwell on the past. See, I am doing a new thing!
Now it springs up; do you not perceive it?
ISAIAH 43:18,19, NIV

Without God's merciful, saving grace, we are completely lost in our wickedness. We cannot hope to have fellowship with Jesus unless He removes our sin and renews our innocence before Him. Charles Spurgeon stated it well.

You might notice that God doesn't promise to improve our nature or mend our broken hearts. No, He promises to give us new hearts and right spirits. Human nature is too far gone to ever be mended. It's not a house that is a little out of repair, with an occasional roof shingle missing and a little plaster broken down from the ceiling. No, it's rotten throughout and totally decayed, for the worm has eaten every single timber. From the roof to its foundation, it is completely unsound and ready to fall. If it was only a little out of repair, it might be mended, but it's too far gone. God will not attempt to simply repair the walls and repaint the door. He will not beautify, but He determines that old house needs to be entirely swept away. He will build a new one.

Be careful not to hold on to the "old self," friend. It would be like trying to live out your life in a condemned shack. It will collapse on you in time. Jesus said, "If any man be in Christ, he is a new creature: old things are passed away; behold, all things are become new" (2 Corinthians 5:17). Is there anything old you still haven't given up? Choose today to let go and allow Jesus to make you completely new!

EXODUS 6; LUKE 9; JOB 23; 1 CORINTHIANS 10

A Cry for the Lost

The great day of the LORD is near—near and coming quickly. Listen!
The cry on the day of the LORD will be bitter, the shouting of the warrior there.
ZEPHANIAH 1:14, NIV

The day Jonathan Edwards preached the inspired sermon, *Sinners in the Hands of an Angry God*, the Spirit of God allowed a holy fear to engulf the crowd. Yet, the unction behind that message was a cry for the lost—as Edwards had come to a divine insight regarding the agony of such separation from God.

How dreadful is the state of those that are daily and hourly in danger of His great wrath and infinite misery! But this is the dismal case of every soul...that has not been born again, however moral and strict, sober and religious, they may otherwise be. Think about that, whether you are young or old! I believe that there are many right now that will actually be the subjects of this very misery for all eternity. Maybe they are now at ease, listening to all these things without much disturbance, flattering themselves that they are not the persons, promising themselves that they will escape. If we knew that there was one person, only one, in the whole congregation, that was to be the subject of this misery, it would be an awful thing! The rest of the congregation would no doubt bitterly cry over him! But, alas! Instead of one, how many is it likely will remember this message—in hell?

Oh, that we, too, would open our hearts to the truth of this message, that our hearts might cry forth unto God in ceaseless intercession for the souls of lost humanity.

The Danger of Pride

But he gives us more grace. That is why Scripture says: "God opposes the proud but gives grace to the humble."
JAMES 4:6, NIV

We should always be willing to evaluate ourselves in order to prevent pride from gaining any foothold in our hearts. John Wesley (1703-1791) suggests a simple test.

If your pride has been hurt, it will become evident. Perhaps you are not so teachable or advisable as you once were. Maybe you are no longer so easy to be convinced or persuaded. Do you have a much better opinion of your own judgment, and are you now more attached to your own will? You once were glad to be admonished or reproved: but that time is past. Formerly one might have guided you with a thread, and now one cannot turn you with a rope. And you now consider a man your enemy because he tells you the truth. Oh let each of you calmly consider this, and make sure it never becomes your own picture!

Nothing can destroy a solid Christian witness like pride. Everyone struggles with it at one time or another, but pride is dangerous; it will damn your soul to hell. It alienates you from others by making you ready to reject any thought that contradicts your own opinions.

Remember, the Lord is looking for those who are humble, teachable, pliable. Those people are the ones He can use. The haughty will be passed by. Humble yourself in the sight of the Lord, for the flower of humility grows on the grave of pride.

EXODUS 8; LUKE 11; JOB 25—26; 1 CORINTHIANS 12

A Pulpit in Paradise

But the other answering rebuked him, saying, Dost not thou fear God,
seeing thou art in the same condemnation?
LUKE 23:40

If he were given a pulpit in paradise, I believe the thief's message would be something like this:

There are times when God will stick you right next to Jesus. Much of my life was spent in selfish and riotous living. I was a lover of pleasure more than a lover of God. Yet, there I was, right next to Jesus on a day that all eternity would remember.

Don't allow the opinions of others to silence the cry of your heart. Some were ridiculing Him. Others were calling Him a fake. Many were laughing. But I couldn't allow the feelings of others to dictate what my own heart was saying. Friend, you must never allow the opinions of others to silence the cry of your heart. If Jesus has convicted you of your sinful lifestyle, then don't let anyone else talk you out of repenting.

Finally the words came that changed eternity: "It is finished" (John 19:30); "Father, into thy hands I commend my spirit" (Luke 23:46). Moments later, pain racked my body once again as the Roman soldier broke my legs to speed my death. Then I was in paradise. You see, the right decision I made *on* the cross changed my destiny—ushering me into heaven and the arms of my Savior. But never forget—like the thief who was crucified on the other side of Jesus—you, too, can be *close* to Jesus yet never make it to heaven. Don't delay your coming to Him.

EXODUS 9; LUKE 12; JOB 27; 1 CORINTHIANS 13

I've Got That Joy

You have made known to me the path of life; you will fill me with joy in your presence, with eternal pleasures at your right hand.

PSALM 16:11, NIV

I'm so thankful that the Lord created in us the capacity to experience joy. The opposite of sadness and sorrow, to be joyful is to be exceedingly *glad*. Sadly, many people live each day void of joy, as though it were a luxury too costly for them, or a privilege they simply don't deserve. I love the way Robert Murray McCheyne describes it.

There is no joy like divine joy. It is infinite, full, eternal, pure and unmingled. It is light, without any cloud to darken it. It is calm, without any breath to ruffle it. Clouds and darkness may surround, storms and fire may come and go, but within Him all is peaceful and unchangeable. Remember, all things happen according to the good pleasure of His will. He has preordained whatever comes to pass. Nothing catches God by surprise. If you have come to Christ, you can consider any circumstances with a calm, holy joy, knowing that your Father's will and purposes alone will stand.

There is also joy in the presence of the angels over one sinner who repents, more so than over the ninety-nine who need no repentance. I have no doubt that this is one of the great elements of His joy—seeing souls brought into His favor. God loves to save; He delights in mercy.

Freely you have received, freely give. Make it your purpose today to share His joy with someone who knows no joy. In doing so, you will bring your Father great joy as well.

EXODUS 10; LUKE 13; JOB 28; 1 CORINTHIANS 14

You Can Overcome the World

*In fact, everyone who wants to live a godly life in
Christ Jesus will be persecuted.*
2 TIMOTHY 3:12, NIV

George Whitefield shares a candid, unpopular truth that many Christians would rather avoid, but all Christians need to hear.

Persecution is inevitable for the godly. If we never experience evil spoken of us, how can we know whether we can endure contempt, and seek only that honor which comes from above? If we never have persecutors, how can we ever exercise our passive graces? How can all of those Christian precepts be put into practice? How can we love, pray for, and do good to those who spitefully use us? How can we overcome evil with good? In short, how can we know we love God better than life itself?

I do not mean to imply that all are persecuted to the same degree. No, this would be contrary both to Scripture and experience. Not all Christians are called to suffer every kind of persecution. But, all Christians should be *willing* and *prepared* for it. Some may live in more peaceful times of the church than others, yet all Christians, in all ages, will find by their own experience that they must in some degree or other, suffer persecution.

Jesus said, "I have told you these things, so that in me you may have peace. In this world you will have trouble. But take heart! I have overcome the world" (John 16:33, *NIV*). Friend, if we stay close to Jesus, hidden in His shadow, we will also overcome the world.

EXODUS 11:12-21; LUKE 14; JOB 29; 1 CORINTHIANS 15

An Extra Day to Pray!

Our Father which art in heaven, Hallowed be thy name.
Thy kingdom come. Thy will be done in earth, as it is in heaven.
Give us this day our daily bread. And forgive us our debts,
as we forgive our debtors.
And lead us not into temptation, but deliver us from evil:
For thine is the kingdom, and the power, and the glory, for ever. Amen.
MATTHEW 6:9-13

Though it doesn't happen often, leap year provides us with the wonderful opportunity of an extra day to pray. I could think of no more perfect passage than this discourse by E. M. Bounds, who is best known for his ceaseless praying, and his many writings on prayer.

As every day demands its bread, so every day demands its prayer. No amount of praying done today will suffice for tomorrow's praying. On the other hand, no praying for tomorrow is of any great value to us today. Today's manna is what we need; tomorrow God will see that our needs are supplied. This is the faith which God seeks to inspire. So leave tomorrow, with its cares, its needs, its troubles, in God's hands. There is no storing of tomorrow's grace or tomorrow's praying; neither is there any laying up of today's grace to meet tomorrow's necessities. We cannot have tomorrow's grace, we cannot eat tomorrow's bread, we cannot do tomorrow's praying.[1]

When Jesus said, "Give us this day our daily bread," I believe He was teaching us to live one day at a time. Rejoice therefore in this day of extra provision, and pray. Also, take a few moments to read today's special Bible texts on prayer from the book of Matthew.

1. Leonard Ravenhill, comp., *A Treasury of Prayer* (Minneapolis: Bethany House Publishers, 1961), p. 124.

MATTHEW 6:5-8; MATTHEW 7:7-11; MATTHEW 18:19,20; MATTHEW 21:22

The Final Word

*And entering in, He said to them, "Why make a commotion
and weep? The child has not died, but is asleep." And taking the child by
the hand, He said to her, "Talitha kum!" (which translated
means, "Little girl, I say to you, arise!")*
MARK 5:39,41, NASB

To intercede is to step in on behalf of someone else. Though his little girl lay dead, with mourners weeping all around, Jairus went after Jesus! He knew those mourners didn't have the final word, and Satan didn't have the final word...only Jesus did!

Jesus messed up every funeral He ever went to. He didn't see the casket or the flowers. He *is* the Final Word. His voice pierces the darkness and penetrates death itself.

Perhaps you have experienced what seems to be a death to your spiritual walk. Are there times when you feel cold and all alone? Remember, as happened with Jairus's daughter, when Jesus is present He will speak to you. He might speak to someone else about helping you, but He is going to speak to *you* to get up, and it will be up to you to rise in obedience. He will speak revival into your life, but it will be up to you to respond.

Most of us know someone who is spiritually dead. Skeptics have spoken words of death over the situation saying, "He's just too far gone to be saved," or even, "Revival will never come to our church." Friend, I encourage you today to be like Jairus, to go after the One who has the final word. The words of Jesus supersede anything negative that man has spoken. His word dissolves generational curses. The voice of Jesus commands peace in the midst of the storm. Remember, when Jesus steps on the scene—everything changes!

EXODUS 12:22-51; LUKE 15; JOB 30; 1 CORINTHIANS 16

Pressing On

The LORD is nigh unto all them that call upon him, to all that call upon him in truth. He will fulfil the desire of them that fear him: he also will hear their cry, and will save them.

PSALM 145:18,19

David Brainerd, missionary to the American Indians in the 1700s, was passionately devoted to seeking God. Many of his journal entries reveal a man who was first "after God's own heart," as we see here.

> I was enabled in secret prayer to raise my soul to God, with desire and delight. It was indeed a blessed time. All my past sorrows seemed kindly to disappear, and I "remembered no more the sorrow, for joy." O, how sweetly, and with what an affectionate tenderness the soul confides in the Rock of Ages, knowing He will "never leave it nor forsake it," and that He will cause "all things to work together for good!" I longed that others should know how good a God the Lord is. My soul was full of tenderness and love—even to the greatest of my enemies. I longed that they should share in the same mercy. I loved the thought that God should so do as He pleased with me—and everything else. I felt peculiarly serious, calm, and peaceful, and felt encouragement to press after holiness as long as I live, whatever difficulties and trials may be in my way. May the Lord always help me to do so! Amen, and amen.

Our desire should be first and foremost to know God, and by so doing, His power and passion for the lost will flow through our lives. Make it your determined purpose today to press on after holiness—letting nothing steal your desire to know Him.

EXODUS 13; LUKE 16; JOB 31; 2 CORINTHIANS 1

Born unto Trouble

*Praise be to the God and Father of our Lord Jesus Christ,
the Father of compassion and the God of all comfort, who comforts us
in all our troubles, so that we can comfort those in any trouble with
the comfort we ourselves have received from God.*

2 CORINTHIANS 1:3,4 NIV

While church planting in Argentina, my wife, Jeri, suffered a difficult miscarriage. Her doctor released her, unaware she had been pregnant with twins. One fetus remained in her fallopian tube, causing her excruciating pain and threatening her life. We rushed her to a hospital in another city, for emergency surgery, just in time. Throughout that agonizing trial, Jeri had such peace and comfort in God that it dramatically affected her nurse. Within days, Jeri led her in prayer as the two of them knelt together on the floor of the restroom! Jeri's suffering had been used of God to draw her nurse closer to Jesus.

Consider these words of Phillip Doddridge:

Since "man is born unto trouble, as the sparks fly upward," (Job 5:7)...we should all expect to meet with trials and afflictions. You should endeavor to secure your armor and position yourself to encounter those trials which will be your destiny as a Christian. Prepare to receive your afflictions, and endure them. In this view, when you see others under a burden, consider that you may be called out to the very same difficulties, or others equal to them. Endeavor at once to comfort them and to strengthen your own heart, or rather pray that God would do it.

Friend, today you may be faced with your own trials, or the suffering of others. Keep this scripture in mind as you, too, endeavor to lead others to the God of all comfort, making the most of every opportunity.

EXODUS 14; LUKE 17; JOB 32; 2 CORINTHIANS 2

Some Loud, Some Soft

That if thou shalt confess with thy mouth the Lord Jesus, and shalt believe in thine heart that God hath raised him from the dead, thou shalt be saved. For with the heart man believeth unto righteousness; and with the mouth confession is made unto salvation.

ROMANS 10:9,10

The Early Church was in revival! Teaching and discipleship had begun as thousands were being added to the ranks. The book of Acts describes a woman named Lydia who was a seller of cloth, and a worshiper (see 16:14). When she came to hear Paul preach, his teachings made sense, her heart was opened and she responded without a lot of commotion or manifestation.

Andrew Murray once said, "There are those to whom the fountain springs up from within, quietly streaming forth." On the other hand, says Murray, "There are some Christians who are not content unless they have special, mighty visitations of the Spirit—the rushing mighty wind, floods outpoured and the baptism of fire—these are their symbols."

The latter is evident in the life of the Philippian jailer (see Acts 16:26-30). "What must I do to be saved?" was the cry of a trembling sinner convinced of the danger he was in. The account of his conversion illustrates salvation during a traumatic episode. His initial salvation was marked by great emotion.

As you set out to fulfill the Great Commission, remember never to measure salvation by someone's emotional response. Some come slowly and surely to the place of being saved, others come with extreme emotion. Learn to recognize God in both the loud and the soft, and be blessed—whichever way He chooses to come.

EXODUS 15; LUKE 18; JOB 33; 2 CORINTHIANS 3

Get a Better Grip

*And we know that the Son of God has come, and has given us understanding,
in order that we might know Him who is true, and we are in Him who is
true, in His Son Jesus Christ. This is the true God and eternal life.*

1 JOHN 5:20, NASB

Do you have a burning desire to know Jesus more deeply than
ever? As a believer, you should. According to Robert Murray
McCheyne, it is a desire easily within the believer's reach.

> The only way to hold fast is to believe more and more. Grasp
> a deeper acquaintance with Christ—with His person, work,
> and character. Every page of the Gospel unfolds new features
> in His character, every line of the epistles discloses new depths
> of His work. Get faith and you will get a firmer hold.
>
> A plant that has got a single root may be easily torn up by
> the hand, crushed by the foot of the wild beast, or blown
> down by the wind; but a plant that has a thousand roots
> struck down into the ground can stand. Faith is like that root.
> Every new truth concerning Jesus is a new root struck down-
> wards. Believe more intensely—a root may be growing in a
> right direction, but if it doesn't grow deep, it is easily torn up.
> Pray for deep-rooted faith. Pray to be established, strength-
> ened, settled.

McCheyne speaks from experience. His own life was devoted to
knowing Christ in this way. He concludes:

> Take a long intense look at Jesus—often. If you wanted to
> remember a man again, who was going away, you would take
> an intense look at His face. Look then at Jesus—deeply,
> intensely—till every feature is carved upon your heart.

Pardon for the Greatest Sinners

All that the Father gives Me will come to Me,
and the one who comes to Me I will by no means cast out.
JOHN 6:37, NKJV

"Go for souls and go for the worst!" Such was the directive that filled the heart of General William Booth, the founder of the Salvation Army. Likewise, no soldier who claims to be in the ranks of Christ's army should forsake that divine focus. Jonathan Edwards burned with this same passionate understanding of the cause of Christ.

> Christ *will not refuse* to save the greatest sinners—who in a right manner come to God for mercy—for this is His work. It is His business to be a Savior of sinners; it is the work for which He came into the world; and therefore He will not object to it. He did not come to call the righteous but sinners to repentance (Mark 2:17). Sin is the very evil which He came into the world to remedy. The more sinful a man is, the more he has need of Christ. The sinfulness of man was the reason of Christ's coming into the world; this is the very misery from which He came to deliver men. The more they have of it, the more need they have of being delivered.

Christ will not reject even the foulest of sinners. In the presence of an admittedly sinful people, Samuel said, "Far be it from me that I should sin against the LORD by ceasing to pray for you" (1 Samuel 12:23, *NASB*). Friend, God hears. Never cease in your praying and pleading for the souls of men—no matter how hopeless they seem. Remember: The sickest patients are the ones most in need of a physician.

EXODUS 17; LUKE 20; JOB 35; 2 CORINTHIANS 5

Material Pleasures

Jesus said to him, "If you wish to be complete, go and sell your possessions and give to the poor, and you shall have treasure in heaven; and come, follow Me." But when the young man heard this statement, he went away grieved; for he was one who owned much property.

MATTHEW 19:21,22, NASB

A man in his sixties once approached me after a meeting and handed me a large contribution. "Preacher," he said, "this is for you to go to the mission field." Curious, I asked the man about himself. He began to weep as he told me how God had called him to missions as a young man, but he thought he should work just a little longer to set some money aside. Forty years later he was very wealthy indeed but had neglected the call of God. Unable to accept his gift, I advised him to use the money to finally obey God himself.

Bishop Samuel Wilberforce (1805-1873) served the Lord in ministry to the upper class and royalty of England. Sadly, his observations are still true of many Christians today.

> There are many powerful influences at work, which are hostile to our spiritual development. Life is lived easily. Cheap gratifications—within the reach of almost all of us—abound everywhere. Our styles of living are strongly flavored with abundant material comforts and physical pleasures. All this tends to soften the spirit, making it reluctant to venture to the place of high communing, where reverence is bred. The valley is so pleasant, its air so soft, its flowers so many, its attraction so enticing that few are willing to climb the mountainside and brace their nerves in its sharper airs.

As Christians, we are not called to a life of softness, but a life of service. If your heart is truly in pursuit of God, be careful not to value comfort more highly than calling.

A Personal Baptism

Then remembered I the word of the Lord, how that he said, John indeed baptized with water; but ye shall be baptized with the Holy Ghost.

ACTS 11:16

This passage from the memoirs of Charles G. Finney details an encounter he had with the Holy Spirit of God:

> I returned to the front office and found that the fire I had made of large wood was nearly burned out. But as I turned and was about to take a seat by the fire, I received a mighty baptism of the Holy Ghost. Without any expectation of it, without ever having the thought in my mind that there was any such thing for me, without any recollection that I had ever heard the thing mentioned by any person in the world—the Holy Spirit descended upon me in a manner that seemed to go through me, body and soul. I could feel the impression, like a wave of electricity, going through and through me. Indeed it seemed to come in waves and waves of liquid love; for I could not express it in any other way. It seemed like the very breath of God. No words can express the wonderful love that was shed abroad in my heart. I wept aloud with joy and love. I literally bellowed out the unutterable gushings of my heart. These waves came over me, one after the other, until I cried out, "I shall die if these waves continue to pass over me. Lord, I cannot bear anymore." Yet I had no fear of death.

My friend, this was the secret of Charles Finney's success as a preacher. God had set him on fire in private, making him ready to burn freely in public. The result was the conversion of thousands. Seek for your own personal baptism. There is more of God than what we have.

EXODUS 19; LUKE 22; JOB 37; 2 CORINTHIANS 7

I'm Warning You

And the LORD said, My spirit shall not always strive with man.
GENESIS 6:3

A warning is a notice of approaching or probable danger. To warn someone is to caution them against anything that may prove injurious.

For example, a farmer might sternly warn you to "get out of bed during harvest time! If you don't pull out the combine and sweep the fields while the harvest is ripe, you're going to not only lose the harvest but lose your family's income for the upcoming months. If you don't harvest the grain outside, you won't have any grain for bread inside."

Many of us as parents may have the opportunity to warn a small child to "look both ways when you cross the road! Son, if you chase after that soccer ball when it bounces out into the street like you just did, without looking both ways for traffic, you could get hit by a car and possibly be killed!"

The sharp commanding voice of a military officer would ring out the warning, "Troops, if you don't keep your eyes on the enemy, if you don't pay close attention to every possible form of attack, we are all liable to be killed on the battlefield!"

The Word of God is full of warnings of a much more permanent nature. This one is clear and to the point. If you don't do what you are supposed to do—if you don't get right with God, if you don't make things right with your neighbor, if you don't get your house in order, if you don't think seriously about your spiritual condition—there is coming a day when it will be too late.

EXODUS 20; LUKE 23; JOB 38; 2 CORINTHIANS 8

When Others Suffer

*Do not merely look out for your own personal interests, but also
for the interests of others.*
PHILIPPIANS 2:4, NASB

I will never forget the time I fell three stories from a construction site, severely breaking my right arm. The bone shattered in half and the ragged ends scraped back and forth on each other, causing horrible pain. In retrospect, at that moment I don't remember being hungry, thirsty or sleepy. No, every nerve in my body was swiftly responding to the area that was injured. That, after all, is how God created our bodies to function. As Thomas Watson describes, God intended the Body of Christ to function in a very similar manner.

A godly man takes it to heart when he sees others suffering. There are certain trees whose leaves contract, shrink up and seemingly hang their heads whenever another leaf is cut or touched. There should be a similar spiritual sympathy among Christians. When other parts of God's church suffer, others feel it also, as though they themselves were suffering. Queen Esther enjoyed the king's favor, and all the delights of the court, yet when a bloody warrant was signed for the death of the Jews, she mourned and fasted, and risked her own life to save theirs.

Just as our physical bodies let us know when they need attention, the Spirit of God touches our hearts with the needs of others in the Body of Christ. May we always endeavor to function as we should, being swift to respond through prayer, fasting, blessing—or whatever manner the Holy Spirit directs.

EXODUS 21; LUKE 24; JOB 39; 2 CORINTHIANS 9

Missing Mercy

*Fools mock at making amends for sin, but goodwill is found
among the upright.*
PROVERBS 14:9, NIV

"And as it is appointed unto men once to die, but after this the judgment" (Hebrews 9:27). What an eternally damning error it is to mock the mercy of God! Mercy, by definition, is undeserved forgiveness. To mock something is to view it as insignificant or worthless. This is how many people view the mercy of God. Let's look at how John Bunyan viewed the danger of mocking mercy.

> I have often thought of the Day of Judgment, and how God will deal with sinners on that day. I believe it will be managed with sweetness and fairness, with excellent righteousness as to every sin, circumstance and aggravation thereof. Men that are damned will feel such conviction as the righteous judgment of God comes upon them. They will feel deserving of hell-fire, they themselves will conclude that there is all the reason in the world why they should be shut out of heaven and go to hell.
>
> It will tear them that they have missed of mercy and glory and obtained everlasting damnation through their unbelief. It will tear their own souls; they will gnash upon themselves; for that mercy was offered to them in the first place and they were damned for rejecting it.

These are haunting words that should be read and heeded. As today's scripture clearly states, we will all face the judgment of God. Obtaining mercy today will prepare us for the judgment tomorrow.

EXODUS 22; JOHN 1; JOB 40; 2 CORINTHIANS 10

Seeking a Savior

I cried unto God with my voice, even unto God with my voice;
and he gave ear unto me.
PSALM 77:1

Charles Spurgeon used to tell the story of an incident that took place in one of John Wesley's meetings. It seems the Methodists would meet regularly in a certain barn. Not uncommon to Wesley's meetings, there were some local villagers intent on disrupting the service. Afraid to break through the door in this particular attempt, they resolved instead to place one of their number inside who would open the door to them during the sermon so they could carry out their wicked plan.

The elected perpetrator went in before the service began and concealed himself in a large sack in a corner of the barn. When the Methodists began to sing, he liked the tune so well that he chose not to get out of the sack until he had heard it through.

When the song ended, prayer followed. During that prayer, God so worked on the man in the sack that he began to cry for mercy. Hearing the moaning and weeping, the good people looked around for its source. The congregation was astonished to find in their midst a sinner in a sack, seeking his Savior.

That night the door was not opened to the mob after all—for he who intended to do so was suddenly convicted and converted.

I am always amazed at the way God does things. This story is proof, once again, that man's best-laid plans often melt like wax in the presence of the Lord.

Delight in the Lord

Delight thyself also in the LORD;
and he shall give thee the desires of thine heart.
PSALM 37:4

Isaac Barrow (1630-1705) said, "Praise and thanksgiving are the most delectable business of heaven; and God grant they may be our greatest delight, our most frequent employment upon earth!" Consider further, the admonition of F. B. Meyer:

> We must not spend all our lives in cleaning our windows or in considering whether they are clean, but in sunning ourselves in God's blessed light. That light will soon show us what still needs to be cleansed away and will enable us to cleanse it with unerring accuracy. Our Lord Jesus is a perfect reservoir of everything the soul of man requires for a blessed and holy life. To make much of Him, to abide in Him, to draw from Him, to receive each moment from His fullness is, therefore, the only condition of soul-health. But to be more concerned with self than with Him is like spending much time and thought over the senses of the body (sight, taste, touch, smell, hearing), and never using them for the purpose of receiving impressions from the world outside. Look often to Jesus. Delight thyself in the Lord.

All joy and reason for being lies in the first part of our text: Delight thyself in the Lord. Far too often we place more value on the latter part—the desires of our heart. Guard yourself today and always, that you may be found in "the most delectable business of heaven."

EXODUS 24; JOHN 3; JOB 42; 2 CORINTHIANS 12

Finally and Forever Saved

To whom God would make known what is the riches of the glory of this mystery among the Gentiles; which is Christ in you, the hope of glory.
COLOSSIANS 1:27

I have often made the statement, "Jesus should be the first thing on your mind in the morning and the last thing on your mind at night. If you don't eat, breathe, and sleep Jesus, I question your salvation." The Bible says we are the Bride of Christ. That means we should be consumed with thoughts about the groom. Some have asked why I speak so strongly about that. Let's take a look at how the great preacher William Plumer explained it.

> But if Christ be found in us the hope of glory...if we have taken Him to be our prophet, priest, and kin...if His name is to us as ointment poured forth...if He is precious to our souls...if we esteem His reproach greater riches than the treasures of earth...if we had rather suffer than sin...if we rest the whole weight of our salvation on His righteousness...if we delight in His ordinances...if we esteem all His precepts concerning all things to be right...if we count His service a privilege...if we faint for the longing we have for His grace and presence...if we hate all iniquity, even the thought of foolishness...if we strive to perfect holiness in the fear of God...if we weep over our shortcomings...if we greatly long to be made like Christ...then we are Christ's servants and friends, and we shall be finally and forever saved.

Friend, have you ever seen a sad bride? If we are the bride of Christ, then we should be looking forward to His coming. How else will Christ be found in us? Live expectantly, with your eyes focused firmly on the Groom.

EXODUS 25; JOHN 4; PROVERBS 1; 2 CORINTHIANS 13

Therefore, since we have so great a cloud of witnesses surrounding us, let us also lay aside every encumbrance, and the sin which so easily entangles us, and let us run with endurance the race that is set before us.
HEBREWS 12:1, NASB

Most Christians are like a man who was toiling along the road, bending under a heavy burden, when a wagon happened by and the driver kindly offered to help him on his journey. He joyfully accepted the offer, but when seated in the wagon, continued to bend beneath his burden, which he still kept on his shoulders. "Why do you not lay down your burden?" asked the kind-hearted driver. "Oh!" replied the man, "I feel that it is almost too much to ask you to carry me, and I could not think of letting you carry my burden too."

And so Christians, who have given themselves into the care and keeping of the Lord Jesus, still continue to bend beneath the weight of their burdens, and often go weary and heavy-laden throughout the whole length of their journey.

This story is found in Hannah Whitall Smith's book, *The Christian's Secret of a Happy Life*. I found her parallels amusing, pointed and memorable. She concludes:

The greatest burden we have to carry in life is self; the most difficult thing we have to manage is self. In laying off your burdens, therefore, the first one you must get rid of is yourself. You must hand yourself, with your temptations, your temperament, your frames and feelings, and all your inward and outward experiences, over into the care and keeping of your God, and leave it *all* there.

EXODUS 26; JOHN 5; PROVERBS 2; GALATIANS 1

Come, Cry Out, and Crown Him

Then came she and worshipped him, saying, Lord, help me. But he answered and said, It is not meet to take the children's bread, and to cast it to dogs.
MATTHEW 15:25,26

There is so much to learn from today's text. The woman in this story was from the land of Canaan. The Canaanites were a people marked for divine judgment because of their rampant idolatry. That is why Jesus made the distinction between the Canaanites and the people of Israel, to whom He had been sent. What I love about this portion of Scripture is the mother's unwillingness to give up. She came, she cried out, and her persistent faith paid off. Too often we come and cry out to Jesus under the influence of the spirit of "instant gratification." How many of us, if in the same predicament, would have given up and walked away?

We must all pursue Jesus as this woman did. She openly acknowledged her personal need for mercy, saying first, "Have mercy on *me*," and then, "My daughter is severely demon-possessed" (v. 22, *NKJV*, emphasis added). Though our churches and families desperately need revival, we must always be more aware that *we* need revival. Humbly cry out to Jesus, "Revive *me*, Lord. Refresh *my* soul, Holy Spirit."

There is one further notable observation about the character of this woman. When she cried out, "Have mercy on me, O Lord, Son of David!" she recognized Jesus for who He was—the Messiah. With her words, she crowned Him Supreme Authority! Those weren't the words of someone who merely hoped Jesus could help her; they were the proclamation of a mother in need of a miracle from the throne of God. Whatever your needs may be, remember Who it is you are coming to, crying out to and believing in!

EXODUS 27; JOHN 6; PROVERBS 3; GALATIANS 2

The Captain in Complete Control

Since you are my rock and my fortress,
for the sake of your name lead and guide me.
PSALM 31:3, NIV

You know, it had to be a rather peculiar moment in Noah's life when God told him to build an ark because it was going to *rain*. God said, "For after seven more days I will cause it to rain on the earth forty days and forty nights, and I will destroy from the face of the earth all living things that I have made" (Genesis 7:4, *NKJV*). Noah had never seen or heard of rain. It had never rained on the earth before. Yet he didn't question God; he just obediently followed God's instructions, built the boat and got in it. Wouldn't life be simpler these days if we could hear, accept and obey God's directions that easily? I like what William Jay had to say about it back in the 1700s.

> We are not certain of what a day or even an hour holds for us. We cannot pierce through the future's uncertainties. But we can think of God's all-knowing ability and say, "With Him I leave myself; with Him I leave my loved ones; with Him I leave my business; with Him I leave everything that can befall me." Christians may put themselves and all their concerns on board this ship and give God the entire command of it. Let's not, under any circumstances, call Him away from the helm, but leave Him to manage it all.

Noah didn't even know where the boat was going to end up or how it was going to get there. It was all in the hands of his Captain! Oh friend, walk in that security today! Enjoy this journey as a mere passenger, looking to the Lord to direct every step of the course.

EXODUS 28; JOHN 7; PROVERBS 4; GALATIANS 3

Control Your Thoughts

Finally, brethren, whatever is true, whatever is honorable, whatever is right, whatever is pure, whatever is lovely, whatever is of good repute, if there is any excellence and if anything worthy of praise, let your mind dwell on these things.

PHILIPPIANS 4:8, NASB

What is ruling your thoughts today? Perhaps this excerpt from the writings of the Methodist minister Louis Albert Banks will give you something to think about.

> Many fail to hold themselves responsible for the character of their thoughts, seeing them as unreal or fanciful, not taking them seriously. But our thoughts *do* affect our character.
>
> Mammoth Cave in Kentucky, famous for its splendid masonry of solid rock, is the result of nature's slow, silent process. The steady dripping of water from the cavern's roof forms enormous pillars. One drop of water, falling from the ceiling, deposits its sediment. Others follow, each drop adding its contribution until the icicle of stone begins to grow, ultimately reaching the rock beneath, becoming a massive pillar.
>
> Each one of our hearts displays a similar process. A thought may stir only momentarily, but can sink into the soul, unconsciously making its deposit. Other thoughts follow, forming habits of thought, erecting within us monuments of purpose or pillars of abomination. Our characters are affected forever, made of petrified thoughts.

Are there any unwanted columns of petrified thoughts in your life? Ask the Lord to show them to you, forgive you of them, break them down and free you from them—today.

EXODUS 29; JOHN 8; PROVERBS 5; GALATIANS 4

What's on Your Mind?

But I say unto you, That whosoever looketh on a woman to lust after her hath committed adultery with her already in his heart.
MATTHEW 5:28

What Jesus was telling us in this scripture is not difficult to understand. Did you know, for example, that men and women are often guilty of the *spirit* of murder, though they have never physically taken a life? How? When a married man fantasizes about what life would be like with another woman making him breakfast, playing with his kids and going to bed with him at night, he has first, in his mind, removed his wife from the picture. That is the spirit of murder! Jesus was telling us that to think lustful thoughts about another is to have actually committed the act of adultery. The same applies to wives, as well. I offer you the continued explanation of Rev. Louis Albert Banks.

Thoughts allowed in the heart soon steer the will. We won't be responsible for the vile thoughts that approach if we don't welcome or harbor them. We are responsible only for the way we treat these evil suggestions. Drive them from the door, refuse them and they will soon tire of trying to enter.

Fill the mind with pure, good meditations, and bolt the entrance from evil thoughts. An empty mind is a constant invitation for evil thoughts to enter and control. The mind will corrupt itself and generate evil thoughts just because it is empty.

Impure thoughts will soon destroy us, while godly thoughts will lead us to the perfect will of God. Friend, renewing our minds every day on God's Word isn't a pleasant suggestion, it's a survival tactic.

Three Strikes, You're In

And they overcame him by the blood of the Lamb, and by the word of their testimony; and they loved not their lives unto the death.
REVELATION 12:11

Overcomers aren't born, they are reborn in Christ. It is important to note that all three of these elements (not just one or two), are used to define an overcomer.

The Blood of the Lamb. It dripped down that rugged Cross onto the cursed soil of Golgotha to redeem a fallen race. If you are born again, your sins have been washed away by the Blood of the Lamb. However, you must be cleansed, restored and renewed daily. You need to be able to plead the Blood every time you face the adversary of your soul.

The word of their testimony. A testimony is an up-to-date account of what Jesus has done and *is doing* in your life. It should not be limited to something that happened years ago, but also should be evidence of your faith and His working in your life—today. Compromise of any kind destroys your testimony. You will never have the power to overcome the enemy if you are willingly falling prey to his devices. Holy living will preserve your testimony and give you the second tool needed to overcome.

They loved not their lives unto death. This kind of total devotion to Christ is considered part of the normal Christian life in the Bible and throughout Church history. Those who were martyred for their faith could never be accused of loving the comforts of this world more than their Lord. Weak convictions and weak commitment will cause you to be defeated. The attitude of an overcomer is: "Jesus has washed me in His Blood. I love Him with all of my heart, soul and strength, and I will not deny Him—though it cost me my life."

From Other Fishermen

And he saith unto them, Follow me, and I will make you fishers of men.
MATTHEW 4:19

I have been asked before why I so enjoy the writings of Christian leaders who are dead and gone. For one thing, if they are dead they can't backslide, and therefore their testimony is all the more proven. Further, I believe it is the same passion that J. H. Jowett demonstrated in the following piece. His words convey my reasons well.

Other men will never make us fishermen, but they may make us *better* fishermen. Let us turn to the expert fishermen and see if their ways and methods can give us helpful counsel. John Wesley was a great fisher; can we learn anything from him? Dr. Alexander Whyte made a patient and laborious study of Wesley's journals. Is that not a splendid discipline for anyone who wishes to become skillful in the great ministry? What did Wesley preach about? And how did he fit his message to the changing circumstances of his varying spheres? The Salvation Army has a great body of expert fishers. They lack many things, but they catch fish. How do they do it? What was the secret of Finney and Moody? And what is it about Torrey which constrains the people to become disciples of Christ? Let us eagerly pick up any hints these highly endowed and experienced men may be able to give us.

If you want to learn how to catch fish, take lessons from great fishermen. Hang around Jesus, follow His teachings and examples in the Word. After all, He is the greatest fisher of men!

EXODUS 32; JOHN 11; PROVERBS 8; EPHESIANS 1

Wait on His Promises

"For the mountains may be removed and the hills may shake, but My lovingkindness will not be removed from you, and My covenant of peace will not be shaken," says the LORD who has compassion on you.
ISAIAH 54:10, NASB

Chiefly remembered for his work, *Golden Treasury of the Children of God*, German-born Karl Heinrich von Bogatzky (1690-1774) was an evangelist at heart. Though his father groomed him for military life, he instead pursued the ministry and was greatly successful, wherever he went (as a soldier of God), in leading men to Christ. He spent his last years writing hymns and books of devotion. His words here reflect a man who truly knew his God and trusted Him to the uttermost.

The nearer to heaven, the higher the mountains, the deeper the valleys, and the sharper the conflicts. But be not discouraged; it is only for the trial of our faith. God gives also more strength, carries us through all, as He has done from the beginning, and suffers none to be ashamed who trust in Him. Sometimes we may seem to be tempted above measure and are afraid of being confounded; but far from it; it is quite impossible that we should. Here are the plain words of the Lord. Take hold of them and wait on His time; for since the world stood, none have been confounded in anything who have waited for His promise; and surely He will not make you the first instance of the failure of His word. By no means.

Oh, friend, take comfort in these words. Take comfort in God's great promises for He will never leave you nor forsake you.

EXODUS 33; JOHN 12; PROVERBS 9; EPHESIANS 2

Ten Looks at Christ

You were taught, with regard to your former way of life, to put off your old self, which is being corrupted by its deceitful desires; to be made new in the attitude of your minds; and to put on the new self, created to be like God in true righteousness and holiness.

EPHESIANS 4:22-24, NIV

"Self-help" has swiftly become the cure-all of the masses, persuading us to seek within our own hearts the answers to life's many problems. As Robert Murray McCheyne points out, that philosophy is severely flawed.

Learn much of your own heart; and when you have learned all you can, remember that you have seen but a few yards into a pit that is unfathomable. "The heart is deceitful above all things, and desperately wicked: who can know it?" (Jeremiah 17:9).

That stated, McCheyne directs our focus to the One who created us—the only one from which our help comes.

Learn much of the Lord Jesus. For every look at yourself, take ten looks at Christ. He is altogether lovely. Such infinite majesty, yet such meekness and grace, and all for sinners—even the chief! Live much in the smiles of God. Bask in His beams. Feel His all-seeing eye settled on you in love, and repose in His almighty arms. Cry after divine knowledge, and lift up your voice for understanding. Seek her as silver, and search for her as for hidden treasure, according to Proverbs 2:4. Let your soul be filled with a heart-ravishing sense of the sweetness and excellency of Christ and all that is in Him. Let the Holy Spirit fill every chamber of your heart and there will be no room for folly or the world or Satan or the flesh.

As David said, "My help cometh from the LORD" (Psalm 121:2). Look to the Lord every day, for He alone has all the answers to your questions.

EXODUS 34; JOHN 13; PROVERBS 10; EPHESIANS 3

No man can serve two masters: for either he will hate the one, and love the other; or else he will hold to the one, and despise the other. Ye cannot serve God and mammon.

MATTHEW 6:24

In order to walk with God, you must do two things: Let go of the hand of evil and take hold of the hand of God.

Let go of the hand of evil. SHAKE IT LOOSE! The old life is like an old flame that doesn't want to go out. Don't allow Satan to make you homesick for the way you were. He is a liar. He will try to romance you. Before you were saved you probably received what I call "articles of affection" from him. To walk with God you must get rid of the emblems of your relationship. Don't sit down and compromise by saying, "We can just be friends." You cannot reason with evil. He has one plan—to steal, kill and destroy. But Jesus came to destroy the works of the devil!

Take hold of the hand of God. Holding God's hand is visible. People recognize that you're walking with God when you openly witness and testify of your relationship. Your life is clean and others can see the difference.

When you hold God's hand, it is also intimate. You must be very close to someone to abide under his shadow. If you draw near to God, by His side, He will draw near to you, by your side. When you hold God's hand you are going somewhere. You are no longer walking aimlessly without direction. Rather, you are walking purposefully with your eyes set on eternity with the Lover of your soul.

He Is Wonderful!

For unto us a child is born, unto us a son is given: and the government
shall be upon his shoulder: and his name shall be called Wonderful,
Counsellor, The mighty God, The everlasting Father, The Prince of Peace.
ISAIAH 9:6

It is easy to understand why many have referred to Charles Spurgeon as the Prince of Preachers. His eloquence in expressing his passion for Jesus is well demonstrated in this piece.

Trace the course of the Savior's life, and all throughout He is wonderful. Isn't it marvelous that He submitted to the taunts and jeers of His enemies—that He allowed His accusers to surround Him, like dogs encircling Him? Isn't it amazing that He bridled His anger when blasphemy was uttered against His sacred person? Had you or I possessed His matchless might, we might have dashed our enemies down the brow of the hill. We probably would never have submitted to the shame and spitting. No, we would have looked at them, and with one fierce look of wrath, dashed their spirits into eternal torment.

But He bore it all, keeping His noble spirit—the Lion of the Tribe of Judah, but bearing still the lamb-like character. The humble man before His foes, a weary man, and full of woes. Jesus of Nazareth was the King of Heaven and yet He was a poor, despised, persecuted, slandered man. While I believe it, I never can understand it. I bless Him for it, love Him for it, I desire to praise His name forever for His infinite willingness to suffer for me. But I can never pretend to understand it. His name must all His life long be called *Wonderful*.

Dipped in the Blood

No temptation has overtaken you but such as is common to man;
and God is faithful, who will not allow you to be tempted beyond what
you are able, but with the temptation will provide the way of escape also,
that you may be able to endure it.

1 CORINTHIANS 10:13, NASB

Born in 1600, William Bridge took his obscure place in history as a nonconformist divine. Reading this excerpt from some of his works makes it is easy to see how he may have ruffled the feathers of the elite in his day.

> Think not to comfort or relieve yourself in temptation with mere philosophical or moral reasons. For the disease of temptation is stronger than that remedy. Temptations answered by reason will return again; but temptations dipped in the Blood of Christ will return no more, or not with such violence and success. You see how it is with a candle that is blown out, it is easily lighted again; but if you put it into water, then it is more difficult to light. So temptations blown out with resolutions and moral reasons do easily return; but not so when quenched in Christ's Blood.

Just days before the Lord miraculously delivered me on October 28, 1975, I was suffering with the effects of drug poisoning so severe I knew I was going out of my mind. A hospital physician filled me in on the benefits of their drug therapy treatment, which would help me "deal with my addiction." Fortunately, I knew enough to run out of that place. Days later, I was delivered—washed in the Blood of the Lamb! No more temptations! No more addictions!

Friend, you too will succeed by heeding Rev. Bridge's advice. We were never intended to merely "deal" with temptation but to overcome it by the Blood of the Lamb!

EXODUS 37; JOHN 16; PROVERBS 13; EPHESIANS 6

The Inner Sanctuary

The Holy Ghost this signifying, that the way into the holiest of all was not yet made manifest, while as the first tabernacle was yet standing.
HEBREWS 9:8

Christ has opened the Most Holy Place to all believers. The rending of the veil was a sign that a new covenant had been established, and now we can all enter into the Holy of Holies by the blood of the Lamb. However, as Andrew Murray describes in his exposition on the book of Hebrews, *The Holiest of All*, there are still those of us who have not been brought in.

Many believers never experience this life of the inner sanctuary—the more complete and abiding nearness to God. They have, in the outer court, seen the altar and received the pardon of sin. They have entered upon the service of God and seek to do His will, but the joy of His presence as their abiding portion they know not. Very often, they do not know that there is a better life, an entering within the veil, a real dwelling in the secret of God's presence. They need the Holy Spirit to work in them the conviction that to them the way into the Holiest hath not yet been made manifest. Oh let us, if we have not yet entered in, give ourselves to pray for the discovery that there is an inner chamber; and that there is still the veil of the flesh—the life of the carnal Christian—that prevents the access. Only the Spirit that came from the throne when Jesus had rent the veil will bring us in.

Have you entered into the inner sanctuary? If not, ask the Holy Spirit to show you, and draw you in.

EXODUS 38; JOHN 17; PROVERBS 14; PHILIPPIANS 1

Step Back and Look Up

Set your affection on things above, not on things on the earth.
COLOSSIANS 3:2

Like many of his contemporaries, the English clergyman George Swinnock (1627-1673) was marked as a nonconformist. His affection was not set on the praise of man but on pleasing God. This passage, for example, demonstrates his understanding of the heart of the Father.

There are two lessons where God may choose to use affliction to wean us from the world.

First, that your affections would not be focused on earthly possessions. That which is created may become our idol by nature, but infinite wisdom makes it our grief, so it does not become our God. When children have too much freedom, they are mindless of home—but when abused by strangers, they hasten to their parents. The world is as a purgatory that it might not be our paradise. Every loss we suffer because of this world causes our affections to retreat and calls off our heart from the eager pursuit of these withering vanities.

Second, that you choose the good part that will never be taken from you. Man's heart will be fixed on searching for hope and happiness. God may therefore put out our candles that we may look up to the sun. It wasn't until the prodigal met with a famine that he regarded his father.

Are you facing things that seem difficult or even, at times, hurtful? Step back and look up. Set your affection above, on God alone. Ask Him to bring divine revelation to the situation. You may discover that your temporary affliction was necessary in order to bring you to a better place.

EXODUS 39; JOHN 18; PROVERBS 15; PHILIPPIANS 2

For you have been called for this purpose, since Christ also suffered for you, leaving you an example for you to follow in His steps.
1 PETER 2:21, NASB

The Crusade of the Christ Child was marked by **submission**. Jesus was submitted, yielded to the leadership of His heavenly Father. Do you follow that example?

His Crusade was marked by **servanthood**. Jesus knew from where He came and where He was going, (John 13:3). Because of this, He had no problem being a servant to all. Your certainty of where you come from and where you are going will enable you to be a servant in like manner.

The Christ Child's crusade was marked by **seriousness**. Jesus took life very seriously. He was sober-minded, not given to silliness or idleness. Are you following that pattern?

His Crusade was marked by the **supernatural**. Everywhere He went, signs and wonders followed. Are you following Him? Are signs and wonders following you?

The Crusade of the Christ Child was marked by a **specific purpose**. Jesus came to save that which was lost and destroy the works of the devil. He came to save you. Have you sought Him for His will—His specific purpose for your life?

His Crusade was marked by **sacrifice**. He came to give something for the sake of something else. Do you live a life of sacrifice?

His Crusade ended in **supremacy** (Revelation 5:5). If you continue to follow the Lord, you too are destined to win! In the end, you will reign with Him for eternity.

You are my hiding place; you shall preserve me from trouble; you shall
surround me with songs of deliverance.
PSALM 32:7, NKJV

There are times when Christians go through tremendous attacks.
These are seasons when it seems the devil is at every door and God's
presence can't be felt. Scared and bewildered as the enemy assails,
some wrestle with depression and even consider death an inviting
option. But I've got good news! There is a refuge. Consider what the
Puritan minister John Owen wrote over three centuries ago.

> Christ is a "hiding place." Imagine someone caught on top of
> a hillside during a storm with lightning and squalling winds.
> He would want nothing more than to find a hiding place
> until the tempest was over. Consider a boat at sea, when fierce
> winds have driven it from all its anchors. With nothing to
> keep it from being split open on the next rock, a safe harbor—
> a hiding place—is the great desire and expectation of the poor
> ones in that boat. Is this the condition of the soul? Do strong
> temptations beat upon it, ready to hurry it down into sin and
> folly, so that it has no rest from them? With one blast imme-
> diately succeeding another—the soul begins to faint, to be
> weary, give over, and say, "I'm going to die, I can't hold out
> much longer!" Fly to His bosom, retreat into His arms. Expect
> relief by faith in Him, and you will be safe.

Don't give in, friend. Don't compromise. Rely on God's Word—
His promise to you. Remember: "No weapon that is formed against
you shall prosper" (Isaiah 54:17, *NASB*). He alone is our hiding place,
our strong tower, our almighty Father!

LEVITICUS 1; JOHN 20; PROVERBS 17; PHILIPPIANS 4

Be of Good Courage

And Caleb stilled the people before Moses, and said, Let us go up at once,
and possess it; for we are well able to overcome it.
NUMBERS 13:30

One of my favorite statements by Dwight L. Moody is, "If God be your partner, make your plans large." Proverbs 3:6 instructs us to acknowledge God in all our ways and He will direct our paths. Unfortunately, our undertakings often do not include God. As a result, we see ourselves for what we are: tiny and incapable. This passage by Moody penetrates to the core of the matter.

> Courage is necessary to success in Christian work. I have yet to find a man who is easily discouraged that amounts to anything anywhere. If a minister is easily discouraged his people soon find it out and lose their courage, also. If a Sunday school teacher hasn't any courage, his class will find it out and leave him. About the most worthless set of people you can find is a lot of faint-hearted Sunday school teachers. If we are to have any success, we must be of good courage, and we must also meditate upon, and believe in, and obey the word of God. God hasn't any use for a man who is all the time looking on the dark side. What he wants is a man who isn't afraid. "Be of good courage," says He, "fear nothing; believe that I am willing to use you, and then I will use you."

When Caleb, at 80 years old, proclaimed, "we are well able to overcome it," he knew the great God, Jehovah, was with them. Caleb knew who his partner was. As a result, he planned to succeed. Friend, if God is your partner, be of good courage. Nothing is impossible for Him!

LEVITICUS 2—3; JOHN 21; PROVERBS 18; COLOSSIANS 1

Crumbling Walls

Except the LORD build the house, they labour in vain that build it: except the LORD keep the city, the watchman waketh but in vain.
PSALM 127:1

From the cradle to the grave we are busy constructing a building called "our house." None of us had a choice about where to build; we were born into certain circumstances, and that is where our foundation was laid. Early on we started building walls for privacy and protection from others. Fears and phobias resulting from bad experiences caused us to build the walls ever thicker. But not every building that looks good is stable. You see, Jesus Christ is a master builder and architect. He knows how to construct lives and He knows the foundations we are built upon.

Jesus is not only a master builder, He's also in the demolition business. He can tear down our temporary structures in order to build something that will last for eternity. The life of Saul of Tarsus (see Acts 9) is a clear testimony of this fact. Saul had spent his life building a "house" that would be the pride of any Pharisee and would surely catch the eye of the God of his fathers. However, in one swift motion the Master Builder leveled the house Saul had built, and in three days He reconstructed a temple fit for the King of kings.

All that we build is in vain, my friend. Maybe you've built part of your spiritual life on an unstable, sandy foundation. Or perhaps walls of fear and hurt from the past still remain. Ask the Lord to remove the old walls and He will build a new foundation and construct walls that can truly withstand the storms of life.

The Perfect Body

Who, by the power that enables him to bring everything under his control,
will transform our lowly bodies so that they will be like his glorious body.
PHILIPPIANS 3:21, NIV

Distinguished among the most successful preachers of his day, Richard Baxter (1615-1691) was known for his analytical yet heartfelt presentations of the gospel. In this concise analysis of death—and the subsequent resurrection of the saints—Baxter sums up one of the most delightful rewards a disciple of Jesus has to look forward to.

> At death, the souls of the true believers go to Christ and enter into a state of happiness. On the last and final day, the body will be raised and united to the soul, and the Lord Jesus Christ will come in glory to judge the world, to openly acquit and justify the righteous. He will then condemn the ungodly, be glorified in His saints, and admired by all them that believe. And the saints will also judge the world, and they themselves will enter into everlasting glory. Their eternal home will be in heaven, near God and in the presence of His glory. Their company will be only the holy angels and glorified saints and will be perfectly one in God forever. Bodies shall be perfected and made immortal, spiritual, incorruptible and glorious, shining like the stars. No longer to be subject to hunger or thirst, cold or weariness, shame, pain or any of the frailties that now hinder, but the believer will be made like the glorified body of Christ.

There isn't an exercise machine on the planet that can give you the "perfect body." To be physically fit is wise, but to be spiritually fit should be our highest goal. Let us labor fervently to remain in Christ and attain this resurrection!

The Ultimate Peace

Yea, though I walk through the valley of the shadow of death, I will fear no evil: for thou art with me; thy rod and thy staff they comfort me.
PSALM 23:4

English-born Isaac Watts (1674-1748) came to know the Lord at a very early age and set his course toward the ministry. At age four, he began studying Latin, Greek and Hebrew. By 16, he began his studies at an academy in London where he remained three years, "studying with such zeal and application as permanently to injure his health." By age 33, he released a collection of 210 hymns for the church—the first of its kind. He battled for his health the last 36 years of his life in order to continue preaching and writing. How could he continue to drive himself so hard and accomplish so much for the kingdom of God? Because Watts knew his Shepherd. He had followed the Lord's divine leading and had heard His sweet voice.

Let me hear Your voice, Jesus, my Savior, let me hear Your voice walking upon the waters; when I am tossed about upon the waves of distress and difficulty, speak to my soul and say, "It is I, be not afraid."
Jesus can support me in the heaviest distresses, though all the sorrows I fear should come upon me. He can bear me on the wings of faith and hope, high above all the turmoil and commotion of life: He can carry me through the shadow of the dark valley and scatter all the terrors of it.

Watts was intimate with Jesus. That, dear saint, plain and simple, is the ultimate peace. When you remain in close fellowship with the Lord, no matter what valley of death you find yourself in, the Great Shepherd is with you—against whom no foe can stand!

April 4

Rise Up and Pray!

O Lord, hear! O Lord, forgive! O Lord, listen and take action!
For Thine own sake, O my God, do not delay, because Thy city and
Thy people are called by Thy name.
DANIEL 9:19, NASB

Jesus said to His disciples, "Watch ye and pray....The spirit truly is ready, but the flesh is weak" (Mark 14:38). In Romans 13:14, Paul warns us to "make not provision for the flesh, to fulfil the lusts thereof." The flesh lusts after sleep and carnal delights; the spirit desires communion with God.

Robert M. McCheyne recognized this war within, which is why he encouraged his congregation all the more to rise up and pray. He once wrote to them from the mission field:

It is said of John Welch, minister of Ayr, that he would always sleep with a plaid [a blanket] upon his bed to wrap around himself when he arose in the night to pray. He used to spend whole nights in wrestling with God for Zion and for the purity of the Church of Scotland, and he wondered how Christians could lie all night in bed without rising to pray. Oh! We have few Welches now; therefore our church is so dim, and our land a barren wilderness. Dear Christians, I often think it strange that ever we should be in heaven, yet so many in hell, through our soul-destroying carelessness. The Lord pardon the past, and stir you up for the future. I learn that you are more stirred up to pray since I left, both in secret and unitedly. God grant it be so. Continue in it, dear children. Plead and wrestle with God, showing Him that the cause is His own, and that it is all for His own glory to arise and have mercy upon Zion.

Make provision for the spirit, not the flesh, friend. Live prepared for duty, be it day or night.

God's Will for Me

"For I know the plans that I have for you," declares the LORD, "plans for welfare and not for calamity to give you a future and a hope."
JEREMIAH 29:11, NASB

You will never know the will of God for your life while relying on your own finite understanding. Paul exhorts us to be transformed by the renewing of our minds that we may prove what is the good, acceptable and perfect will of God (see Romans 12:2). Why? Because our thoughts are not His thoughts, nor our ways His ways (see Isaiah 55:8,9).

Often, the will of God will not be attained without personal pain. Jesus told the thief on the cross, "Today shalt thou be with me in paradise" (Luke 23:43). What a soothing thought: paradise with Jesus! But then, Jesus died —and the thief was left behind. Suddenly, searing pain flooded the man's body as a Roman soldier took a rod and broke his legs. Note a powerful truth here: There can be a lot of pain between the altar and the promise.

The will of God requires that you press through in order to attain it. Don't give up! In his letter to the Philippians, Paul encouraged them to forget those things which were past and press on toward what was ahead. Giving up halfway there just won't do.

Fulfilling God's will in this life will lead to your promotion in the next. Paul spoke with confidence about what it would be like when his days on earth were through. As he told Timothy, "There is laid up for me a crown of righteousness, which the Lord, the righteous judge, shall give me at that day" (2 Timothy 4:8). Paul suffered much in his body, but he was greatly rewarded for never losing sight of the goal!

No Matter the Source

My son, despise not the chastening of the LORD; neither be weary of his correction: for whom the LORD loveth he correcteth; even as a father the son in whom he delighteth.

PROVERBS 3:11,12

God can, and will, bring about His desires in us—one way or another. At times He may even use those around us to carry out His desire. As Hannah Whitall Smith writes:

> A very good illustration of this may be found in the familiar act of a mother giving medicine to her dearly loved child. The bottle holds the medicine, but the mother gives it—the bottle is not responsible, but the mother. No matter how full her closet may be of bottles of medicine, the mother will not allow one drop to be given to the child unless she believes it will be good for it; but when she does believe it will be good for her darling, the very depth of her love compels her to force it on the child, no matter how bitter it may taste.
>
> The human beings around us are often the bottles that hold our medicine, but it is our Father's hand of love that pours it out and compels us to drink it. The medicine that these human "bottles" hold is prescribed for us and given to us by the Great Physician of our souls—who is seeking thereby to heal all our spiritual diseases. Shall we rebel against the human bottles then? Shall we not rather take thankfully from our Father's hand the medicine they contain and say joyfully, "Thy will be done" in everything that comes to us, no matter what its source may be?

What wonderful medicine to keep in mind the next time we find ourselves rubbed the wrong way! Perhaps, keeping today's text in mind, we will find it was for our own good!

LEVITICUS 9; PSALM 10; PROVERBS 24; 1 THESSALONIANS 3

Awaken the Watchman!

*But if the watchman sees the sword coming and does not blow the trumpet
to warn the people and the sword comes and takes the life of one of them,
that man will be taken away because of his sin,
but I will hold the watchman accountable for his blood.*

EZEKIEL 33:6, NIV

This word from Charles Finney is a hard one, but I would be negligent if I were to omit such an alarming passage from this collection of "daily awakenings."

> If your spiritual ears were opened, you would hear the chariot wheels rolling, the great Judge coming in His car of thunder, the sword of Death gleaming in the air—ready to smite down the hardened sinner. But hear that professedly Christian father pray for his ungodly son. Feeling he *ought* to pray for him regularly he begins, but he hardly knows or thinks what he is praying about. God says, "Pray for your dying son! Cry for him while Mercy yet lingers and pardon can be found."
>
> Where are the Christian parents that pray as for a son sentenced and on death row? They say they believe the Bible, but do they? Do they act as if they believed half of its awful truth about sentenced sinners ready to go down to an eternal hell?
>
> What is wrong with the one who professes Christ but has no spirit of prayer, no power with God? He is an infidel.

Rise up and cry out to God with unceasing petition on behalf of the unsaved! They are blinded to the danger ahead, but you are not. Allow this passage to stir your heart with compassion. You won't be able to reach the entire sin-filled world, but your prayers for mercy will reach the ears of the God who can!

Death of Me

Knowing this, that our old man is crucified with him, that the body of sin
might be destroyed, that henceforth we should not serve sin.
For he that is dead is freed from sin.
ROMANS 6:6,7

If you are going to be a Christian, the death of Me is certain. It is impossible to truly follow a self-denying Christ without first engaging in the denial of self. The term "self-denial" is too often mistaken to mean self-control—simply reining in our will, desires and dreams by some higher element of our being. That, however, is not at all what Jesus meant. We are to live as He did, treating self as nonexistent. He never meant for us to merely control self—but to *die to* self.

The death of Me will be painful. Crucifixion hurts. Since we cannot nail ourselves to the Cross, we find the deed is greatly accomplished by others, and most often, publicly. Regardless, like Paul, we too must die daily and quit allowing Me to crawl off the cross!

Take heart! The death of Me will be rewarding. Jesus, our self-denying role model, promised life "more abundantly" (John 10:10) to those who experience the death of Me. There is not only reward here on earth but eternal reward as well: "For whosoever will save his life shall lose it: and whosoever will lose his life for my sake shall find it" (Matthew 16:25).

Concerning the resurrection of our "old man," the Holy Spirit is faithful to check for a pulse. He will tell us if there are signs of life, and where they are. It is then up to us to take action and bring about the death of Me, "for he that is dead is freed from sin"!

The Riches of the Bible

How sweet are thy words unto my taste! yea, sweeter than honey to my mouth! Through thy precepts I get understanding: therefore I hate every false way. Thy word is a lamp unto my feet, and a light unto my path.
PSALM 119:103-105

William Guthrie (1620-1665), eminent clergyman of the Presbyterian Church of Scotland, was one who had great ability to draw upon the riches of God's Word, and in this passage he turns our thoughts to the same.

> Wondrous book! It humbles the lofty and exalts the lowliest; it condemns the best and yet saves the worst. It engages the study of angels and is not above the understanding of a little child. It heals by wounding and kills to make alive. It is an armory of heavenly weapons, a laboratory of infallible medicines, a mine of exhaustless wealth. Teaching kings how to reign, and subjects how to obey; masters how to rule, and domestics how to serve; pastors how to preach, and people how to hear; teachers how to instruct, and pupils how to learn; husbands how to love their wives, and wives how to obey their husbands. Divinely adapted to our circumstances, whatever these may be, we can say of this book as David said of the giant's sword, "Give me that, there is none like it." Rob us of the Bible, and our sky has lost its sun; and even in the best of other books we have nothing but the glimmer of twinkling stars.

How such a divinely inspired work could merely sit decoratively on a mantel, collecting dust, is beyond my understanding. Many American homes contain a Holy Bible, yet it is unfortunate that many Americans do not realize the value of what they have. As Leonard Ravenhill once said to me, I now say to you of the Bible: "Don't just go through this book, but instead, let this book go through you."

LEVITICUS 13; PSALMS 15—16; PROVERBS 27; 2 THESSALONIANS 1

The Way of the Christian

But thou, O man of God, flee these things; and follow after righteousness,
godliness, faith, love, patience, meekness.
1 TIMOTHY 6:11

In the face of misery, the way of the world is to drown one's sorrows with alcohol, drugs or other distractions. The way of the Christian, however, is to drown one's sorrows in repentant, prayerful tears. The latter, as John Flavel describes, offers eternal—not temporary—relief.

> Go your way, Christian, to your God; get to your knees in the cloudy and dark day; retire from all people and distractions that you may have full liberty with God and there pour out your heart before Him in free, full, and brokenhearted confessions of sin. Judge yourself worthy of hell, as well as of this trouble; justify God in all His smartest blows and beg Him in this distress to put under you the everlasting arms. Entreat one smile, one gracious look, to brighten your darkness and cheer your drooping spirit. Say with the prophet Jeremiah, "Be not a terror unto me: thou art my hope in the day of evil" (17:17). You may be surprised at what relief such a course will afford you. Surely, if your heart is sincere in this course, you shall be able to say with that holy man, "In the multitude of my thoughts which I had within me, thy comforts delighted my soul" (Psalm 94:19).

There is no greater comfort than comes from God, and no other way there but the way of the Christian. Be sincere in your journey, for as Flavel further states, "Sincerity is the holy oil which makes the wheels of the soul run nimbly, even in the difficult paths of obedience."

More of Thy Likeness

Lead me in thy truth, and teach me:
for thou art the God of my salvation; on thee do I wait all the day.
PSALM 25:5

Are you growing in the image of your Creator? According to Horatius Bonar, "A Christian is growing when he elevates his Master, talks less of what he himself is doing, and becomes smaller and smaller in his own esteem; until, like the morning star, he fades away before the rising sun." The following journal entry by missionary David Brainerd will surely awaken a new hunger and thirst in your soul.

> I woke up this morning thirsty for more of God. This evening, I enjoyed a precious season of time in sweet meditations of the Bible; divine things opened with clearness and certainty and had a divine stamp upon them. My soul was also strengthened and refreshed in prayer; I delighted to continue in the duty of praying for my fellow Christians and dear brothers in the ministry, and was blessed by the dear Lord for such pleasure. Oh, how sweet and precious it is to have a clear understanding and tender sense of the mystery of godliness, of true holiness, and of *likeness to the best of beings!* Oh, what blessedness it is to be as much like God as it is possible for a creature to be like his Creator! Lord, give me more of your likeness; I will be satisfied when I awake with it.

That passionate seeking after God is the key, my friend. All else is stale religion. In the words of J. B. Stoney, "The young Christian who is growing is more interesting and more helpful to others than the most advanced one who is stationary." Always stay "young" in Christ, ever-growing, ever-seeking more of His likeness.

Follow the Leader

Then said Jesus unto his disciples, If any man will come after me,
let him deny himself, and take up his cross, and follow me.
MATTHEW 16:24

Childhood games of "follow the leader" provided silly ways to pass the time—but as the children of God we find that follow the leader is not a mere game at all, but a delightfully intimate discipline. Though the stakes are much higher, the "rules" for following Jesus are pretty much the same, as this passage from Andrew Murray illustrates.

His followers must walk in the very path in which He walks. Jesus came and was made like us—we must come and be made like Him. His suffering death is not only substitution and atonement for us. (It is that, thank God! But it is much more.) His death calls to fellowship and conformity. The substitution rests on our identification in Him, and out of that conformity has its growth and strength. The Lamb of God has no salvation nor perfection to give us but His own meek spirit of entire dependence and absolute submission to God. The meekness and humility that was needful for God to perfect in Him are as needful for us. We must suffer and be crucified and die with Him. Death to self and the world, at the cost of any suffering or self-denial, is the only path to glory the Leader of our salvation has opened up to us.

Be encouraged today, by the words of our glorious Leader: "My sheep hear my voice, and I know them, and they follow me: and I give unto them eternal life; and they shall never perish, neither shall any man pluck them out of my hand" (John 10:27,28). Jesus, lead on!

LEVITICUS 16; PSALM 19; PROVERBS 30; 1 TIMOTHY 1

Cross-Check, Please!

Therefore I say unto you, Take no thought for your life, what ye shall eat, or what ye shall drink; nor yet for your body, what ye shall put on. Is not the life more than meat, and the body than raiment?

MATTHEW 6:25

If you've ever flown on an airline, you're probably familiar with the term "carry-on baggage." Now, there are specific size and weight restrictions for those two burdens you're allowed—and that is a good thing. You simply can't go on with too much carry-on baggage! Yet I've watched as would-be passengers argue with ground personnel as the cargo bay closed and the plane prepared to leave the terminal. The same problem exists spiritually. People try to make it on this flight called Life with way too much baggage.

On most airlines, one of the final instructions the captain announces just before landing ends with the phrase, "Prepare for arrival and cross-check, please." The crew then proceeds to check that all is secure and in order, as the flight has almost reached its final destination.

It won't be long on this flight called Life before we hear the Holy Captain announce: "Ladies and Gentlemen, we are on our final approach to Glory land Intercontinental Airport. We will be landing from the east on Golden Runway #7. Please remain seated with your hands lifted in exuberant praise position as we make our final approach! Pastors, evangelists, Christian workers: Prepare for arrival; cross-check, please!!"

Have you checked your burdens at the Cross today, friend? Don't be left standing at the gate. Free yourself at the foot of the Cross and enjoy the journey!

LEVITICUS 17; PSALMS 20—21; PROVERBS 31; 1 TIMOTHY 2

God Calls Them Jewels

And they shall be mine, saith the LORD of hosts,
in that day when I make up my jewels;
and I will spare them, as a man spareth his own son that serveth him.
MALACHI 3:17

In light of all the garbage God has to listen to on a daily basis, such as cursing, swearing and blaspheming, what a special joy it must be when He hears one of His children singing His praise or testifying of His marvelous works. That one who fears God, loves Him, honors Him and walks in His ways is of special interest to God, as the distinguished English pastor Thomas Watson explains.

What rare persons the godly are: "The righteous is more excellent than his neighbour" (Proverbs 12:26). As the flower of the sun, as the wine of Lebanon, as the sparkling upon Aaron's breastplate, such is the ardent splendor of a person embellished with godliness. The godly are precious, therefore they are set apart for God: "Know that the LORD hath set apart him that is godly for himself" (Psalm 4:3). We set apart things that are precious; the godly are set apart as God's peculiar treasure (Psalm 135:4); as His royal diadem (Isaiah 62:3); the godly are the excellent of the earth (Psalm 16:3); comparable to fine gold (Lamentations 4:2); double refined (Zechariah 13:9). They are the glory of the creation, (Isaiah 60:13). God calls them jewels (Malachi 3:17).

Dear saint, make it your determined purpose today to catch God's eye—be one of His precious, set-apart jewels, sparkling as you reflect His radiance all around. Nothing can snatch you from His hand, "for whoever touches you touches the apple of his eye" (Zechariah 2:8, *NIV*).

LEVITICUS 18; PSALM 22; ECCLESIASTES 1; 1 TIMOTHY 3

Driving the World Mad

And as he thus spake for himself, Festus said with a loud voice, Paul,
thou art beside thyself; much learning doth make thee mad.
ACTS 26:24

History records that Reverend John Wesley was charged with preaching madness. "But you drive them out of their senses—you make them mad," protested his accusers. Wesley responded by declaring that the charge deserved his deepest consideration.

> First, I grant, it is my earnest desire to drive all the world into what you probably call madness (I mean, *Christianity*); to make them just as mad as Paul when he was so accounted by Festus. The counting all things on earth but dung and dross, so we may win Christ...the trampling under foot all the pleasures of the world...the seeking no treasure but in heaven...the having no desire of the praise of men, and the being exceeding glad when men revile us and persecute us, and say all manner of evil against us falsely...the giving God thanks when our father and mother forsake us, when we have neither food to eat nor raiment to put on nor a friend but what shoots out bitter words, nor a place where to lay our head. This is utter distraction in your account; but in God's it is sober, rational religion; the genuine fruit, not of a distempered brain, not of a sickly imagination, but of the power of God in the heart, of victorious love, "and of a sound mind."

It's high time all Christians desire, as Wesley, to indeed drive the world mad. Perhaps we should endeavor to be less "sane" and more "mad about Jesus," in order that we too, could have such a powerful impact.

LEVITICUS 19; PSALMS 23—24; ECCLESIASTES 2; 1 TIMOTHY 4

True Christianity

For consider Him who has endured such hostility by sinners against Himself, so that you may not grow weary and lose heart.
HEBREWS 12:3, NASB

The Imitation of Christ by Thomas à Kempis exposes the true grit of Christianity as few other works have. Take heart as you consider this encouraging discourse about the burden of tribulation and the confidence of divine comfort.

Christ's whole life was a cross and martyrdom—yet do you seek rest and joy for yourself? You are deceived if you seek any other thing than to suffer tribulations; for this whole mortal life is full of miseries and marked on every side with crosses. The higher a person has advanced in the Spirit, so much the heavier crosses he often finds. Nevertheless, this man, though in so many ways afflicted, is not without refreshing comfort, for he understands that great benefit is accrued to him by the bearing of his own cross. All the burden of tribulation is turned into the confidence of divine comfort.

It is not man's natural inclination or ability to bear the cross, love the cross, chastise the body and bring it into subjection; willingly suffer reproach, despise oneself and wish to be despised; endure all adversities and losses and desire no prosperity in this world. You are not able to accomplish anything of this kind alone. But, if you trust in the Lord, strength shall be given you from heaven, and the world and the flesh shall be made subject to your command. Set yourself, therefore, like a good and faithful servant of Christ, to boldly and courageously bear the cross of the Lord, who out of love, was crucified for you.

LEVITICUS 20; PSALM 25; ECCLESIASTES 3; 1 TIMOTHY 5

Then the LORD God called to the man, and said to him, "Where are you?"
GENESIS 3:9, NASB

Where are you from? Adam and Eve were created by God in His own image, placed in a fruitful garden and put in charge of everything there (Genesis 1:27-30). What a start! Reading the story of the prodigal son (Luke 15:11-32), we see that he was raised in a good home, with a father who loved him dearly.

Where have you been? What have you been doing with your life? The prodigal had been blowing it. He had taken his inheritance and squandered it on riotous living. Adam and Eve should have been fellowshiping with the Father, enjoying the good things of God. But instead of dining with Deity, they were off in no-man's-land, dealing with the devil.

Where are you now? Have you lost your spiritual appetite? Are you backslidden, growing worldly in your actions and desires and less troubled about sin? Adam and Eve found themselves cowering in their nakedness, hiding from their Creator behind a bush. The prodigal, who had been partying in the devil's playpen, was now in a filthy pigpen, craving anything to eat.

Where are you going? Adam and Eve suffered severe punishment for their disobedience. The prodigal was warmly welcomed home in his repentance. Ask yourself these questions: Where have I been? Where am I right now with God? Where am I going in my relationship with Him?

Don't Be a Busybody

*But let none of you suffer as a murderer, a thief, an evildoer,
or as a busybody in other people's matters.*
1 PETER 4:15, NKJV

The apostle Paul warned Timothy about being a busybody, instructing him that "No soldier in active service entangles himself in the affairs of everyday life, so that he may please the one who enlisted him as a soldier" (2 Timothy 2:4, *NASB*). William Jay (1769-1853) believed in two great truths: "that if we are saved it is entirely of God's grace; and if we are lost it will be entirely from ourselves." That, perhaps, is why he had such a clear understanding of the consequences of not obeying today's text.

Let me not be entangled in the affairs of this life. Let me keep myself as detached as possible from things that do not concern me. Let me not embarrass myself, as a meddler and busybody, in other men's matters but study to be quiet and to do my own business; and pray for the peace of the country through which I am passing; and be thankful for every advantage I enjoy in my temporary exile; and let my affection be set on things that are above; and my conversation be always in heaven.

In the words of Adam Clarke (1762-1832), "If men were as much in earnest to get their souls saved as they are to prepare them for perdition, heaven would be highly peopled, and devils would be their own companions." Practice minding your own business, friend. This is war, and the enemy is willing to take you any way he can. How dreadful that it be by our own devices—or worse, by default, for our not heeding the Word of God.

LEVITICUS 22; PSALMS 28—29; ECCLESIASTES 5; 2 TIMOTHY 1

Staying Cleansed

There is a generation that are pure in their own eyes,
and yet is not washed from their filthiness.
PROVERBS 30:12

Frederick Brotherton (F. B.) Meyer, born in London in 1847, was a highly regarded Baptist pastor, noted to have preached over 15,000 sermons and to have itinerated in every continent before his death in 1929. As evidenced by this passage, in all his achievements he never lost sight of his personal need of constant cleansing from sin.

Sin is something more than that of which our *conscience* convicts us. Our conscience may excuse or rationalize our sins, or may fail to detect them for want of proper enlightenment, or may be misled by the practices and sentiment of others. There is more sin in us than any of us know. If we think we have passed a day without conscious sin, we have only to wait till an intense light is flashed on our motives and intentions and we shall see specks and flaws. If we do not actually violate known commands, there may be a grievous coming short of the infinite standard of God's perfection. It is very needful, then, for us to be perpetually cleansed in the precious blood of Christ. We must ask to be forgiven for the many sins which we know not, as well as for those we know. The work of confession and forgiveness must therefore go on to life's end applied to each heart and conscience by the Holy Spirit.

Yes, in all of us there is more sin in our lives than we know. Ask the Holy Spirit to show you anything that would grieve the heart of God. Be quick to repent, and stay washed in the precious Blood of the Lamb.

I Give You Rest

Peace I leave with you, my peace I give unto you:
not as the world giveth, give I unto you.
Let not your heart be troubled, neither let it be afraid.
JOHN 14:27

It was Thomas Watson who said, "The godly man, when he dies, enters into peace; but while he lives, peace must enter into him." That can sometimes seem to be a difficult transaction when war is raging all around. However, this illustration by Henry Drummond (1851-1897) may make it a great deal easier to realize.

Two painters each painted a picture to illustrate his conception of rest. The first chose for his scene a still, lone lake among the far-off mountains. The second threw on his canvas a thundering waterfall with a fragile birch tree bending over the foam; at the fork of the branch, almost wet with the white water's spray, a robin sat on its nest. The first [painting] was only stagnation; the last was rest.

Christ's life outwardly was one of the most troubled lives that was ever lived; tempest and tumult, tumult and tempest, the waves breaking over it all the time till His worn body was laid in the grave. But the inner life was a sea of glass. The great calm was always there. At any moment you might have gone to Him and found rest. And even when His enemies were dogging Him in the streets of Jerusalem, He turned to His disciples and offered them, as a last legacy, "My peace."

Today as every day, Jesus says, "Come unto me, all ye that labour and are heavy laden, and I will give you rest" (Matthew 11:28). It is available...and it is your legacy.

LEVITICUS 24; PSALM 31; ECCLESIASTES 7; 2 TIMOTHY 3

April 21

This Is War!

Who is this King of glory?
The LORD strong and mighty, the LORD mighty in battle.
PSALM 24:8

There is a wicked war raging between heaven and hell. The battleground is the mind of man. The spoil of war is your soul. No one is exempt from this conflict. Perhaps this simple acrostic teaching on the word "war" will help you in the fight.

Warning signs—God doesn't want any to perish, but all to come to repentance. He was grieved that He had ever made man on the face of the earth, yet He warned Noah, though no one else believed. God sent angels to bring Lot and his family from Sodom just before its violent destruction. Likewise, the Lord sends His messengers to warn you.

Attack—From the time we are born there are at least three things against us at all times. The world, with temptation all around; the flesh, full of our own selfish cravings; and the devil, who is subtle, slanderous, fierce and deceitful. Some have not heeded the warning signs and have ended up in the midst of a full-fledged attack.

Refuge—A refuge is a shelter or protection from danger. To Noah, God sent the ark. To sinners, God sent Jesus Christ, His only Son. Jesus is our shelter in the storm. He is our Rock, our mighty fortress!

Yes, there is a spiritual war raging. I thank God for the battle—it keeps me alert. Always remember: "The LORD your God is the one who goes with you, to fight for you against your enemies, to save you" (Deuteronomy 20:4, *NASB*).

When Jesus Sees His Image

If a man therefore purge himself from these, he shall be a vessel unto honour, sanctified, and meet for the master's use, and prepared unto every good work.
2 TIMOTHY 2:21

To refine something is to free it from impurities, thus improving and eventually even bringing it to perfection. Alexander Dickson, author of *Beauty for Ashes,* presents one of the best parallels regarding the process of God's refinement in the lives of His children.

> The refiner receives the precious metals fresh from the mines, and finding them mixed with many worthless substances, before they can be of much use to anybody they must be purified, so he puts them in a fining-pot and subjects them to an intense heat. When the whole mass is melted, a separation takes place between the precious and the vile, and the precious becomes more precious because it is pure; and just as soon as the refiner can see his image in the seething gold, its purification is complete. That Refiner is our Kinsman Redeemer.
>
> His own self kindles the fire by which we are melted down and all our sins are burned away; and when He can see His own pure image in our pure hearts, for which He sits watching beside the furnace, then we are sanctified wholly and may be minted into money, or fashioned into vessels "meet for the Master's use."

Do not resent these times of refining. The heat may be intense, but the results will be immense. What a delight it must be for our Lord when He looks down and sees His image reflected in the lives of His own.

LEVITICUS 26; PSALM 33; ECCLESIASTES 9; TITUS 1

Don't Forget to Look Up

She gave this name to the LORD who spoke to her: "You are the God who sees me," for she said, "I have now seen the One who sees me."
GENESIS 16:13, NIV

I once heard a story of a young boy who went with his father to a neighbor's cornfield to hold a bag while his father filled it with stolen ears of corn.

Just before the wicked work was begun, the child noticed that his father climbed up on the fence and looked all around—north, south, east and west—to be sure they were not seen by anybody. The boy, observing his father's precautionary measures, took him gently by the hand and said, "Father, you forgot to look up."

Never was a word more fitly spoken. It fell like a hammer, like a thunderbolt, on the heart of the father, and he went home to steal no more.

It is a shame that such simple, childlike truth has not so penetrated the heart of everyone. As the psalmist David said, "Where can I go from your Spirit? Where can I flee from your presence?" (Psalm 139:7, *NIV*).

Wherever we go and whatever we do, He is there...and He sees. I have often said there are always three witnesses to everything we do—the Father, the Son and the Holy Ghost. We are always being watched. Let us never forget to look up, remembering that Jesus is always looking down. "The eyes of the LORD are in every place, beholding the evil and the good" (Proverbs 15:3).

LEVITICUS 27; PSALM 34; ECCLESIASTES 10; TITUS 2

April 24

Shake and Shake

*Meditate on these things; give yourself entirely to them,
that your progress may be evident to all.*
1 TIMOTHY 4:15, NKJV

Once, while attending Teen Challenge in Missouri, I worked as an apple picker in a nearby orchard. Just holding a ripe apple covered in the chill of early morning dew is terribly tantalizing. Can you imagine me not getting to eat one? I thoroughly enjoyed that fruitful experience. It was a little like what Charles Spurgeon points out about the promises of God.

> Get a promise every day and take it with you wherever you go. Mark it, learn it, and inwardly digest it. Don't do as some men do—who, out of Christian duty, read a chapter every morning, and they read one as long as your arm without understanding it at all. Instead, take out some choice text and pray for the Lord to remind you of it during the day. Do as Luther says: "When I get hold of a promise, I look upon it as I would a fruit tree. I think, There hang the fruits above my head, and if I would get them I must shake the tree to and fro." In the same way, I take a promise and meditate on it. I shake it to and fro and sometimes the mellow fruit falls into my hand. At other times, the fruit is less ready to fall, but I never give up until I get it. I shake and shake all day long. I turn the text over and over again and at last, the fruit drops down and my soul is comforted with it.

Just as no apple has ever tasted as sweet since that experience, the fruit of God's Word will never taste so sweet as when you "pick it" yourself. You can savor the fullness of it the rest of your days.

NUMBERS 1; PSALM 35; ECCLESIASTES 11; TITUS 3

Have Mercy on Me

O LORD, I have heard thy speech, and was afraid:
O LORD, revive thy work in the midst of the years, in the midst of the
years make known; in wrath remember mercy.

HABAKKUK 3:2

The prophet Habakkuk began his prayer in a state of fear. He had heard of all the deeds God had done to the sinful, disobedient nations, and he surely recognized his own sinful condition as well. In order to receive God's mercy you must first recognize your sinful condition.

Further, you must resign your position and humble yourself under God's mighty hand. God resists the proud but is gracious toward the humble. Habakkuk knew this and expressed it when he prayed, "Revive thy work."

God has had mercy upon us. We have an opportunity Habakkuk no doubt longed to see in his day. We have a Savior whose sacrifice made atonement for all our sins. Bleeding and in agony, with the forces of hell raging against Him, the precious Lamb of God asked for mercy...not for Himself but for you and me, saying, "Father, forgive *them*" (Luke 23:34, emphasis added). Now we must respond to that work of atonement in order to receive mercy.

Charles Wesley beautifully expressed his response to God's mercy in the words to his hymn, *Amazing Love*.

And can it be that I should gain an interest in the Savior's Blood? Died He for me, who caused His pain—for me, who Him to death pursued?

Wesley thoroughly understood that mercy is undeserved forgiveness. Let us always rejoice and give thanks that Jesus has given us the opportunity to escape wrath and obtain mercy.

NUMBERS 2; PSALM 36; ECCLESIASTES 12; PHILEMON 1

A Complete Turnabout

And God saw their works,
that they turned from their evil way; and God repented of the evil, that he
had said that he would do unto them; and he did it not.

JONAH 3:10

What are you waiting for?! That is a question to which I may never receive a satisfactory answer. Time and again at the close of countless altar calls—when the air itself is charged with the presence of a merciful, Holy God—there are still those who wait until the last possible moment to repent. If they only realized the eternal difference it would make in their lives, their steps would not be so hesitant.

Repentance, of all things in the world, makes the greatest change. It changes things in heaven and earth, for it changes the whole man from sin to grace, from vicious habits to holy customs, from unchaste bodies to angelic souls, from swine to philosophers, from drunkenness to sober counsels. God Himself, "with whom is no variance or shadow of change" is pleased, by descending to our weak understanding, to say that He changes also upon man's repentance. He alters His decrees, revokes His sentence, cancels the bills of accusation, throws the records of shame and sorrow from the court of heaven, and lifts up the sinner from the grave to life, from his prison to a throne, from hell and guilt of eternal torture to heaven, and to a title to never-ceasing pleasures.

Jeremy Taylor's presentation of the value of repentance concludes with this simple reminder: "If we be bound on earth, we shall be bound in heaven; if we be absolved here, we shall be loosed there; if we repent, God will repent and not send the evil upon us which we had deserved."

NUMBERS 3; PSALM 37; SONG OF SOLOMON 1; HEBREWS 1

Ye Did Run Well

You were running well; who hindered you from obeying the truth? This persuasion did not come from Him who calls you.
GALATIANS 5:7,8, NASB

I am greatly disturbed over what happens to the faith of many believers. Even in the midst of a mighty move of God, many believers in Christ lose their grip on Him. While millions clasp His hand ever tighter, others loosen their hold, seduced by lukewarm teachings and what Paul called "doctrines of devils" in 1 Timothy 4:1.

It is as if the devil comes along with his crowbar and begins to pry believers loose from their Christian foundation. The things they once believed—and even fought for—become less important.

The beliefs that many of our grandfathers and grandmothers stood firm on have become objects of intense scrutiny and question. Faith and the fear of God have been voted on as serious endangerments to the freedom of thought and enlightenment.

Friend, don't let a little scrutiny, a little seduction from the devil cause you to drop your convictions by the wayside. Don't allow the fiery zeal you were once known for to burn down to nothing more than a smoldering ember. Don't allow your love for Christ and fallen mankind, which once motivated you to witness and evangelize, to become like a mere memory of someone else's life.

Take heed to this word from God: "So then, brethren, stand firm and hold to the traditions which you were taught, whether by word of mouth or by letter from us" (2 Thessalonians 2:15, *NASB*).

What Measure?

For we are not bold to class or compare ourselves with some of those who commend themselves; but when they measure themselves by themselves, and compare themselves with themselves, they are without understanding.
2 CORINTHIANS 10:12, NASB

Do you burn with a desire to see this world touched by the flames of Holy Ghost revival? Really? In this excerpt from his book *Revival Praying*, Leonard Ravenhill forces us to examine our standard of measurement.

> In Luke 15, one conspicuous failure in the life of the elder brother was that he measured his own goodness by the badness of his prodigal brother. He should have seen how low he too had sunk in lacking compassion for a lost soul. He should have recognized how low he himself had fallen from the height of concern his father lived on. He should have known that the prodigal son did not need to come home—he had alternatives. He could have floated a loan and gone back to the gaming tables...changed his job...or worse, he could have committed suicide.
>
> Have we Christians dropped into the sin of the elder brother? Are we measuring ourselves by the fireless altars of neighboring churches instead of checking on the praying blaze of our saintly ancestors? The world boasts its atomic power; some cults boast their satanic power; but where are those who boast Holy Ghost power?[1]

Awake, Church! What was set ablaze by the agonizing of our forefathers cannot forever keep our own lamps lit. Like the 10 virgins, we must get our own oil, trim our own wicks and call out to God for the fire! Our standard of measurement need not be our neighbor; our standard should be Christ Himself.

1. Leonard Ravenhill, *Revival Praying* (Minneapolis, Minn.: Bethany House Publishers, 1962), pp. 19-20.

NUMBERS 5; PSALM 39; SONG OF SOLOMON 3; HEBREWS 3

Faith That Doesn't Quit

*And shall God not avenge His own elect who cry out day and night to
Him, though he bears long with them?
I tell you that He will avenge them speedily. Nevertheless, when the Son
of Man comes, will He really find faith on the earth?*
LUKE 18:7,8, NKJV

Prior to telling His hearers the story of the persistent widow (see
Luke 18:1-8), Jesus prefaced the parable by saying, "Men always ought
to pray and not lose heart." I wonder how often our prayers grow faint
in the ears of God. How often do we, as if hoisting a matter up a cliff,
leave off just before reaching the top, simply because we see no
progress? The book, *The Wonders of Prayer,* published by F. H. Revell in
1885, is a "thankful record and tribute to the power of persevering
faith." The following excerpt particularly relates to today's text.

At one of the prayer meetings at the Brooklyn Tabernacle,
Rev. Moody closed by narrating an instance of a persevering
prayer by a Christian wife for her infidel husband. She
resolved to pray for him at noon for eighteen months, and at
the expiration of that time, her knocking not having been
responded to, she exclaimed, "Lord, I will pray for him every
day, and at all hours, as long as life lasts."
   That day the Lord heard her knock and gave her the desire of
her heart in the conversion of her husband. When the Lord saw
her faith would not give up, He sent the answer immediately.

What if she had simply said, "Lord, I've prayed faithfully these
eighteen months, yet there is no change...I give up"? Oh friend, those
months of prayer could have been what placed her husband right at
the brink of salvation! Thankfully, her persistence paid off. Her act of
faith in deciding to pray *even more* for him, was possibly greater than
the faith required to pray the months prior.
   Will the Son of Man find faith? Will He find it in you? Don't give up,
friend. Don't let your prayers grow faint. Rise up with faith that doesn't quit!

NUMBERS 6; PSALMS 40—41; SONG OF SOLOMON 4; HEBREWS 4

Reproached for Christ

*Blessed are ye, when men shall revile you, and persecute you, and shall
say all manner of evil against you falsely, for my sake.
Rejoice, and be exceeding glad: for great is your reward in heaven:
for so persecuted they the prophets which were before you.*
MATTHEW 5:11,12

Dear Christian, I want to remind you of something today: *You are
on the winning team!* That is somewhat paraphrased, but it is frequently how our Lord encouraged the disciples. As Thomas Scott (1747-
1821) was aware, if Jesus was of all things persecuted and reproached,
how can we expect to share in any of the blessings of His identity without partaking of the reproach as well?

> The apostles were fools for Christ's sake; were deemed to be
> "beside themselves;" went through evil report and good report,
> as deceivers and yet true. As the fellows that turned the world
> upside down they were treated as vain babblers and accounted
> the filth of the world and the refuse of all things. Jesus
> Himself, the brightness of the Father's glory, the Word and
> Wisdom of God, who went about doing good and spoke as
> never man spoke was not only rejected, but despised, as not
> worth hearing, as one that had a devil, as a blasphemer, a
> Samaritan, a madman, a devil himself. The scriptures plainly
> state; "If ye were of the world, the world would love his own:
> but because ye are not of the world, but I have chosen you out
> of the world; therefore the world hates you. Remember the
> word that I said unto you: the servant is not greater than the
> Lord; if they have persecuted Me, they will also persecute you."

Perhaps right now you are passing through a time of difficulty or
persecution. "Rejoice, and be exceeding glad: for great is your reward
in heaven" (Matthew 5:12).

NUMBERS 7; PSALMS 42—43; SONG OF SOLOMON 5; HEBREWS 5

No Time to Kill

Take ye heed, watch and pray: for ye know not when the time is.
MARK 13:33

As I write these words I feel the intensity of the warfare and the necessity to work while it is day. The cost of winning the lost is ringing in my ears. I see the battlefield of life littered with victims—some dead, others barely breathing, blood everywhere. The enemy is unleashing every weapon. I hear the voice of the Lord saying, "This is not the time of peace...there is no time to kill!"

This is the time to fight for the Lord
Not the time for ourselves, our treasures to hoard.
This is the time, deep travailing in prayer
Not the time to lay down His burden of care.
This is the time to harvest the wheat
Not the time to sit down and doze off to sleep.
This is the time of suffering and pain
Not the time to enjoy even more earthly gain.
This is the time to win souls for Him
Not the time to slide back and wallow in sin.
This is the time of enduring the cold
Not the warmth of the Son on bright streets of gold.
Yes, the timepiece we wear, with accurate detail
We race to and fro, we must buy and sell.
Our schedule is tight, with precision we dwell
But His appointment is certain, it's heaven or hell.
To the doctor we run, his schedule to keep
God's time is more precious, don't drift off to sleep!
Keep pace with the Lord, seek out His will
His appointments are urgent, there's no time to kill.

Saints of God, travail with tears over the lost. Work while it is day. When you feel the alarm, rush to make God's appointment to speak to that person. Don't be late—for there's no time to kill!

NUMBERS 8; PSALM 44; SONG OF SOLOMON 6; HEBREWS 6

Do What You Can

*For as the body without the spirit is dead,
so faith without works is dead also.*
JAMES 2:26

Are you doing all that you can for Jesus? It is a question we should ask ourselves frequently. Go with Robert Murray McCheyne into the life of Mary and you will realize a trap many of us fall into.

Mary, the sister of Lazarus and Martha, had been distinguished for sitting at the feet of Jesus, choosing what was good. Now, it is interesting to see this same Mary distinguished not only as a contemplative believer, but also, as an active believer.

Many seem to think that to be a believer is to have certain feelings and experiences, forgetting all the while that these are but the flowers, and that the fruit must follow. The engrafting of the branch is good, the inflowing of the sap good, but the fruit is the end in view. Likewise faith is good, and peace and joy are good, but *holy fruit* is the end for which we are saved.

Many of you, on Sundays, are like Mary, sitting at the Redeemer's feet and hearing His Word. Now I would persuade you to be like Mary in doing what you can for Christ. If you have been bought with a price, then glorify God in your body and spirit, which are His.

Pour out your heart to Jesus, filling the room with the aroma of your praise. Intercede for the unconverted and actively set out to reach them. Live holy, allowing the fragrance of heaven to manifest through your life and draw those around you to Him. Do all that you can for Jesus.

NUMBERS 9; PSALM 45; SONG OF SOLOMON 7; HEBREWS 7

The Friendship of God

A man that hath friends must show himself friendly:
and there is a friend that sticketh closer than a brother.
PROVERBS 18:24

Do you ever look back across your life and wonder what happened to people you were once so close to? As Rev. G. D. Watson describes, even the strongest friendships can part ways, but Jesus is indeed a friend forever.

As children, we all had little friends that we thought would last forever, but in a few years the delicate romance passed away and the friends drifted from us. Then came youth with its friendships that we thought were rooted in granite, but they obeyed the same law of change and fleeting. And then came middle life, with its more thoughtful and serious friendship, which after a while were rent with cruel misunderstandings and unexplained silences and so gradually declined. And then we drift on to the lonely, quiet havens of old age, into which we anchor our riper years, to find that change and decay have characterized all earthly things, including what we once supposed were friendships riveted with steel. Like passing ships at sea we lived awhile in the sight of each other's sails, but we each had to make a different port, and so we slipped over the rim of the sea and lost sight of each other. But God is the dear old faithful friend from whom we never sail away and who always is going our way and making for the same port, and whose interests are always our own.

Have you made Jesus not only your Lord and Savior, but also your best friend? There is no greater love than His. He is the eternal friend, and He is very interested in you.

NUMBERS 10; PSALMS 46—47; SONG OF SOLOMON 8; HEBREWS 8

Season of Seduction

These things have I written unto you concerning
them that seduce you.
1 JOHN 2:26

Everyone who receives Christ as Savior does so during a time of spiritual sickness. You might have been well physically when you received Christ, but your soul was ailing. That is what Jesus meant when early in His ministry He said, "They that are whole have no need of the physician, but they that are sick" (Mark 2:17).

After receiving Christ as Savior, most of us enter into a time I call a *season of strength*. With God we feel invincible, our prayers seem instantly answered, we witness everywhere, our prayers heal the sick and cast out devils. But we must be careful: It is often during our season of strength that Satan will move in with a *season of seduction*.

"Seduction" means to persuade to disobedience or disloyalty; to lead astray, to entice. One of Satan's favorite seductive tools is what I call the *season of sleep and slothfulness*, aimed at getting you to relax, rest and stop being so zealous. It is similar to the *season of spare time*, with its pitfalls of entertaining distractions. And one of the most subtle is the season of *superficial spirituality*—imitating a genuine relationship with God.

No one is immune to one of these attacks, but like Jesus, you can be immune to its effects. Seek the counsel of the Great Physician, for as William Gurnall said, "Heaven overlooks hell, and God at any time can tell you what plots are hatching there against you." Always be sure you are in an active relationship with the Lord and not a season of seduction with the devil.

*But now they desire a better country, that is, an heavenly: wherefore God
is not ashamed to be called their God: for he hath prepared for them a city.*
HEBREWS 11:16

"*I Can't Wait to Get to Heaven*" is a heart's cry set to music by Keith
Green before he actually made that final journey on July 28, 1982. In
the opening of that song, Keith points out an exciting contrast when
he says: "Jesus Christ has been preparing a home for me, and for some
of you, for two thousand years. And if this world took six days, and
that home took two thousand years—hey, man, this is living in
a garbage can compared to what's going up there!"[1] Think about that,
friend, what a wake-up call!

Jonathan Edwards, born 250 years before Keith Green, related
a very similar concept in one of his sermons.

> Labor to be much acquainted with heaven. If you are not
> acquainted with it, you will not be likely to spend your life as
> a journey there. You will have no sense of its worth, nor will
> you long for it. Unless you are much familiar in your mind
> with heaven, it will be exceedingly difficult for you to keep
> your hearts loosed from the things of earth, and thereby be
> ready to part with them for the sake of that better good.
> Labor therefore to obtain a realizing sense of a heavenly
> world, to get a firm belief of its reality, and to be very much
> conversant with it in your thoughts.

Our minds should be much more occupied with heaven and the
One waiting for us there than with the things surrounding us down
here. Think about heaven right now and get excited about it. See you
there!

1. Keith Green, "I Can't Wait to Get to Heaven," The Prodigal Son, produced by Bill Maxwell, released August
15, 1983, (Pretty Good Records).

NUMBERS 12—13; PSALM 49; ISAIAH 2; HEBREWS 10

Prayer Is Alive

So then faith cometh by hearing, and hearing by the word of God.
ROMANS 10:17

Prayer can never be reduced to a mere system or method. Prayer is alive. It is multifaceted. Its effect is immeasurable. Leonard Ravenhill was one who would daily spend five hours or more in prayer to God. He considered it the highest calling of a Christian, above preaching or anything so visible. Because of his great devotion, he had gathered a wealth of understanding as to this magnificent, transforming communion with almighty God.

One great value of reading the Word of God is that it is faith-feeding, for "faith cometh by hearing, and hearing by the word of God." Notice that it does not say that faith cometh by reading or that faith cometh by seeing. Faith comes by hearing. The soul has "ears" (Galatians 3:5). Jesus Christ said, "He that hath an ear, let him hear what the Spirit saith." (It is present tense, for the Spirit still speaks to the inner ear of the heart.) In the place of prayer, the soul also has eyes which "see." In the place of prayer, the soul has aspirations which are sanctified and set aflame and, what is more, kept aflame. Do you wonder that the devil strives with great might and with all that is reasonable—and all that is unreasonable too—to keep us from this soul-hearing, soul-seeing, soul-activating place of prayer?[1]

Natural faith will never produce what faith that comes by hearing the voice of the Spirit deep in your soul will produce. Keep yourself from distractions; fill yourself with His Word and hear His Spirit today.

1. Leonard Ravenhill, *Meat for Men* (Minneapolis, Minn.: Bethany House Publishers, 1962), pp. 30-31.

The Baptism of Fire!

John answered, saying unto them all, I indeed baptize you with water; but one mightier than I cometh, the latchet of whose shoes I am not worthy to unloose: he shall baptize you with the Holy Ghost and with fire.

LUKE 3:16

Ever wonder what the "baptism of fire" John referred to literally meant? This description from *Tongues of Fire*, by William Arthur, will shed some clarity.

Suppose we saw an army sitting down before a granite fort, and they told us that they intended to batter it down; we might ask them, "How?" They point to a cannonball. Well, there is no power in that; it is heavy, but not more than 50 or perhaps 100 pounds. If all the men in the army hurled it against the fort, they would make no impression. They say, "No, but look at the cannon." Well, there is no power in that, a child may ride upon it, a bird may perch in its mouth. It is a machine and nothing more. "But look at the powder." Well, there is no power in that; a child may spill it, a sparrow may peck it. Yet, this powerless powder and powerless ball are put into the powerless cannon—one spark of fire enters it—and then, in the twinkling of an eye, that powder is a flash of lightning, and that ball a thunderbolt which smites as if it had been sent from heaven. So is it with our Church machinery at this day: we have all the instruments necessary for pulling down strongholds, *and O for the baptism of fire!*

Armed with the power of the Holy Spirit, the gates of hell cannot prevail against the Church any more than a granite wall can stand against a cannon-wielding army! We each must brush off the dust, aim the cannons of truth and cry out for the fire of God. Then the walls will indeed crumble and the Church will be the victorious bride she is called to be.

Spirit of Prayer

But ye, beloved, building up yourselves on your most holy faith, praying in the Holy Ghost, keep yourselves in the love of God, looking for the mercy of our Lord Jesus Christ unto eternal life.

JUDE 20,21

In the words of Jonathan Edwards, "Prayer is as natural an expression of faith as breathing is of life; and to say a man lives a life of faith, and yet lives a prayerless life, is every bit as inconsistent and incredible as to say that a man lives without breathing." Charles Finney was equally plainspoken about 100 years later, in this analysis.

> The lack of prayer is evidence of a backslidden heart. When the love of Christ remains fresh in the soul, the indwelling Spirit of Christ will reveal Himself as the Spirit of grace and supplication. He will instill strong desires in the soul for the salvation of sinners and the sanctification of saints. He will often make intercessions in them, with great longings, strong crying and tears, and with groaning that cannot be uttered in words, for those things that are according to the will of God. If the spirit of prayer departs, it is a sure indication of a backslidden heart, for while the first love of a Christian continues he is sure to be drawn by the Holy Spirit to wrestle much in prayer.

Oh, friend, if you are not in this position, take heed lest you find yourself in it one day. If, however, this passage describes you, may it serve as an alarm! Stir yourself to pray for forgiveness for forsaking your first love. Then, when your joy and delight is restored in the Lover of your soul, expect the spirit of prayer to be ignited within you—the very breath of your relationship.

NUMBERS 16; PSALMS 52—54; ISAIAH 6; HEBREWS 13

The Master's Plan

I say: My purpose will stand, and I will do all that I please.
ISAIAH 46:10, NIV

Are your ways pleasing to you or are they pleasing to the Lord? Have you asked Him lately? Many people have a "master plan" for their lives. By that I don't mean the short-term goals people set, but rather, the long-term dreams—where they want to go, who they want to be—the things that dominate (or master) their life's planning and preparation.

Have you thought about the One who has had a plan for your life since before you were born? The Bible says, "For Thou didst form my inward parts; Thou didst weave me in my mother's womb. Thine eyes have seen my unformed substance; and in Thy book they were all written, the days that were ordained for me, when as yet there was not one of them" (Psalm 139:13,16, *NASB*). Have you yet resigned yourself to recognize that you are not your own, that there is One greater who also has a plan for your life? The Lord says, "Call to Me, and I will answer you, and I will tell you great and mighty things, which you do not know" (Jeremiah 33:3, *NASB*). Why? " 'For I know the plans that I have for you,' " declares the LORD, 'plans for welfare and not for calamity to give you a future and a hope' " (Jeremiah 29:11, *NASB*).

Rather than having a master plan for your life, you need to plan for the Master of your life. Take the advice of Robert Murray McCheyne: "It has always been my aim, and it is my prayer, to have no plan as regards myself—as I am well assured that the place where the Savior sees meet to place me must ever be the best place for me."

NUMBERS 17—18; PSALM 55; ISAIAH 7; JAMES 1

Thy Will Be Done

The carnal mind is enmity against God; for it is not subject to the law of God, nor indeed can be. So then, those who are in the flesh cannot please God.

ROMANS 8:7,8, NKJV

Thomas Watson began this passage with a warning to believers to loose themselves from terrestrial things, becoming crucified to the world. He points out that, like a child who has his toys removed from him in order to gain his attention, when we have our earthly pleasures removed, we become resentful and disobedient toward God.

He who is a lover of the world can never pray this prayer heartily: "Thy will be done." His heart boils with anger against God; and when the "world" is gone, his patience is gone too.

If we would have our wills submit to God, let us not look so much on the dark side of the cloud as the light side; that is, let us not look so much on the *sting* of affliction, as the eternal *good* of affliction.

Samson did not only look on the lion's carcass but on the honeycomb within it (see Judges 14:8). Affliction is the frightful lion, but see what honey there is in it: affliction humbles, purifies, fills us with the consolations of God; here is honey in the belly of the lion; could we but look upon the benefit of affliction, stubbornness would be turned into submissiveness, and we should gladly say, "Thy will be done."

Pray to God that he would calm our spirits and conquer our wills. It is no easy thing to submit to God in affliction; there will be uprisings of the heart. Therefore let us pray that when God inflicts righteously, we may bear it patiently.

Where Is Thy Sting?

So when this corruptible shall have put on incorruption, and this mortal shall have put on immortality, then shall be brought to pass the saying that is written, Death is swallowed up in victory. "O death, where is thy sting?"

1 CORINTHIANS 15:54,55

This encouraging discourse by Horatius Bonar (1808-1889) will surely cause the Blood-washed soul to rejoice!

"O death, where is thy sting?" He that has the power of death is the devil, that old serpent, who torments us here. Sin gave him his sting, and the law gave sin its strength. But now that sin has been forgiven and the law magnified, the sting is plucked out. The stinging begins at birth; and our life throughout is one unceasing battle with death until, for a season, death conquers and we fall beneath his power. But the prey shall be taken from the mighty and his victims rescued forever. Now sin has passed away, what has become of death's sting—its sharpness, its pain, its power to kill? It cannot touch the immortal and the incorruptible!

Ah, this is victory! We do not simply escape from the enemy, we conquer him. This is open and triumphant victory that not only routs and disgraces the enemy but swallows him up. This victory is achieved in righteousness and on behalf of these who had once been "lawful captives."

And the Victor, who is He? Not we, but our Brother-King. His sword smote the enemy, and under His shield we have won. But the wreath of victorious battle is His, not ours. We are not the conquerors, but the trophies.

Thank You, Lord, that You are the Victor over all!

NUMBERS 20; PSALMS 58—59; ISAIAH 9:8—10:4; JAMES 3

Simon vs. Peter

*You have no part or portion in this matter,
for your heart is not right before God. For I see that you are in the gall of
bitterness and in the bondage of iniquity.*
ACTS 8:21,23, NASB

Did you know that a man can adhere to the church and still have sin lurking in his heart? When Simon the sorcerer heard Philip preach, he was drawn to Jesus, baptized, and began following Philip everywhere. But God knows the true motives of our hearts. Simon soon came face-to-face with Peter. The Bible tells us that when Simon offered the apostles money for the gift of the Holy Spirit, the true motives of his heart were revealed. Peter, perceiving that Simon's relationship with God was at issue, responded urgently, saying, "Repent of this wickedness of yours, and pray the Lord that if possible, the intention of your heart may be forgiven you" (Acts 8:22, *NASB*).

Simon was seeking promotion without the price. Promotion only comes from the Lord. As William Gurnall said, "The sweet bait of religion has drawn many to nibble at it who are offended with the hard services it calls to. It requires another Spirit than the world can give or receive to follow Christ fully." Peter tried to get Simon to recognize his error, but there was no humility or shame on Simon's part. Some historians record that after Simon's "day in court" with Peter, he went back to his old ways and became a bitter opponent of Christianity.

We must individually pray for God to cleanse us and make us pure. The first thing that must be done with sin is to repent of it, the second is to seek forgiveness, and then we may follow Christ *fully*.

NUMBERS 21; PSALMS 60—61; ISAIAH 10:5-34; JAMES 4

Like Sheep Going Astray

*Then he said, "I beg you therefore, father, that you would send him to my
father's house, for I have five brothers, that he may testify to them, lest they
also come to this place of torment."*
LUKE 16:27,28, NKJV

The rich man Lazarus knew his five brothers were sure to follow him
in his fate. Richard Baxter (1615-1691) had this to share about man's
foolish tendency to thoughtlessly follow the multitude who do evil.

> I remember an incident a gentleman told me he once saw
> upon a bridge over a river. A man was driving a flock of fat
> lambs, when something met them and hindered their pas-
> sage. In reaction, one of the lambs leaped upon the wall of the
> bridge and, his legs slipping from under him, fell into the
> stream. Seeing him, the rest, one after another, leaped over
> the bridge into the stream and were all, or almost all,
> drowned. Those that were behind did not know what was to
> become of them that were gone before, but thought that they
> might venture to follow their companions regardless. As soon
> as they were over the wall and falling headlong, the case was
> altered.
>
> And so it is with unconverted carnal men. One dies beside
> them and drops into hell, and another follows the same way.
> Yet, they will go after them because they think nothing of
> where they are going. Oh! But when death has once opened
> their eyes and they see what is on the other side of the wall,
> even in the other world, then what would they give to be
> where they were?

"Beloved, follow not that which is evil, but that which is good"
(3 John 1:11). Be careful, friend, to always follow the Savior, who
knows where He is going and how to lead us.

NUMBERS 22; PSALMS 62—63; ISAIAH 11—12; JAMES 5

He Will Be with You

No one will be able to stand up against you all the days of your life. As I was with Moses, so I will be with you; I will never leave you nor forsake you.
JOSHUA 1:5, NIV

Bramwell Booth was the son of General William Booth, founder of the Salvation Army. An intimate son, friend and colaborer, Bramwell was well acquainted with God's provision as he saw the needs of the hopeless met. I want to encourage you with this passage from a man who knew that God keeps His promises.

Dark valleys of bitter loneliness are often better for us than the greener pastures. A certain queen, once sitting for her portrait, commanded that it be painted without shadows. "Without shadows!" said the astonished artist. "I fear your Majesty knows not of the laws of light and beauty. There can be no good portrait without shading." Nor can there be a solid Christian without stormy trial or sorrow. There may, perhaps, remain a stunted, unfruitful infant life—but a man in Christ Jesus, a Soldier of the Cross, a leader of God's people, without tribulation there can never be. Patience, experience, faith, hope, love, may not actually grow from tribulations, but are helped by them to grow.

Oh, believe that by every blow of disappointing sorrow God permits into your life, He is striving to bring you to the measure of the stature of a man in Christ Jesus. Work with Him, fully knowing that He will not forsake you. He penetrated to the heart of every form of sorrow and left a blessing there. He silently watched every kind of earthly grief and found its antidote. He will be with you.

NUMBERS 23; PSALMS 64—65; ISAIAH 13; 1 PETER 1

Just Like a Child

*And Jesus called a little child unto him, and set him in the midst of them,
and said, Verily I say unto you, Except ye be converted, and become as
little children, ye shall not enter into the kingdom of heaven.*
MATTHEW 18:2,3

Though some in this world have memories of a delightful childhood, many others have only fleeting or painful reminders of their
race toward maturity. Perhaps this passage by Hannah Whitall Smith
will more clearly define those elements of childlikeness to which Jesus
was referring.

> Now, what are the characteristics of a little child, and how does
> it live? It lives by faith, and its chief characteristic is freedom
> from care. Its life is one long trust from year's end to year's end.
> It trusts its parents, its caretakers, its teachers, sometimes even
> people who are utterly unworthy of trust, out of the abounding
> trustfulness of its nature. And this trust is abundantly
> answered. The child provides nothing for itself, and yet every-
> thing is provided. It takes no thought for tomorrow and forms
> no plans, yet all its life is planned out, and its paths made ready.
> It goes in and out of its father's house with an unspeakable ease
> and abandonment, enjoying all the good things therein, with-
> out having spent a penny in procuring them. Pestilence may
> walk through the streets of its city. Famine and fire and war
> may rage, but under its father's tender care the child abides in
> utter unconcern and perfect rest. It lives in the present moment
> and receives its life unquestioningly as it comes to it day by day
> from its father's hands.

The Father is calling to you to lay it all down, run to His arms and
be led by His hand...just like a child.

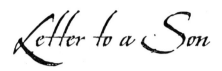

*But I discipline my body and bring it into subjection, lest, when I have
preached to others, I myself should become disqualified.*
1 CORINTHIANS 9:27, NKJV

Susannah Wesley's children's high repute in the history of English
households is largely attributed to their early domestic training.
Reading the lesson of this letter to a son, it is easy to see why.

I am concerned for you (who were even before your birth dedicated to the service of the sanctuary), that you may be instru-
mental, if God shall spare your life, in bringing many souls to
heaven. Take heed, therefore, in the first place, of your own
soul, lest you yourself should be a castaway.... You must not
think to live like the rest of the world.... For my part, I cannot
see with what face clergymen can reprove sinners or exhort
men to lead a good life when they themselves indulge their
own corrupt inclinations, and by their practice contradict
their doctrine. If the Holy Jesus be indeed their Master, and
they are really His ambassadors, surely it becomes them to live
like His disciples; and if they do not, what a sad account they
must give of their stewardship! I exhort you, as I am your
faithful friend; and I command you, as I am your parent, to use
your utmost diligence to make your calling and election sure;
to be faithful to your God; and after I have said that, I need not
tell you to be industrious in your calling.

Such a great cloud of witnesses has gone before us, testifying to
the ability to live holy lives. What keeps us then, from the disciplines
that will prevent our being disqualified? Are you dealing with such a
hindrance today?

NUMBERS 25; PSALM 68; ISAIAH 15; 1 PETER 3

Raising the Dead

*And he gave her his hand and raised her up; and calling
the saints and widows, he presented her alive.*
ACTS 9:41, NASB

Sometimes (even in the midst of revival), we can find ourselves feeling spiritually dead. I want you to consider the story about Tabitha (see Acts 9:36-42), a disciple known for her kindness and charity. She was a good person, loved by all who knew her. However, right in the midst of a great revival, Tabitha fell sick and died.

Spiritually speaking, some of you may feel as dead as Tabitha was. Perhaps you've become dry, lost your hunger for the things of God, and now you feel you'll never have that fire for God again. Take comfort, friend! Like Tabitha, you too are in the perfect position for a miracle.

Tabitha had friends who had been touched by God in that revival. They knew it was too late for a doctor, but not too late for Jesus! They were ready to believe God for a miracle. They didn't bury her right away. Instead they sent for Peter. When Peter brought Tabitha in contact with the resurrecting power of Jesus Christ, she sat up, raised to life again!

You may think all hope is gone, friend, but do not allow yourself to be buried by your circumstances. Keep holding on, because your miracle is on the way! Even though you may feel spiritually deceased, there are intercessors—some known and many unknown to you—who are going after Jesus on your behalf, just like Tabitha's friends did for her.

Jesus said He would never leave you nor forsake you. Believe His promises. Ask Him to touch you, to revive you, to renew you. He will raise you to life again.

NUMBERS 26; PSALM 69; ISAIAH 16; 1 PETER 4

In His Presence

When Moses came down from Mount Sinai with the two tablets of the
Testimony in his hands, he was not aware that his face was radiant
because he had spoken with the Lord.
EXODUS 34:29, NIV

Before he had quite turned 16 years old, William Jay began preaching.
He is said to have delivered no less than 1,000 sermons by the time he
reached 21 years of age. Perhaps the very thing that drew the people to
listen was the afterglow of God's glory emanating from him after
spending time in God's presence.

> Resemblance to God results from our intimacy with Him. "Evil
> communications corrupt good manners." But while a compan-
> ion of fools shall be destroyed, he that walks with wise men
> shall be wise. We soon assume the manners and absorb the spir-
> it of those with whom we are most familiar, especially if the
> individual is distinguished as someone we esteem and dearly
> love. Upon this principle, the more we have to do with God, the
> more we shall grow into His likeness and "be followers of Him
> as dear children." When Moses descended from communion
> with God, his face shone; and although he was not aware of the
> luster himself, the people could not look directly at him
> because of the glory of his countenance, and he was compelled
> to hide his face under a veil. The Christian, too, may be
> unaware of such radiating brilliance; but it will appear unto all
> men—who will take note that he has been with Jesus.

How many around you every day are suffering in darkness?
Remember, light dispels darkness. Jesus is the Light of the world. The
more time you spend in His presence, the more His light shines
through you to those still walking in darkness, to lead them home.

NUMBERS 27; PSALMS 70—71; ISAIAH 17—18; 1 PETER 5

Known in Heaven

For as the new heavens and the new earth, which I will make, shall remain before me, saith the Lord, so shall your seed and your name remain.
ISAIAH 66:22

In all the following after God, dying to self, studying the Scriptures, fervent prayer and fasting, there are still inquiries like this one that require particular consideration. Many questions cannot be answered completely until we see Jesus face-to-face. However, note how D. L. Moody covered this subject.

> Many are anxious to know if they will recognize their friends in heaven. In Matthew 8:11, we read: "And I say unto you, That many shall come from the east and west, and shall sit down with Abraham, and Isaac, and Jacob, in the kingdom of heaven." Here we find that Abraham, Isaac and Jacob, who lived so many hundreds of years before Christ, had *not* lost their identity. And if you will turn to that wonderful scene that took place on the Mount of Transfiguration, you will find that Moses (who had been gone from the earth 1,500 years) was there; Peter, James and John recognized him; he had not lost his name. Further, God says in Isaiah, "I will not blot your names out of the Lamb's book of life."
> We have names in heaven; we are going to bear our names there; we will be known.

Though this is another question that we will know the answer to more fully once we are in heaven, I believe Moody has made an interesting case. Once again, we see that none of us are here by accident. God knows each one of us by name. He created us in His image, but each one of us is unique, individual and known in heaven.

Heavenly Affections

And as we have borne the image of the earthy,
we shall also bear the image of the heavenly.
1 CORINTHIANS 15:49

"I have learned more from John Howe than from any other author I ever read. There is an astonishing magnificence in his conceptions." So said Robert Hall, nearly 100 years after Howe's death. It is Howe's "magnificence in his conceptions," presented in concise, to-the-point language, that has continued to touch successive generations. The following advice is no exception.

> Do not think that Christ came into the world and died to procure the pardon of your sins and so translate you to heaven, while your hearts should still remain cleaving to the earth. He came and returned to prepare a way for you and then call, not drag you, to that place—that by His precepts, promises, example and Spirit, He might form and fashion your souls to that glorious state and make you willing to abandon all things for it.

When you put your affection toward something, you are passionate toward whatever that thing is. What has your affection? What means more to you than anything else? Is it a house? Is it a boat? Is it a car? Is it a relationship? Is it the way you look? Are you more concerned how people look at you than how God sees you?

Determine in your heart to shake off the affections of the world, and become infatuated with Jesus. "Set your affection on things above, not on things on the earth" (Colossians 3:2).

Come Home Before Dark

I must work the works of him that sent me,
while it is day: the night cometh, when no man can work.
JOHN 9:4

"Jesus Loves Me" is a song many children learn while very young. Though the words are true, there is more to Christianity than just *love*. I have taken the liberty to write several more verses, one of which is: "Jesus will judge me, this I know, for the Bible tells me so. If I choose to live in sin, hell awaits me in the end."

People today are living in self-inflicted darkness. Having allowed the devil to blind them, they live consumed in sin. But God said He would not always contend with our self-indulgences and neglect of godly things (see Genesis 6:3).

As the text states, "night cometh." There is coming a time when you'll no longer be able to make things right with your fellow man. You may think you have plenty of time for restoration, but only God knows the number of a man's days. We must learn to "give roses" while people live. Now is the time to mend relationships. Now is the time to let God revive your family and draw your loved ones together.

There is coming a time when you won't be able to fulfill your purpose in life. Many hustle around, fulfilling the plan they have for their own lives. However, God is the One with the plan; we must check with Him to find out what it is. What a tragedy to find that we spent so much time improving our talents, but no time improving our relationship with God. We must work while it is day and be sure to come home before dark.

What Prayer Has Done

Confess your faults one to another, and pray one for another, that ye may be healed. The effectual fervent prayer of a righteous man availeth much.
JAMES 5:16

Anglican minister Jeremy Taylor (1613-1667) was acutely aware that man is nothing...God is everything...and prayer changes things.

The prayers of men have saved cities and kingdoms from ruin, raised the dead to life, stopped the violence of fire, and shut the mouths of wild beasts. Prayer has altered the course of nature—caused rain in Egypt and drought in the sea, made the sun go from west to east, the moon to stand still, and rocks and mountains to walk. Prayer cures diseases without medicine, makes medicine to do the work of nature, nature to do the work of grace, grace to do the work of God and does miracles of accident and event. Yet prayer, that does all this, is of itself nothing but an assent of the mind to God. It is a desiring of things fit to be desired and an expression of this desire to God. Our unwillingness to pray is nothing else than our not desiring what we ought to passionately long for—or if we do desire it, choosing rather to miss our satisfaction and pleasure than to ask.

What a travesty for anyone to subdue prayer when so much good comes from so little struggle. As William S. Plumer (1802-1880) stated, "Past answers to prayer should encourage us to come the more boldly to the Throne of Grace." Friend, it would be impossible to record what all prayer has done, but remember, there is no limit on what prayer can do!

The Smitten Rock

In that day there shall be a fountain opened to the house of David and to the inhabitants of Jerusalem for sin and for uncleanness.
ZECHARIAH 13:1

Here we have a type of Christ. Just as the rock was smitten and brought forth water, so Christ is the smitten rock, as His Blood has been poured out for our sin. Robert Murray McCheyne completes this analogy in one of his sermons.

> So it is with Christ. He was smitten of God and afflicted. He bore the wrath of God; and therefore His Blood gushed forth and cleanses from all sin.

Jesus said, If any man thirst, let him come to Me and drink. Friend, there is a vast supply.

> The water gushed forth abundantly when Moses smote the rock (see Numbers 20:11). It was no scanty stream—it was enough for all the thousands of Israel. So it is with the blood of the Savior. It is no scanty stream. There are no sins it cannot wash out—there is no sinner beyond its reach—there is enough here for all the thousands of Israel. It was a constant supply: "They drank of that spiritual Rock that followed them: and that Rock was Christ" (1 Corinthians 10:4). So is it with Christ. He is a rock that follows us. He is like rivers of water in a dry place. You may wash, and wash again.

As McCheyne's description clearly reveals, just like the rock to the Israelites, so is the Rock, our Redeemer! King David said, "Wash me thoroughly from mine iniquity, and cleanse me from my sin" (Psalm 51:2). Don't hesitate to be cleansed; don't hesitate to drink from the Rock of our salvation!

NUMBERS 32; PSALM 77; ISAIAH 24; 1 JOHN 2

Evidence of Strength

*Therefore I take pleasure in infirmities, in reproaches, in needs, in persecutions,
in distresses, for Christ's sake. For when I am weak, then I am strong.*
2 CORINTHIANS 12:10, NKJV

There are times when we should be as the towering oak tree, boldly withstanding the forces of nature. At other times, we should be as the weeping willow, allowing our branches to humbly hang to the ground. Consider the distinction Charles H. Spurgeon makes.

Sometimes tears are base things; the offspring of a cowardly spirit. Some men weep when they should instead pray a thing through, and many a woman weeps when she should instead resign herself to the will of God. Many of those salty drops are but an expression of childlike weakness. It would be better if we could wipe such tears away and face a frowning world with a constant countenance.

But oftentimes, tears are the very evidence of strength. There are periods when they are the noblest thing in the world. The tears of repentance are most precious; a cup of them worth a king's ransom. It is no sign of weakness when a man weeps for sin. Such weeping shows that he has strength of mind; but even more importantly, that he has strength imparted by God, which enables him to renounce his lusts and overcome his passions, and to turn unto God with full purpose of heart.

Paul had often experienced that strength, saying of his many trials, "the Lord stood with me and strengthened me" (2 Timothy 4:17). Never be afraid to shed such tears as this, friend. They are indeed the evidence of strength—God's strength working in our weakness.

NUMBERS 33; PSALM 78:1-37; ISAIAH 25; 1 JOHN 3

May 25

Going After God

*The Pharisees therefore said to one another, "You see that you are not
doing any good; look, the world has gone after Him."*

JOHN 12:19, NASB

Some may look at Nicodemus as a cowardly sneak, afraid to be
seen with Jesus. Though there may have been an element of fear, his
goal was to spend quality time with the Lord. We must break away and
make time to be with Jesus. No schedule is more important. If you go
after God, He will meet you. If you get serious with God, He will get
serious with you.

Like Nicodemus, if you make time for Jesus, Jesus will make time
for you. Slip away from the crowd—get up in the still of the night—and
go sit with Him. Remember, Jesus took time to explain things to
Nicodemus, and He'll take time to explain things to you.

Nicodemus came empty, humble and unassuming. He had a troubled heart. Deep down he longed for answers to some of life's most
important questions. He had ears to hear. He listened, he pondered
and his life was forever changed! If you desire to go after God, shake
the pride, lose the intellect and get rid of the attitude. Come to Jesus
empty enough for Him to have room to fill you.

If you desire to go after God, you don't have to have all the
answers. Begin by being honest about the questions lurking deep
inside your heart. Don't allow the devil to sidetrack the issue. You're
going after the Creator of the universe! Let nothing stand in your way.
Your times of communion will be sweet treasures that will change your
life forever.

NUMBERS 34; PSALM 78:38-72; ISAIAH 26; 1 JOHN 4

What Have You Found?

Then Peter and the other apostles answered and said,
"We ought to obey God rather than men."
ACTS 5:29

Scottish-born John Welch was a man devoted to prayer, and quite intimate with God. His ministry changed the eternal destiny of many. However, such meetings as he preached eventually became outlawed. Continuing to preach, refusing to submit to any other authority over the Church than Christ, Welch was soon incarcerated and exiled. Condemned of high treason for spreading the gospel, he wrote:

> Who am I that He should first have called me and then constitute me a minister of the glad tidings of the gospel of salvation these years already, and now last of all, to be a sufferer for His cause and Kingdom?

In Welch's day, the government was attempting to control every aspect of the Church. Welch lived and was willing to die convinced of two things:

> First, that Christ is the head of His church. Secondly, that she is free in her government from all other jurisdiction except Christ's. These two points are the special cause of our imprisonment.

Welch was anticipating losing his life over these two points. What an attitude! How many of us today are willing to lay down our lives with such a focused heart? Friend, hold fast to what you believe and do not be swayed by the opinions of others, for as Jesus said, "He that loseth his life for my sake shall find it" (Matthew 10:39).

NUMBERS 35; PSALM 79; ISAIAH 27; 1 JOHN 5

Like a Tree

For he will be like a tree planted by the water, that extends its roots by a stream and will not fear when the heat comes; but its leaves will be green, and it will not be anxious in a year of drought nor cease to yield fruit.
JEREMIAH 17:8, NASB

Are you growing as a Christian? Do you sometimes feel there is no fruit to be found in your life? I believe you will be encouraged by what pastor and author Phillips Brooks so beautifully illustrates in this passage.

Our life is like the life of a tree, which may seem full of immediate apparent failure; it is always dropping back after each rich summer to the same barrenness that it had last winter. It keeps no leaves or fruit and stands again and again stripped of every sign of life that it has put forth. And yet, as we see when we watch it with a larger eye, it has gathered all those apparent failures into the success of one long, continuous growth; it hasn't lost the strength of those old summers but gathered them into its own enlarged girth and sturdier strength. What seemed to perish and die has really only added to its growth, and makes the noble tree mature.

And so it is with our hopes and plans, our endeavors, resolutions and thoughts, which seem to fade and perish. If we have Christ living in us, we have really been made to grow into new strength, which is not merely a thing of the future but a thing of the present.

Sink your roots ever deeper into the soil of God's Word. Hold fast to His teachings, bask in His light and be watered by His love. He is working His perfection in you, and one day you will be able to see the results.

NUMBERS 36; PSALM 80; ISAIAH 28; 2 JOHN 1

Share Your Struggle

One generation shall praise thy works to another, and shall declare thy mighty acts. I will speak of the glorious honour of thy majesty, and of thy wondrous works. And men shall speak of the might of thy terrible acts: and I will declare thy greatness.

PSALM 145:4-6

There is not only great joy in testifying of what the Lord has brought us through, there is also great benefit to others, as the English minister Timothy Rogers noted. In fact, in referring to the sixth verse of the text, "I will declare," he makes it clear that it is actually a part of Christian duty.

> After we are delivered from the dreadful apprehensions of the wrath of God, it is our duty to be publicly thankful. It is for the glory of our Healer to speak of the miserable wounds that once pained us; and of that kind hand that saved us when we were brought very low. It is for the glory of our Pilot to tell of the rocks and of the sands; the many dangers and threatening calamities that He, by His wise conduct, made us to escape. To see us safe on the shore may cause others that are still afflicted and tossed with tempests to look to Him for help; for He is able and ready to save them as well as us. We must, like soldiers, when a tedious war is over, relate our combats, our fears, our dangers, with delight and make known our experiences to doubting, troubled Christians and to those that have not yet been under such long and severe trials as we have been.

The Bible tells us that "faith cometh by hearing, and hearing by the word of God" (Romans 10:17). When God delivers our foot from the snare, that indeed is the Word in action. Build someone's faith today—even the one who may be unsaved—by sharing what God has done for you.

DEUTERONOMY 1; PSALMS 81—82; ISAIAH 29; 3 JOHN 1

A Noah Wanna-Be

These are the generations of Noah: Noah was a just man and perfect in his generations, and Noah walked with God.
GENESIS 6:9

Noah is one of my personal heroes. To describe him, one could use a simple acrostic of his name that would define his relationship to God. Noah was **n**ear, **o**bedient, **a**vailable and **h**oly. I want to be like Noah.

Noah lived his life **near** to God. In this scripture, "walked with God" literally means he stayed in habitual fellowship with God. The psalmist describes a secret place, near to God, as being under the shadow of the Almighty. Always remember, one has to be awfully close to someone to abide in their shadow.

Noah was a man **obedient** to the commands of God. Even in the New Testament Noah is hailed as an example of obedience (see Hebrews 11:7). Though it had never before rained on the earth, by faith, Noah built an ark exactly to God's specifications.

Noah was a man who made himself **available** to God. Only a man interested in the heart of God would have received the instructions as Noah did. He wasn't so caught up in his own affairs that he had no time for God.

Noah was a man who lived **holy** unto the Lord. The whole reason the Lord's eye rested with delight upon Noah is that he lived holy in the first place. When God was sorely grieved that He had made man on the earth, there was one who brought relief to His sorrow. Noah found grace, because Noah lived holy. In today's world, choose to be a Noah. He's an example we can all follow.

DEUTERONOMY 2; PSALMS 83—84; ISAIAH 30; JUDE 1

He Shed Real Blood

For I am not ashamed of the gospel of Christ: for it is the power of God unto salvation to every one that believeth; to the Jew first, and also to the Greek.
ROMANS 1:16

I've read that most adults in the United States believe in God. But judging by the fruit of this wicked generation, it is apparent that many of them adhere to a mere idea of God—as a tolerant, understanding, sugar-daddy. General William Booth, the on-fire founder of the Salvation Army, held instead to the clear-cut revelation of our holy God as set forth in the gospel.

> The old-fashioned Gospel tells man he is thoroughly bad and under the power of the devil. It drags out the very hidden things of iniquity to the light of the great judgment throne, and denounces sin without mercy and warns men of eternal wrath to come, unless they repent and believe in the only Savior. The goodness of the Gospel does not consist in the suppression of all but sweet sounds of love, but in plain, straightforward, ceaseless announcement of the whole truth. It is the Gospel of a crucified Savior who shed real blood to save men from a real guilt and a real danger, and a real hell. He lives again—to give a real pardon to the really penitent, a real deliverance from the guilt and love of sin to all who really give up to Him a whole heart and trust Him with a perfect confidence.

William Booth not only believed in God, but also intensely followed Him. He understood that Jesus shed real blood, and the least he could do was give his life for others in return.

DEUTERONOMY 3; PSALM 85; ISAIAH 31; REVELATION 1

Nothing Like It

Even the Spirit of truth; whom the world cannot receive,
because it seeth him not, neither knoweth him:
but ye know him;for he dwelleth with you, and shall be in you.
JOHN 14:17

I believe this passage by Samuel Chadwick (1860-1932) will be a refreshing blessing to you today.

There is no life like the life filled with the Spirit. It is beyond the power of speech to set forth its glory and its might. Filled with all the fullness of God, energized and sustained by His indwelling, more than a conqueror in His strength, sharing His ministry, rejoicing in His glory, it transcends human power to describe; but it is every man's privilege to realize it in his own soul. The Spirit waits to enter and abide; to take possession and endue with life and power.

Mendelssohn once visited the Cathedral at Gribourg, and having heard the great organ went into the organ loft and asked to be allowed to play it. The old organist, in jealousy for his instrument at first refused, but was at length prevailed upon, and allowed the stranger to try what was claimed to be the greatest organ in Europe. After standing by in an ecstasy of delight and amazement, he suddenly laid his hands on the shoulders of the inspired musician and exclaimed, "Who are you? What is your name?" "Mendelssohn," replied the player, and with tears the old man exclaimed, "And can it be I had so nearly refused to let Mendelssohn touch this organ?"

The Holy Spirit asks possession of your nature with all its possibilities and powers. Only He can fill your life and evoke from it all its melody and power. To be filled with the Spirit is to live the life of God.

DEUTERONOMY 4; PSALMS 86—87; ISAIAH 32; REVELATION 2

Search Me, God!

*Search me, O God, and know my heart: try me, and know my thoughts: and
see if there be any wicked way in me, and lead me in the way everlasting.*
PSALM 139:23,24

There are various degrees of searches we allow the Lord to perform. David wanted nothing to stand between him and God. He knew
God could search below the surface to the deep areas of his heart.

Some of us, however, presume that we can keep God from going
any further than the surface. Blind to our truly sinful state, we vainly
present to God our outward credentials. This *surface search* is worthless
because we know how to put on our religious "makeup." While we
shroud ourselves with creature comforts, God is grieved over the true
condition of our hearts.

The *spot search* is a little more intense, but not much. It simply
means we have allowed God to inspect certain areas of our heart—but
not all areas. Those who submit only to spot searching fidget and
squirm, eventually walking away when the Lord exposes the area of
their greatest struggle.

The *cellar search* is the search David was talking about. It is the only
search that can prepare the way for total cleansing and eternal fruit.
Jesus wants to go into the basement of our lives. He wants access to the
creaky, musty corners of our inner man. He wants to expose those
things that have been hidden in darkness. He knows the source of our
surface problems and will show us how to clean house and keep it
clean!

David knew the value of the depth to which God can search a
heart. Will you invite the Lord as David did, to do a cellar search? It is
the only one that brings about true fulfillment once it's completed.

DEUTERONOMY 5; PSALM 88; ISAIAH 33; REVELATION 3

A Heart Disengaged

But lay up for yourselves treasures in heaven, where neither moth nor
rust doth corrupt, and where thieves do not break through nor steal: for
where your treasure is, there will your heart be also.
MATTHEW 6:20,21

Early in our walk with God, my wife and I learned to live eternity-conscious. It was a good lesson because, as missionaries, we have many times had to quickly sell all we owned and relocate. It was never a difficult task because Jeri and I were not attached to things. As Thomas Boston, the Scotch Presbyterian divine wrote, living eternity-conscious is something we can all learn to practice.

> When you lie down at night, compose your spirit as if you were not to wake up in the morning. And if you awake in the morning, consider that new day as your last, and live accordingly. Surely the night will come, of which you will never see the morning, or that morning of which you will never see the night; but which of your mornings or nights it will be, you know not.
>
> Let the mantle of worldly enjoyments hang loose about you, that it may be easily dropped when death comes to carry you into another world. When the corn is forsaking the ground, it is ready for the sickle; when the fruit is ripe, it falls off the tree easily. So, when a Christian's heart is truly weaned from the world, he is prepared for death, and it will be easy for him. A heart disengaged from the world is a heavenly one, and then we are ready for heaven when our heart is there before us.

Friend, loose yourself from all that binds you here. Be ready to move in the "twinkling of an eye!"

DEUTERONOMY 6; PSALM 89; ISAIAH 34; REVELATION 4

An Omnipresent God

You comprehend my path and my lying down,
and are acquainted with all my ways.
PSALM 139:3, NKJV

Where would we be without the Lord? Too often this question is taken lightly, when instead it should be frequently dwelt upon and deeply considered. Dr. Thomas Chalmers of Scotland (1780-1847) wrote a comforting perspective on the subject of the omnipresence of God.

His eye is upon every hour of my existence. His Spirit is intimately present with every thought of my heart. His inspiration gives birth to every purpose within me. His hand impresses a direction on every footstep of my goings. Every breath I inhale is drawn by an energy which God deals out to me. This body, which upon the slightest derangement would become the prey of death, or of woeful suffering, is now at ease, because He at this moment is warding off from a thousand dangers and upholding the thousand movements of its complex and delicate machinery.

In the silent watches of the night, when my eyelids have closed and my spirit has sunk into unconsciousness, the observant eye of Him who never slumbers, is upon me.

Friend, when we take time to dwell upon the omnipresence of God, suddenly He becomes much larger than the limits of our finite minds. Greater reverence, worship and honor will begin to pour forth from the depths of our being when we truly see where we would be without the Lord.

Learn to Die

For whether we live, we live unto the Lord; and whether we die, we die unto the Lord: whether we live therefore, or die, we are the Lord's.
ROMANS 14:8

Lady Jane Grey was merely 17 years old in 1553, when she was reluctantly placed on the throne of England following the death of Edward VI. It is said she would have made an excellent queen, though her reign was brutally cut short after only nine days. Her cousin, Mary Tudor, rallied an army to march on London, imprisoned Grey for treason and had her beheaded. I found it interesting that from her short life, such lasting counsel was produced.

> Labor always to learn to die. Deny the world, defy the devil, despise the flesh, and delight yourself only in the Word. Be penitent of your sins, and yet despair not. Be steady in faith, and yet presume not. Desire with St. Paul to be dissolved and to be with Christ, with whom, even in death, there is life. Be like the good servant, and even at midnight be waking, lest, when death comes stealthily upon you like a thief in the night, you, with the evil servant, be found sleeping, and lest, for lack of oil, you be found like the five foolish women, and like him that had not on a wedding-garment, and then was cast out from the marriage.

Lady Grey's earthly reign was brief, but I believe her calling and election to an eternal crown were quite certain. Let us also labor in this same manner, saints of God. As missionary Jim Elliot said before he was martyred in the jungles of Ecuador, "When it comes your time to die, be sure that's all you have to do."

DEUTERONOMY 8; PSALM 91; ISAIAH 36; REVELATION 6

Great Expectations

And I John saw the holy city, new Jerusalem, coming down from God out of heaven, prepared as a bride adorned for her husband.
REVELATION 21:2

Have you ever become overwhelmed at the deluge of distractions all around, knowing that if you could just get away from it all for a couple of days, everything would be all right? Yet, how many times have those short getaways gone all wrong? Accommodations fall through, cars break down, flights get canceled, kids get sick. I imagine we've all been there. The Scottish minister John Welch had even greater expectations which kept his life focused.

I expect that new heaven and new earth, wherein dwells the righteousness and wherein I shall dwell forevermore. I look to get entry into the new Jerusalem, at one of those twelve gates whereupon are written the names of the twelve tribes of Israel. I know that Christ Jesus has prepared room for me; why may I not then, with boldness in His Blood, step into that glory, into which my Head and Lord have gone before me? Jesus Christ is the Door and the Porter; who then shall hold me out? Will He let them perish for whom He died? Will He let that poor sheep be plucked out of His hand for which He has laid down His life? Who shall condemn the man whom God has justified? Who shall lay anything to the charge of the man for whom Christ has died, or rather risen again?

Friend, learn to look past all the disappointments in life. Put your hope in heaven and you won't be devastated when things fall through.

DEUTERONOMY 9; PSALMS 92—93; ISAIAH 37; REVELATION 7

Prepare to Meet Thy God

Therefore thus will I do unto thee, O Israel:
and because I will do this unto thee, prepare to meet thy God, O Israel.
AMOS 4:12

Matthew Henry, the English minister and commentator, is widely recognized for his *Exposition of the Old and New Testament*. In this passage, however, Henry's expository skills are focused on his reader, for their eternal benefit.

Are you, dear reader, already prepared? The very warning to prepare implies the possibility of our not being prepared. And by whom is this warning given? By no less authority than God Himself. Does it not behoove you then, to inquire whether an admonition so startling may be applicable to you? Do you imagine that should you now be set before the glorious Judge, you might only be dumb and confused? Remember that in the mighty power of God alone you cannot stand. You must be purified by the Blood of Jesus before you can present yourself for acceptance to a God of infinite purity. Your soul must be born anew of the Holy Spirit before you can enter Heaven! Determine whether you are thus renewed and prepared! Remember, without holiness no man shall see God. If you be ready, pray for grace to stay ready. If you are not ready, oh! Stop, think, pray—that you may repent, prepare and be saved.

Friend, if you were on an airplane at about 30,000 feet, and both engines just blew up, as you plummeted to your death would you need to spend those seconds repenting, or worshiping? You should be able to worship and say, "Jesus, I'm coming home!" That is living prepared. Get the sin out, live holy, stay prepared!

DEUTERONOMY 10; PSALM 94; ISAIAH 38; REVELATION 8

The Gaze of God

But to this man will I look, even to him that is poor and of a contrite spirit, and trembleth at My word.

ISAIAH 66:2

There is much to be sought out in this simple passage of scripture. To begin with, the word "look" in this text refers to an intense look. It suggests one gazed upon, regarded with pleasure, shown favor and cared for.

How does one catch God's eye? Let's consider to whom He will look. First, to the one who is *humble*. Henry Scougal, author of *Life of God in the Soul of Man*, explained that "True humility is not to think low of oneself, but to think rightly, truthfully of oneself." Friend, if you want God to look at you, get down off the "throne" and choose to become honest with yourself. God gives grace to the humble.

Also, God will look to the one who is *contrite of spirit*. Are you broken? The spirit of man here has to do with the center or heart of man's personal activities; the source where his actions derive their origin. The heart of man is the part that makes you do what you do.

Oh, to know the fear of the Lord! God says He will look also to the one who *trembles at His Word*. Do you have an awesome respect for His Word? Are you extremely careful, hastily obeying what you learn? His Word is His advice, counsel, sayings, business, judgments. Proverbs 16:6 tells us that "by the fear of the LORD men depart from evil."

Have you felt the gaze of God lately? It is something you want to feel at all times. God has clearly set out the criteria for living. It is up to each of us to follow the pattern.

DEUTERONOMY 11; PSALMS 95—96; ISAIAH 39; REVELATION 9

Aim to Be Perfect

Likewise reckon ye also yourselves to be dead indeed unto sin, but alive unto God through Jesus Christ our Lord. Let not sin therefore reign in your mortal body, that ye should obey it in the lusts thereof.
ROMANS 6:11,12

Christianity is a life change—a *continual* life change. In the example of Christ, we have been given a goal at which to aim, and as Charles Finney explains, it is that *aim* which distinguishes a true follower of Jesus.

Aim at being perfect. Every young convert should be taught that if it is not his purpose to live without sin, he has not yet begun to be a Christian. What is Christianity, but supreme love to God and a supreme purpose of heart or disposition to obey God? If there is not this, there is no Christianity at all.

It should be our *constant* purpose (aim) to live wholly to God and obey *all* His commandments. We should live so that if we were to sin, it would be an inconsistency, an exception, an individual case, in which we act contrary to the fixed and general purpose of our lives.

That is the essence of the true Christian walk, not to see what we can get away with, but instead, to see what we can stay away *from*. In following that course, it is easier to live a holy life, focused on our example—Jesus.

I heard it said once that "he who fails to plan, plans to fail." That saying would apply well to Finney's teaching. If you do not plan to aim high, toward the example you've been given, then your aim will fail. Jesus is the only target. Aim to be like Him, knowing that even if you miss the mark from time to time, He will help you steady your aim in order to succeed in the future.

DEUTERONOMY 12; PSALMS 97—98; ISAIAH 40; REVELATION 10

A Heart That Never Strays

Listen, my son, and be wise, and keep your heart on the right path.
PROVERBS 23:19, NIV

There are keys to this walk with Christ. The Word of God reveals vital clues to aid us in missing the mark. As John Flavel so well stated, how we keep our hearts is most crucial to how our walk continues.

Keep the Word, and the Word will keep you. As the first receiving of the Word *regenerated* your hearts, so the keeping of the Word within you will *preserve* your hearts. "Let the word of Christ dwell in you richly" (Colossians 3:16); let it *dwell*, not tarry with you for a night. And, let it dwell richly or plentifully in all that is of it; in its commands, promises, threats; in all that is in you, in your understandings, memories, consciences, affections, and then it will preserve your hearts. It is the slipperiness of hearts, in reference to the Word, that causes so many slips in our lives. Conscience cannot be influenced with forgotten truths. Keep the Word in your heart, and it will keep both heart and life upright. "The law of his God is in his heart; none of his steps shall slide" (Psalm 37:31); or if they do, the Word will recover the straying heart again. "And Peter remembered the word of Jesus...and wept bitterly" (Matthew 26:75). We never lose our hearts till they have first lost the effectual and powerful impression of the Word.

Endeavor to keep your heart in check today and always. Guard it, protect it, hide the Word of God there, and your heart will not so readily deceive you (see Jeremiah 17:9).

DEUTERONOMY 13—14; PSALMS 99—101; ISAIAH 41; REVELATION 11

Holy Tears

My friends scorn me: but mine eye poureth out tears unto God. O that one might plead for a man with God, as a man pleadeth for his neighbour!
JOB 16:20,21

Have you ever considered that crying out to God with holy tears has a way of cleansing our spiritual eyes? Well, just as a physical tear washes the physical eye of any disturbing substance, so a heavenly tear cleanses us of spiritual impurities.

What's more, holy tears affect the lives of others. The struggles of coping with everyday life, the seemingly endless barrage of filth, the lack of spiritual leadership in the pulpit and countless other problems have laid waste the dry hearts of the masses. But the moisture of a heavenly tear is a God-sent shower to the spiritually barren. In fact, your tears can fall on the parched, cracked soil of people's hearts, preparing the way for the life-producing seed of His Word.

Do you long to see a deep, holy move of the Spirit? Do you want to see God come down in a way that would cause everyone to proclaim, "This is the presence of the Lord"?

I remember reading a story about William Booth, challenging a group of hard-preaching but ineffective evangelists. His message to them was simple: "Try tears, try tears."

Put into practice the words of Richard Baxter, "Go to poor sinners with tears in your eyes, that they may see you believe them to be miserable, and that you genuinely pity their case. Let them perceive it is the desire of your heart to do them good." Is there someone today who needs to hear your heartfelt words of comfort and encouragement?

Take a Stand!

Stand fast therefore in the liberty wherewith Christ hath made us free,
and be not entangled again with the yoke of bondage.
GALATIANS 5:1

To *stand* is to endure; to sustain; to resist without yielding or receding. Today's text brings up an issue I have seen ruin so many Christians. It is a problem the English Congregational preacher J. H. Jowett exposed with great clarity.

> There are some people who never seem to take a stand. They are always changing their ground. They shift, and budge, and slip, and slide. Life is just a dodging of difficulties and never a magnificent facing of the foe. In these high and critical matters those who yield an inch will soon surrender a mile. They are swayed by loose opinions and not by fixed convictions. Or perhaps they are moved by sentiments and not by ideals. A comfortable feeling is more to be desired than a holy war. Indeed, they do not know anything important enough to warrant the shedding of their blood. To them, there is nothing more precious than quietness. Emblazoned on their dainty picnic banner is the legend, *"Anything for a quiet life!"* And "anything" means indefinite surrender. While on Jesus' blood-red banner are the burning words, *"Anything for a right life!"* And "anything" means not only the yielding of comfort, but even the offering up of life itself!

We are living in a day when Christians are beginning to make a bold stand for their beliefs. Will you be numbered among them? Will you be counted as one who stood strong until the end?

DEUTERONOMY 16; PSALM 103; ISAIAH 43; REVELATION 13

Just a Little While

For our light affliction, which is but for a moment, worketh for us a far
more exceeding and eternal weight of glory.
2 CORINTHIANS 4:17

Friend, consider these words of F. B. Meyer. May they bring you
comfort in your time of adversity.

There is a limitation to our suffering. It is only for a little
while; but every moment has been fixed by the immutable
purpose and love of God. The hour of darkness is timed with
an exact measurement. You shall not suffer one moment
more than is absolutely necessary for your perfecting of God's
glory; and for every moment there is an ample supply of grace.

But remember also that in Christ, God has called you to
His Eternal Glory. You heard that call years ago, and have
been following it through days of evil and nights of pain. But
the gifts and calling of God are without repentance, and He is
waiting to fulfill his eternal purpose. What a banquet that
will be when God will satisfy the expectations of those whom
He has called to partake of it!

Further, the suffering is being used in ways you little
understand to perfect, establish and strengthen you. It is
from sick chambers and torture rooms that God brings forth
his veteran hosts in the day of battle. Think not so much of
affliction as of the love of Christ, and the blessedness of being
like Him and with Him for ever.

I've heard it said that God will pull you through anything, if you
can withstand the pull. Remember, He is the one doing the pulling! He
is with you, He won't forsake you.

DEUTERONOMY 17; PSALM 104; ISAIAH 44; REVELATION 14

Fly Higher

*If then you have been raised up with Christ, keep seeking the things above,
where Christ is, seated at the right hand of God.*

COLOSSIANS 3:1, NASB

I've frequently had new Christians come up and ask for counsel because they just don't get along like they used to with their family, or old friends or colleagues. Usually, it is because of a process that Richard Baxter described well in one of his sermons.

> When once you are truly crucified to the world, you will have the honor and the comfort of a heavenly life. Your thoughts will be daily steeped in the celestial delights of heaven, while other men's are steeped in the gall and vinegar of this world. You will be above with God, when your carnal neighbors converse only with the world. Your thoughts will be higher than their thoughts and your ways than their ways, as the heaven where your conversation is, is higher than the earth. When you take flight from earth in holy devotions, they may look at you and wonder at you, but cannot follow you; for where you go they cannot come till they are such as you.

Don't compromise! Yes, old friends may notice a difference in you; they may even choose not to hang around you as much. But on Judgment Day, you will stand before God, not man. Do not allow the opinions of others to steal from you the heavenly prize. Once you are truly crucified to the world, you will find there is no greater joy than pure communion with God. Daily spread your wings and fly higher than you dared the day before! Remember, one day, your family and friends may follow you.

DEUTERONOMY 18; PSALM 105; ISAIAH 45; REVELATION 15

Toward Full Obedience

But this thing commanded I them, saying, Obey my voice, and I will be your God, and ye shall be my people: and walk ye in all the ways that I have commanded you, that it may be well unto you.
JEREMIAH 7:23

Over a period of several years, I had the honor to spend quality time with the great revivalist, Leonard Ravenhill. One of his classic statements to me was, "You can pour all the ingredients of Christianity into a funnel, and out the bottom will come obedience." He believed that obedience to God was the most important aspect of the Christian life. I agree. One of Leonard's favorite writers, William Gurnall, put it this way:

Such is the mercy of God in Christ to His children—He accepts their weak endeavors, joined with sincerity and perseverance in His service, as if they were in full obedience. Who would not serve such a Lord? Servants sometimes complain of their masters for being rigid and strict. They can never please them; not even when they do their utmost: but this cannot be said about God. Be faithful to do your best, and God is so gracious that He will pardon your worst. When a traveler has his eye set towards the place he is going, though he still be far from it, he continues on until he reaches the destination. So stands the Christian's heart to all the commands of God; he presses on to come nearer and nearer to full obedience; such a soul shall never be put to shame.

Whatever God has asked you to do, wherever He has asked you to go, whomever He has asked you to witness to, be obedient. Faithfulness to God is the key to the blessings of God.

DEUTERONOMY 19; PSALM 106; ISAIAH 46; REVELATION 16

And your ears will hear a word behind you, "This is the way, walk in it,"
whenever you turn to the right or to the left.
ISAIAH 30:21, NASB

The Lord has given each of us crystal-clear directions on how to
live. I call them the "rules of the road."

Do justly. This means being honest, honorable and conscientious
toward others, ourselves and toward God. Paul followed this direction
stringently, saying of himself, "And herein do I exercise myself, to have
always a conscience void of offence toward God, and toward men"
(Acts 24:16).

Love mercy. Mercy is underserved forgiveness. Most of us would
testify that we 'love' mercy when it is shown to us. But we often fall short
when it comes to treating others with mercy (see Matthew 18:21-35).

Walk humbly with thy God. This one has two parts. The first is
to devote oneself to the purpose of knowing God. The second has to
do with personal discipline, and chiefly, ridding yourself of pride.

**Observance of His road signs will ensure safe passage to your
destination.** Determine in your heart to follow these road signs. God
has explained many times the reward of those who do. "Wherefore it
shall come to pass, if ye hearken to these judgments, and keep, and do
them, that the LORD thy God shall keep unto thee the covenant and
the mercy which he sware unto thy fathers" (Deuteronomy 7:12).

Our destination is heaven. Jesus is the only way. He has given us
His Word (road signs) to follow. Adhering to His rules will ensure our
safe arrival.

Satan's Wiles

Neither give place to the devil.
EPHESIANS 4:27

We have all heard the saying, "Give the man an inch, he'll take a mile." This is never more true than when we refer to the effect of evil in our lives. When Satan comes with his sinful enticements, we can be assured that he has spiritual death in mind. We must not give him an inch. One of my favorite devotional writers of all time, William Jay, says:

> There are many reasons why we should not give place to the devil. One is because his designs are always bad. He may transform himself into an angel of light. And he may endeavor to introduce his evils and mischiefs under misleading names, representing covetousness as "laying up for the children," and pride as "dignity," and revenge as a "becoming spirit," and trimming in Christianity as "prudence," and conformity to the world as "winning others." Thus we are hardened through the deceitfulness of sin. But we ought not to be ignorant of Satan's devices. We read of his depths and his wiles—and God, in His Word, tears off all his disguises and shows us at once that his aim is only to ensnare, enslave, rob, degrade, wound and destroy us. The more you give way, the more advantage he has over you. It will always be found much more easy to keep him out, than to let him out.

Take heed to William Jay's council and don't even give the devil an inch!

DEUTERONOMY 21; PSALMS 108—109; ISAIAH 48; REVELATION 18

Neither by the blood of goats and calves, but by his own blood he entered in once into the holy place, having obtained eternal redemption for us.
HEBREWS 9:12

Jesus Christ came for one reason: to take away the sin of the world. He shed His Blood on Calvary, not so we could have a new house, new car and nice clothes. He bled and died to take away our sins. Sin is what crucified our Savior and is what will cripple our walk with Him.

J. G. Pike was known for his godly counsel to young disciples. He wrote this about sin:

> Sin is unspeakable, hateful and loathsome, because it is committed against God. It offends the blessed majesty of heaven, insults the Father, wounds the Son and grieves the Spirit.
>
> Sin is so vile that it can never be pardoned or washed away but by the Blood of the Son of God. Should all the creatures of the earth, and all the angels of heaven, have offered themselves as a sacrifice to divine justice, all could not have expiated one sin or atoned for one transgression. Or had the Son of God himself sought man's happiness by supplication only, there is no reason for supposing He could have been heard. He must suffer, or man eternally must die. We should be filled with eternal abhorrence of that which murdered Jesus on Calvary, and which, but for His death, would have murdered our soul with everlasting destruction.

Ask God to give you a hatred for your sin. Remember, it was sin that crucified our Savior, and it is sin that will cripple you.

DEUTERONOMY 22; PSALMS 110—111; ISAIAH 49; REVELATION 19

June 18

Violent Revival

And from the days of John the Baptist until now the kingdom of heaven suffereth violence, and the violent take it by force.
MATTHEW 11:12

Your salvation was won by the violence of the Cross. Jesus came, lived a perfect life and died a violent death. He was bruised; He was crushed; He was punctured; He was whipped; He was ridiculed; He was spat upon; He was scorned; He was abused; His hands and feet were pierced; He was subjected to the most violent death of His day—crucifixion. He has done His part.

Your salvation depends on your waging violent warfare against sin. It is time to do your part. Friend, if you are sick of sin and how it has laid waste to your life, then you must wage war. War is public. The violent man goes to war with his sins. He doesn't make excuses for them, he annihilates them. He slays them with the sword; burns them without mercy. They are the enemy. He will not settle for compromise or negotiate a treaty. No dealing with the devil. The violent man submits to God, resists the devil and the devil flees.

The salvation of your family and friends depends on your waging violent warfare on their behalf. Call it storming the gates of hell! You must be in a violent fight for the souls of lost loved ones. Be in violent intercessory prayer. Get violent against the strongholds of the enemy when it comes to taking your friends and your nation back for God! And remember, stay alert. Warfare is characterized by activity. Never look for peace while you proclaim war.

DEUTERONOMY 23; PSALMS 112—113; ISAIAH 50; REVELATION 20

Which One Are You?

O foolish Galatians! This only I want to learn from you:
Did you receive the Spirit by the works of the law, or by the hearing
of faith? Are you so foolish? Having begun in the Spirit,
are you now being made perfect by the flesh?
GALATIANS 3:1-3, NKJV

Paul the apostle was having a difficult time with the church in Galatia. They had received the truth, were living for God, and for some reason began to fall away. He was dealing with both the carnal man and the spiritual man. Notice how Andrew Murray differentiates between the two.

> I cannot with too much earnestness urge every Christian reader to learn well the two stages of the Christian. There are the carnal, and there are the spiritual; there are those who remain babes, and those who are full-grown men. There are those who come up out of Egypt, but then remain in the wilderness of a worldly life. The call to holiness, the call to cease from the life of wandering and murmuring, and enter into the rest of God, the call to the life of victory over every enemy and to the service of God in the land of promise, is not obeyed. They say it is too high and too hard. There are those who follow the Lord fully and enter the life of rest and victory. Let each of us find out where we stand, and taking earnest heed to God's warnings, with our whole heart press on to go all the length in following Jesus, in seeking to stand perfect and complete in all the will of God.

Members of the church in Galatia had made a serious mistake. They had allowed the world's philosophy to weave its way into the fabric of their lives. Don't make the same mistake. Carnal or spiritual, the choice is yours.

DEUTERONOMY 24; PSALMS 114—115; ISAIAH 51; REVELATION 21

The Messiah

Now when they heard this, they were pricked in their heart, and said unto Peter and to the rest of the apostles, Men and brethren, what shall we do?
ACTS 2:37

When the brilliant British composer George Frideric Handel was composing his most famous oratorio, he was found openly sobbing with his face resting upon the table, his body shaking. Before him lay the score, open at the place where it is written: "He was despised; He was rejected" (Isaiah 53:3).

The value that Jesus Christ placed on our souls shot like an arrow into Handel's heart. The unspeakable cruelty He endured, the sheer agony of the cross, all because He cared for our souls. It shook the very foundation of Handel's soul, and for that reason, he was able to pen one of the greatest musical works of all time, known as Handel's *Messiah.*

I believe everyone should have a personal encounter with the Messiah. On the Day of Pentecost, over 3,000 were added to the church after hearing the blessed redemption story. They were not content with just hearing a message, they had to meet the Messiah. George Frideric Handel was not content with just another musical score to sing, he too had to meet the Messiah.

We are at the verge of the greatest spiritual awakening this world has ever seen. The religious emblems that hang in our churches are going to suddenly take on new meaning. People today will no longer be content with just hearing a message...they will want to meet the Messiah. Is that your heart's desire?

DEUTERONOMY 25; PSALM 116; ISAIAH 52; REVELATION 22

Too Much to Ask?

*And thou shalt love the Lord thy God with all thy heart, and with all thy
soul, and with all thy mind, and with all thy strength:
this is the first commandment.*

MARK 12:30

I'll never forget the first time I understood that God loved me. I
had fallen deep into sin and had lost all hope in life. It was then that I
began to understand the depth of God's love. I learned about His sacrifice, about the Blood of Jesus and the pain of Calvary. My heart was
broken by the message. I thought to myself, *What could I give in return?*
The answer came through His Word. It was the first commandment.
God wanted my love.

Our response to God should echo the writings of Thomas Watson:

It is nothing but your love that God desires. The Lord might
have demanded your children to be offered in sacrifice; he
might have bid you cut and lance yourselves, or lie in hell a
while; but He only desires your love, He would only have this
flower. Is this a hard request, to love God? Was ever any debt
easier paid than this? Is it any labor for the wife to love her
husband? Love is delightful. What is there in love, that God
should desire it? Why should a king desire the love of a woman
that is in debt and diseased? There are angels enough in heav-
en to adore and love Him. What is God the better for our love?

It's hard to comprehend the fact that God desires any part of us.
After all, He's the Creator of the universe; in reality He owns it all. Just
as we desire to be loved, God's deepest desire is for His children to
praise and adore Him. Is that too much to ask?

DEUTERONOMY 26; PSALMS 117—118; ISAIAH 53; MATTHEW 1

June 22

Sleeping over Hell

God is angry with the wicked every day.
PSALM 7:11

In Dundee, Scotland, back in the early 1800s, it was common to hear Pastor Robert Murray McCheyne speak on this very subject. He was concerned that members of his congregation did not fully understand God's abhorrence of evil. By hearing of God's anger, perhaps the membership would begin witnessing to the unconverted, warning them of the wrath to come.

> God is angry with unconverted souls. Their sins are continually before Him and, therefore, He is continually provoked by them. The smoke of their sins is continually rising into His nostrils. He that believes not the Son, the wrath of God abides on him. Not only is God angry every day, but every moment of the day. There is not a moment of an unconverted man's life but God's wrath abides on him. When he is at his work or at play, sleeping or waking, in church or at market, the sword of God's wrath is over his head. Unconverted souls walk and sleep over hell.
>
> God's anger is like a river dammed up. It is getting higher and higher, fuller and deeper, every day against every soul that is out of Christ.

With this in mind, you should be diligent in sharing the gospel with your unconverted friends, regardless of their reactions toward us. Don't allow their anger to stop you. Better by far to get angry and hear the gospel down here than to fall into the hands of an angry God up there!

DEUTERONOMY 27—28:19; PSALM 119:1-24; ISAIAH 54; MATTHEW 2

So teach us to number our days, that we may apply our hearts unto wisdom.
PSALM 90:12

Can you believe this year is already halfway over? Doesn't it seem like just yesterday we were celebrating the new year? I don't know about you, but it seems to me that life is moving faster than ever before.

The Bible describes life pretty much the way we're feeling it. We're not the first ones to say that time flies. As a matter of fact, this terminology is as old as the Bible. Look at how God's Word portrays our short time here on earth:

It's a dream that flies away (Job 20:8).
It's a shadow that disappears (1 Chronicles 29:15).
It's a cloud that vanishes (Job 7:9).
It's a flower that dies (Job 14:1,2).
It's as grass that withers (1 Peter 1:24,25).
It's a vapor that vanishes (James 4:14).
It's as a mere breath, as nothing (Psalm 39:5).
It's as a phantom (Psalm 39:6, *NASB*).
It's as a sigh (Psalm 90:9, *NASB*).
It's as the wind that passes (Psalm 78:39).

Yes, the year is half gone. If the Bible describes our life in these terms, how much more diligent should we be to make wise use of the days we have.

DEUTERONOMY 28:20-68; PSALM 119:25-48; ISAIAH 55; MATTHEW 3

Back to the Drawing Board

I will give them an undivided heart and put a new spirit in them; I will remove from them their heart of stone and give them a heart of flesh.
EZEKIEL 11:19, NIV

Ever wonder why it's not good enough that we become an *improved* creation...why simply fixing the 'old' us doesn't work? According to the Word of God, we are to be totally transformed. I found Charles Spurgeon's conclusions about this transformation to be quite clear and profound.

Notice that God doesn't promise to remodel our nature or to mend our broken hearts. No, the promise is that He will give us new hearts and right spirits. Human nature is too far gone to ever be mended. It isn't a house that is a little out of repair, with an occasional shingle missing from the roof and a little plaster broken from the ceiling. No, it's rotten throughout, every single timber has been eaten by the worm, from the roof to the foundation. There is no soundness, it is ready to fall.

God will not attempt to mend by repairing the walls and repainting the door. He will build a new one. If it was only a little out of repair, it might be mended, but it's too far gone. Concerning man's depravity, the whole head is sick and the whole heart is faint. From the sole of the foot to the crown of the head, it is all wounds, bruises and festering sores. The Lord, therefore, does not attempt the repairing of this thing. Instead He says, "I will give you a new heart, and a right spirit will I put within you. I will take away the heart of stone, I will not try to soften it, and I will let it be as stony as it ever was. But I will take it away, and I will give you a new heart, and it shall be a heart of flesh."

Keep Moving

"A little sleep, a little slumber, a little folding of the hands to rest," then your poverty will come as a robber, and your want like an armed man.
PROVERBS 24:33,34, NASB

Have you ever been riding a bicycle when suddenly a gust of wind began blowing against you? You had built up momentum but were now being resisted by an uncontrollable force. You may also remember how hard it is to resume peddling once you've stopped. I've been in this position, my friend, and learned the importance of perseverance.

The Puritan writer, Richard Sibbes, illustrates the importance of perseverance in another easy to understand manner:

> As watermen rowing against the stream, if they do not row, but rest ever so little, the stream carries them back again, and they cannot recover themselves but with great difficulty. So it is in this Christian race. A little interruption of duty causes three times as much pain and effort to recover our former estate. Therefore, we are to take up a holy resolution not to be interrupted in good duties.

Reverend Sibbes was warning his congregants about becoming lax in their spiritual exercises. If he were alive today, he would issue a stern warning against substituting television time for Bible study, sporting activities for prayer, and so on. He would firmly but lovingly exhort us to not allow anything to deter us from going after God with all our strength. The moment we begin to slack off is the moment we begin to backslide, instead of moving forward with the Holy Spirit's momentum.

DEUTERONOMY 30; PSALM 119:73-96; ISAIAH 57; MATTHEW 5

Every Hour of the Day

Be ye therefore followers of God, as dear children;
and walk in love, as Christ also hath loved us, and hath given himself for
us an offering and a sacrifice to God for a sweetsmelling savour.
EPHESIANS 5:1,2

The following words by Hannah Whitall Smith are strong, but they should be heeded by everyone who calls himself a Christian.

Some Christians seem to think all the requirements of a holy life are met when they are active and successful in Christian work. Because they do so much for the Lord in public, they feel a liberty to be ugly and ungodly in private. But this is not the sort of Christian life I am depicting. If we are to walk as Christ walked, it must be in private as well as in public, at home as well as abroad; and it must be every hour all day long, and not at stated periods or on certain fixed occasions. We must be just as Christ-like to others as we are to our minister, and just as "good" in our home as we are in our prayer meeting.

An angry, worrying, gloomy, doubting, complaining, demanding, selfish, cruel, hard-hearted, self-indulgent, sharp-tongued or bitter-spirited Christian may be very earnest in his or her *work*, and may have an honorable place in the church; but they are not *Christ-like Christians*. They know nothing of the realities of true Christianity, no matter how loud their professions may be.

Though Jesus understands our shortcomings, His desire is for us to overcome them, not just live with them. Make it a habit to take a serious look at your life and ask the Lord to show you any areas where you are not walking in the love of Christ. He will help you change, if you allow Him.

DEUTERONOMY 31; PSALM 119:97-120; ISAIAH 58; MATTHEW 6

The Name Christian

And the disciples were called Christians first in Antioch.
ACTS 11:26

We live in a nation where the majority call themselves Christian. By definition, the name "Christian" means "a person who believes in Jesus Christ, and lives according to His teaching." If this is the case, and it is, then millions of people need to quit calling themselves by that name. Only the ones who faithfully follow Jesus and are committed to doing His will for their lives should have the right to call themselves a Christian.

Have you ever wondered why the early followers of Jesus were suddenly given this new name? William S. Plumer gives us a brief explanation.

At first, Christians were called disciples, believers, or brethren. In Antioch was first felt the need of a name, which should suit both Jewish and Gentile converts, and which should briefly set forth their religious belief. There were inspired men ministering in that church, who may have been divinely directed to give the name. There was great need of a new name, to embrace all the converts. Some think this is according to that prophecy in Isaiah 62:2, that the people of God, under the gospel, should "be called by a new name, which the mouth of the LORD should name." It early became a form of professing love to the Lord Jesus to say, "I am a Christian."

How wonderful it would be for us to return to the original meaning of this title. To say "I am a Christian" would be to say, "I am in love with my Lord Jesus."

DEUTERONOMY 32; PSALM 119:121-144; ISAIAH 59; MATTHEW 7

Now Is the Time

*"At the acceptable time I listened to you, and on the day of salvation
I helped you"; behold, now is "the acceptable time," behold, now is
"the day of salvation."*
2 CORINTHIANS 6:2, NASB

Everyone should sense the urgency of the days in which we live. While there is a mighty move of God sweeping the world, there is also an ominous fear gripping the hearts of millions. You can read about it in the headlines and hear about it on the evening news. The Bible says, "Seek the LORD while He may be found, call upon Him while He is near" (Isaiah 55:6). We are living in a season of grace. God has chosen to bless, not curse. He has chosen mercy, not judgment. But, my friend, this could change at any moment.

Now is the time to allow the light of the gospel of Christ to shine into the deep, dark inner recesses of your heart.

Now is the time to break up the topsoil of your heart and allow the precious Word of God to enter like a seed falling on a freshly tilled garden.

Now is the time to drop your heavy burdens at the foot of the Cross, take His yoke upon you, and learn of Him.

Now is the time to cast all your cares upon Jesus, because He cares for you. Many people spend so much time musing over past mistakes that they miss the opportunity right before them. Others are so preoccupied in taking care of tomorrow that they bypass their opportunity today.

When God comes near in His great mercy, don't miss your opportunity. Tomorrow is a date that can only be found in a fool's calendar. Now is the day of salvation. Don't put it off. Go after God. Pursue Him for revival in your own life and in the lives of those around you.

DEUTERONOMY 33–34; PSALM 119:145-176; ISAIAH 60; MATTHEW 8

June 29

Forward Focus

Brethren, I do not regard myself as having laid hold of it yet; but one thing I do: forgetting what lies behind and reaching forward to what lies ahead, I press on toward the goal for the prize of the upward call of God in Christ Jesus.
PHILIPPIANS 3:13,14, NASB

As a minister, I have had the opportunity to be with many people in the last moments before they died. During those times, the conversation was never trite and silly, but deep, meaningful and related to the life to come.

As an evangelist, I spend my life endeavoring to help people focus on eternity. Everywhere I go, the majority of mankind is focused on this temporal, material world. If only more ministers warned of the consequences and the judgment to come. If only the world could see how fleeting this life really is.

Robert Hall was a mighty man of God, with his eyes fixed on eternity. His warning is so relevant today.

After death is the judgment. What is to shield you in judgment from the stroke of vengeance? Have you been hearing the calls of the gospel without regarding them? Have you not applied the truth to yourselves? Oh, remove yourself now from the snares of the world. Shut your eyes on the scenes of time, on which they must soon be closed forever. Converse with the world to come, endeavor to yield to the power of it. Look at the things which are not seen. Walk, as it were, upon the borders of the ocean of eternity and listen to the sound of its waters till you are deaf to every sound besides.

Oh friend, do not take his warning lightly. Feel the urgency. Keep a forward focus. Live eternity-conscious.

JOSHUA 1; PSALMS 120—122; ISAIAH 61; MATTHEW 9

June 30

Canceled Debt

Blessed is he whose transgression is forgiven, whose sin is covered.
PSALM 32:1

Do you have any idea how clean you are before God? When Jesus saved you, He completely forgave every sin you have ever committed. You had built up quite an indebtedness. There was no way to pay it, and then God wiped the slate clean. Joseph Alliene gives us a glimpse of the forgiveness of sins.

God no longer charges sin to the sinner's account. If a man owes a debt, and it is canceled, that means there are no charges against him. When God pardons a transgressor, He cancels the sinner's debt.

Pardon renders the sinner free from the charge of transgression, as if he had never sinned. This forgiveness is full, covering every offense; and is free, without money, without price. This completeness of forgiveness is described throughout the scriptures. It is said, "Thou wilt cast all their sins into the depths of the sea" (Micah 7:19). The sin is then removed and hidden, as if buried forever in the depths of an unfathomable ocean. God removes sin to the greatest possible distance from the soul. "As far as the east is from the west, so far hath he removed our transgressions from us" (Psalm 103:12). God Himself expresses, "Though your sins be as scarlet, they shall be as white as snow" (Isaiah 1:18).

Our sin was a debt He did not owe and we could not pay. Yet He canceled it!

As a Thief in the Night

For yourselves know perfectly that the day of the Lord
so cometh as a thief in the night.

1 THESSALONIANS 5:2

Let's establish two facts today: The day of the Lord is coming, and His coming will be terrible (dreadful). Now, anywhere the word "thief" is used in the Bible to describe the return of Jesus, the term refers to *secrecy*, not violence. Here are five characteristics of a thief:

- An experienced thief cases out his target far in advance of his hit.
- A thief lurking in the shadows will let you walk right by him. If you're not looking for him, you won't see him.
- A thief doesn't mind waiting for those in the house to be fast asleep with the light out. When you're asleep, you're unprepared.
- A thief doesn't warn you of his coming; he just appears.
- A thief takes care of his business quickly, quietly and then disappears. You never had a chance.

As I read these characteristics of a thief, it's not difficult to see why Jesus chose this analogy to indicate His return to earth. He wanted His hearers to live in a state of total readiness. He consistently warned of laziness and lukewarmness. He never ceased to challenge His followers to stay alert.

My friend, the Lord is coming back as a thief in the night. Stay alert! Stay wide awake! Be ready!

Captive to the Word

I have rejoiced in the way of thy testimonies, as much as in all riches.
PSALM 119:14

For many years I lived according to the dictates of my own heart. I was a rebellious man and did what was right in my own eyes. Because there was no standard to live by, no God to govern, no eternal purpose to achieve, I found myself wandering aimlessly. But then one autumn morning, a minister shared with me the mercy of Jesus. His love broke through and changed me forever. Shortly thereafter, the minister brought me my first copy of God's holy Word. It was love at first sight. In it I found the perfect will of God for my life.

William Cowper, a pastor who lived according to the Word and will of God, wrote:

> The testimony of God is His Word. The "way" of His testimony is the practice of His Word and doing of that which He hath declared to be His will. David found not this sweetness in hearing, reading, and professing the word only, but in practicing of it. The only reason why we do not find the comfort that is in the Word of God is because we do not practice walking according to it. It is true, at first it is bitter to our natural man, which loves carnal liberty, to render itself as captive to the Word. Much effort must be taken before the heart be totally surrendered; but when it is once begun, it brings such joy.

I have absolutely no regrets about having given my life over to the will of God. Have you totally surrendered your life to God's will? Are you captive to the Word?

JOSHUA 4; PSALMS 129–131; ISAIAH 64; MATTHEW 12

J u l y 3

If Everybody Was Blind

A man's pride shall bring him low:
but honour shall uphold the humble in spirit.
PROVERBS 29:23

The following words were preached by one of the most powerful
evangelists America has ever known. Charles Finney, a lawyer turned
preacher, stated his case with clarity and conviction. Imagine yourself
sitting in a courtroom under his piercing eyes. Pride is on the witness
stand. Finney lifts his voice and begins the cross-examination.

Recollect all the instances you can in which you have detected
yourself in the exercise of pride. Vanity is a particular form of
pride. How many times have you detected yourself in consulting vanity about your dress and appearance? How often have
you spent more time decorating your body to go to church
than you have about preparing your mind for the worship of
God? You have gone to the house of God caring more how
you appear outwardly in the sight of mortal men than how
your soul appears in the sight of the heart-searching God. You
have in fact set up yourself to be worshipped by them, rather
than prepared to worship God yourself. It is in vain to pretend now that you don't care anything about having people
look at you. Be honest about it. Would you take all these
pains about your looks if everybody was blind?

These riveting words should be preached behind every pulpit in
America. Millions in our nation attend church on a weekly basis and
are more concerned about man's opinion than God's. Finney's right.
There would be a major shift in priorities if everybody was blind!

Fire Works!

He shall baptize you with the Holy Ghost, and with fire.
MATTHEW 3:11

Throughout the Word of God we find an array of emblems or symbols of His presence. One symbol of God's presence is fire. By definition, fire is the effect of combustion—that is, anything that is capable of igniting, such as wood, hay and stubble. We too, are combustible in a spiritual sense. God knows it and that's why He sends *fire*.

Fire consumes: "For the LORD thy God is a consuming fire" (Deuteronomy 4:24). To consume means to destroy. For example, if a landowner has some acreage full of harmful weeds and useless crabgrass, he may set fire to that field, consuming the debris while fertilizing the ground at the same time to make it useful.

Fire purifies: Malachi 3:2,3 describes our Lord as a refiner's fire purifying us from unrighteousness. A refiner's fire refers to the separation of dross from useful or even precious metal. Such a fire is hot enough to melt the worst of the rubbish from our past lives.

Fire softens: The fire of God's presence can melt the stoniest sin-hardened heart. "I will take the stony heart out of their flesh, and will give them an heart of flesh" (Ezekiel 11:19,20). Has your life been touched by the *fire* of God? Has the old been burned off to make way for the new? Are you living close to the refiner's fire?

Yes, my friend, on this 4th of July, we need the fire of God. Fire works!

JOSHUA 6:6-27; PSALMS 135—136; ISAIAH 66; MATTHEW 14

Christ Saw the Devil

But He turned and said to Peter, "Get behind Me, Satan!
You are a stumbling block to Me; for you are not setting your mind
on God's interests, but man's."
MATTHEW 16:23, NASB

Have you ever been rebuked by the Lord? I have. There have been times in my life when I blurted out an idea or a plan without ever consulting the Lord. Shortly thereafter, Jesus spoke sharply to me that the idea was not from Him. Today's text shares an instance of that happening to Peter. Jonathan Edwards expounds on this startling rebuke from the Lord.

> This may seem like an instance of harshness in reproving Peter, yet I humbly believe that this is by many taken wrong. This is indeed no instance of Christ's severity in His treatment of Peter, but on the contrary, of His wonderful gentleness and grace. Jesus was not laying the blame of what Peter had then said, or imputing it to him, but to the devil that influenced him. Christ saw the devil secretly influencing Peter to play the part of a tempter to his Master. Therefore Christ turned around to Peter, whom the devil was then using, spoke to the devil and rebuked him. It does not charge what is imperfect in them to *them*—but to sin that dwells in them, and to Satan that influences them.

My friend, at times God must speak harshly to us. What a far worse fix Peter would have found himself in if Jesus had not rebuked the source of his error. We must learn not only to receive His correction, but even more, to rejoice in it. After all, He's only trying to line us up with His perfect will.

JOSHUA 7; PSALMS 137—138; JEREMIAH 1; MATTHEW 15

Money, Money, Money

He who is gracious to a poor man lends to the LORD,
and He will repay him for his good deed.
PROVERBS 19:17, NASB

I have had the privilege of working all over the world. My travels have taken me to some of the most poverty-stricken areas on this planet. My heart breaks as I see the stark contrast between those who have and those who have not. In America, it is common for a family to spend $50 on a meal in a restaurant, while in other nations, that is more than a month's wages. Why is it so easy for us to give a restaurant $50 for one hour of carnal gratification, and so difficult to give a missions offering of $50 that brings eternal rewards? It seems I am not alone in my views on money. As a matter of fact, the Bible speaks clearly of how we should handle our finances. Robert Murray McCheyne spoke to the idol of money in much the same way as I do today.

> If you have felt the love of God, you must dash down the idol of money. You must not love money. You must be more open-hearted, more open-handed to the poor. God be praised for what has been done: but you must do far more. You must give more to missions, to send the knowledge of Jesus to the world. How can you grasp your money in hand so greedily, while there are hundreds of millions perishing? You that give tens must give your hundreds. You that are poor must do what you can. Let us resolve to give the tenth of all we have to God.

The truth of the matter is that God owns it all. We're just stewards of a portion of God's great wealth. Who are we to argue when He wants to give a little away?

JOSHUA 8; PSALM 139; JEREMIAH 2; MATTHEW 16

Joy Has a Language

Through Him then, let us continually offer up a sacrifice of praise to God, that is, the fruit of lips that give thanks to His name. And do not neglect doing good and sharing; for with such sacrifices God is pleased.
HEBREWS 13:15,16, NASB

I will never forget what the Lord has done for me. Every one of us has a testimony. If we have been set free and delivered from sin in our lives, we should be exuberant in our praise and thanksgiving to God.

Joy was one of the first Christian characteristics that welled up in my life after receiving Christ as Savior. It was hard to explain. It was joy unspeakable. All I could do was lift my hands and glorify God through enthusiastic praise. I have learned the same lesson Matthew Henry taught more than 200 years ago.

> Let us be much in the exercise of holy joy, and employ ourselves much in praise. Joy is in the heart of praise, and praise is the language of joy. Let us engage ourselves to these. God has made joy and praise our duty. All the other parts of our duty to God will be pleasant to us when we abound ourselves in joy and praise towards God. Let us not crowd our spiritual joys into a corner of our hearts, nor our thankful praises into a corner of our prayers, but give scope and vent to both. Let us live a life of delight in God, and love to think of Him as we do of one whom we love and value.

If we truly value our relationship with God, if we honestly esteem Him as the Savior of our soul, if He is the one who has set us free, then the most natural response should be the praise of our lips.

A Forgiving Mood

And you, that were sometime alienated and enemies in your mind by wicked works, yet now hath he reconciled in the body of his flesh through death, to present you holy and unblameable and unreproveable in his sight.
COLOSSIANS 1:21,22

To forgive is to cease to feel resentment against. It also means to grant relief from payment. Forgiveness is not something to be presumed, but rather something to be pursued. Herein lies the guilt of many people. Millions upon millions have died and fallen into the hands of the righteous Judge, presuming that He was going to understand their plight on earth and forgive them regardless of whether or not they pursued forgiveness. My friend, this is shaky, dangerous territory.

God desires to cleanse everyone from all unrighteousness. The Bible says He forgives all our sins and heals all our diseases (see Psalm 103:3). This means that He wants to forgive, but we must come to Him. Friend, the sooner you seek forgiveness, the better off you are.

When someone is in a forgiving mood it is a great time to repent of wrongdoing. Just as a parent can be forgiving toward the wrongdoing of a child, so our heavenly Father is forgiving towards us. Right now, God is in a mercy mode. Mercy is undeserved forgiveness. None of us knows how long He will continue displaying mercy, but we all know there is coming a time when His mercy will be traded for wrath.

The Bible says that His Spirit will not always contend with man (see Genesis 6:3). We live now in the dispensation of grace and mercy. Don't take it for granted. It won't be like this forever.

A Cross and a Crown

And when he had called the people unto him with his disciples also,
he said unto them, Whosoever will come after me, let him deny himself,
and take up his cross, and follow me.
MARK 8:34

Every Christian must bear his own cross. Every believer must bear his own burden. What God has chosen for you to do is not necessarily what He has spoken to someone else. We must all, as individuals, follow Jesus down the path He has chosen for us. This road is often rocky, full of challenges and trials, but the purposes of God are far greater than our present difficulties. His eyes are focused on the destination. Pastor Theodore L. Cuyler, having passed through many personal trials, wants to lift our eyes off the present circumstances and lift them up to see God's purpose.

> The trial that purifies our character must be something more than a pin scratch. It must try us; it must cut keenly, or it does not deserve the name "trial." For example, it is hard to be poor while some others are pocketing a large income. It is hard to lie on a sick bed and suffer while godless mirth goes laughing past our door. It is hard to lose our one tiny baby while our neighbor's table is surrounded by a group of rosy-cheeked children. It is hard to drink the very cup that we prayed might pass from us.

Yes it is hard, but necessary. It is of vital importance for us to remember that God has a goal. His ways are not our ways, His thoughts are not our thoughts. God is so much greater. So trust Him today. Endure the trial. Rejoice in the Lord. I believe without a doubt, the heavier the cross down here, the more glorious the crown up there!

I Will Come Again

And if I go and prepare a place for you, I will come again, and receive you unto myself; that where I am, there ye may be also.

JOHN 14:3

The promises of God are the promises of a perfect gentleman. When God says He's going to do something, He will do it. He said He would send us a Savior, and He did. He promised His Holy Spirit to fill and comfort us, and the promise came to pass. Now we anticipate, like little children at Christmas, the fulfillment of another great promise of God. Jesus said, "I will come again."

The great American evangelist D. L. Moody preached often of this great and glorious day.

There are three great facts foretold in the Word of God. First, that Christ would come; which has been fulfilled. Second, that the Holy Ghost would come; which was fulfilled at Pentecost, and the Church is able to testify to it by its experience of His saving grace. Third, the return of our Lord again from heaven: for this we are told to watch and wait "till He come."

Look at the account of the last hours of Christ with His disciples. What does Christ say to them? He says, "I will come again and receive you unto myself." If my wife were in a foreign country, and I had a beautiful mansion all ready for her, she would much rather I come for her than have me send someone else to bring her. So the Church is the Lamb's wife; He has prepared a mansion for His bride, and He promises that He will come Himself and take us to the place He has been preparing all this while.

JOSHUA 12—13; PSALM 145; JEREMIAH 6; MATTHEW 20

The Four Calls of God

So the last shall be first, and the first last: for many be called, but few chosen.
MATTHEW 20:16

The Outward Call. This is the voice of the Shepherd, saying, "Come home." It happens when the Word of God is preached, the arrows of the Lord pierce the heart, and the Holy Spirit convicts the lost soul. The Bible says, "For many be called, but few chosen" (Matthew 20:16). The truth of this scripture is that few choose to be chosen.

The Inward Call. This is the deeper call. The first call gets your attention; the second, your adoration. The outward call brings men to a profession of Christ, the inward to a possession of Christ. The outward call tells you who He is; with the inward call He tells you who you are.

The Forward Call. Once a person has answered the outward call and obeyed the inward call, he is ready to put his heart thoughts into action. It is one thing to tell the Lord that we will go wherever He wants us to go, while it is quite another to actually fulfill our commitment. Jesus said, "Go into all the world and preach the gospel." This is the forward call. It's not optional.

The Upward Call. This is the final call. Jesus is coming back for a spotless Bride. It is the call the first three are in preparation for. As Paul wrote to Timothy, "Henceforth there is laid up for me a crown of righteousness, which the Lord, the righteous judge, shall give me at that day: and not to me only, but unto all them also that love his appearing" (2 Timothy 4:8).

Don't miss the upward call.

JOSHUA 14—15; PSALMS 146—147; JEREMIAH 7; MATTHEW 21

Cause for Cheerfulness

Serve the LORD with gladness: come before His presence with singing.
PSALM 100:2

Allow me to ask some very pointed questions. Do you serve God with a joyful heart? Do you follow Him because you want to, or is it because you feel that you have to? Do you obey Jesus out of love or fear? Is there an attitude of cheerfulness in your spirit during the good times and the bad, or do you only exude joy when things are going your way? Let the words of Thomas Watson challenge you.

We glorify God by walking cheerfully. It is a glory to God when the world sees within a Christian what can make him cheerful in the worst times. The people of God have grounds for cheerfulness. They are justified, and instated into adoption. This creates inward peace, and whatever storms are without, we consider what Christ has wrought for us by His Blood, and wrought in us by His Spirit. It gives cause for great cheerfulness, and this cheerfulness glorifies God. When God's servants hang their heads, it looks as if they do not serve a good Master. This reflects dishonor on God. As the gross sins of the wicked bring a scandal on the gospel, so do the uncheerful lives of the godly. Your serving Him does not glorify him, unless it be with gladness. A Christian's cheerful look glorifies God.

When we hang our heads, as if serving a mean taskmaster, it causes the world to be turned off to Christ. However, if we cheerfully follow Him with a smile on our face, then the unbeliever will have reason to take notice.

JOSHUA 16—17; PSALM 148; JEREMIAH 8; MATTHEW 22

Do We Really Mean It?

When you make a vow to God, do not be late in paying it, for He takes no delight in fools. Pay what you vow! It is better that you should not vow than that you should vow and not pay.
ECCLESIASTES 5:4,5, NASB

I'm sure you've heard the term "jailhouse salvation." It refers to someone who cries out to God when things are going bad and promises God a life of total commitment. When things get better, they back out of their pledge.

Scottish pastor Horatius Bonar spoke directly to this issue over 150 years ago. I find it amazing how accurate his words are today.

> There is a place where many people stumble. During a trial they call on the Lord and vow their life to Him. They say that through bad times and good they will follow Him; on the rough way or the smooth they will walk with Him. By labor, by sacrifice, by watchfulness, by costly gifts, they will prove their love and zeal and devotion! Good words and sincerely spoken! But so were the words of Peter the disciple, "If I should die with You, I will not deny You in any way." He truly felt those words, but when the hour came, the resolution was not to be found. So it is with us. Trials call forth many a high thought and prompts to noble promises. Yet how seldom do these thoughts deteriorate; how often do these intentions die! Peace returns, sunshine brightens over us, our broken strength knits again and we sink back into idleness! The calm hour for which we longed, that we might do something for God, has come, but it finds us nearly as heedless and selfish as before we entered into the storm.

JOSHUA 18—19; PSALMS 149—150; JEREMIAH 9; MATTHEW 23

This poor man cried, and the LORD heard him,
and saved him out of all his troubles.
PSALM 34:6

There are some who go to Christian meetings with an incredible hunger for more of God's presence and power. Their appetite for a sovereign move of God has been a constant preoccupation. They are tired of the mediocre. They want to see God come down in their midst. Their thirst for God has not been quenched and their hunger pains have not been satisfied. A man's desperation for the presence of God should melt all preoccupation with self, notoriety, public image and social status. His hunger and thirst, if genuine, will drive him to eat and drink regardless of the opinions of others. He will be willing to be a fool in the sight of his peers in order to be embraced in the arms of the Lord.

Saint of God, don't allow worldly preoccupations to stand between you and the outpouring of the Holy Spirit. Walk humbly before God. Our Scripture text says that a poor man cried out to God. It is of vital importance for us to go after God with a clear understanding of our spiritual destitution.

Also, be faithful in the small things. Keep your heart guarded and prepared for revival. When true revival breaks out and God begins moving in your church, don't allow pride to enter. Stay broken before the Lord. Be faithful, and one day you may hear Him say, "Well done, good and faithful servant; thou hast been faithful over a few things, I will make thee ruler over many things: enter thou into the joy of thy lord" (Matthew 25:23).

The Upper Room Men

*Blessed are they which do hunger and thirst after righteousness:
for they shall be filled.*

MATTHEW 5:6

What does it mean to truly be hungry after God? We talk about the power of God, but we see little of it in our lives, our churches, our nation. The late Leonard Ravenhill brings our attention to the fact that we need a powerful touch from the Lord like never before, and there is only one way to receive that touch.

God-hungry men find God. As the deer pants after the water brooks, so the Upper-Room crowd panted for the living God. Spiritually naked, they fled to Him so that they might be clothed with the blessed Spirit. Empty, they craved to be filled. Powerless, they tarried until they were endued. Bankrupt and beggar-like, they pled the riches of His grace. This fear-filled crowd became fire-filled messengers. Though swordless, these soldiers of Christ fought the might of imperial Rome and won. Though without ecclesiastical prestige, they opposed the frozen orthodoxy of sterile Judaism and pierced it to the heart. Though not deeply educated, they unblushingly declared the whole counsel of God and eventually staggered the intellectual Greeks.

Without question, the greatest need of this hour is that the Church meet with her risen Lord again, and get an endowment that would usher in the revival of revivals just before the night of nights settles over this age of incomparable corruption.[1]

My friend, those who seek God will find Him.

1. Leonard Ravenhill, *The Upper Room Men* (Minneapolis, Minn.: 1989), p. 19.

JOSHUA 22; ACTS 2; JEREMIAH 11; MATTHEW 25

The First State

> *Remember therefore from where you have fallen, and repent and do the deeds you did at first; or else I am coming to you, and will remove your lampstand out of its place—unless you repent.*
>
> REVELATION 2:5, NASB

Though the author of the following passage is unknown, the divine inspiration for it is quite apparent.

> Our knees then, must bow to Him who walks in the midst of the golden candlesticks. Back we must go until the glorious Lord stands among us in all the majesty of His Holy Person. The Church, which is His by gift of the Father and by His own purchase, comes under His complete control. For too long our remiss ways have shut the gates against the heavenly breathing of this Holy Spirit. Back we must go until the Lord Jesus is gloriously unveiled so that the fragrance of His Holy Presence becomes again the saving power of the Gospel. It is only our full return to the first state of the church which will once again make our worship spiritual and our prayers and devotions fervent and zealous. Those mighty acts wrought by the apostles are possible again but only when those who love Him walk with Him in white. Therefore, He says, "Do the first works"—that is, do as the first Christians did.

Whoever penned these words knew the secret of revival. There must be a passionate love for the Savior before a move of God will ever take place. This love must be daily demonstrated in our prayers and actions. We must return to the first state, that is, when we first fell in love with Jesus Christ.

The Rod of God

Behold, happy is the man whom God correcteth:
therefore despise not thou the chastening of the Almighty.
JOB 5:17

Discipline and affliction is a subject that many Christians refuse to understand. They want to learn of love. They want to pursue peace. They enjoy meditating on mercy. They harbor hope in their hearts, but when it comes to the chastening of the Lord, they quickly change channels. The writings of Joseph Caryl, more than 300 years ago, are relevant for today.

If a man is watchful over his own ways, and the dealings of God with him, there is seldom a day to pass without some rod of affliction upon him. But, through lack of care and watch-fulness, we may lose sight of many mercies, so we do of many afflictions. God may not every day bring a man to his bed, and break his bones, yet we seldom, if at all, pass a day without some rebuke and chastening. "I have been chastened every morning," says the psalmist. "As sure, or as soon, as I rise I have a whipping, and my breakfast is bread of sorrow and the water of adversity." Our lives are full of afflictions; and it is as great a part of a Christian's skill to know afflictions as to know mercies; to know when God smites, as to know when he supports us; and it is our sin to overlook afflictions as well as to overlook mercies.

The very fact that God is allowing affliction is evidence of His love toward you. Remember, He is not wanting to hurt you, rather He wants to heal you. The rod of God may sting for a moment, but the lesson learned will last for eternity.

JOSHUA 24; ACTS 4; JEREMIAH 13; MATTHEW 27

Bonsai Babies

The righteous shall flourish like the palm tree: he shall grow like a cedar in Lebanon. Those that be planted in the house of the LORD shall flourish in the courts of our God.

PSALM 92:12,13

Have you ever seen a bonsai tree? Those tiny trees look as if they were shrunk by some scientific reducing machine. There was an interesting and very practical parallel drawn by Pastor J. R. Miller that I want you to notice.

One of the strange freaks of Japanese horticulture is the cultivation of dwarf trees. The Japanese grow forest giants in flowerpots. Some of these strange miniature trees are a century old, and are only two or three feet high. The gardener, instead of trying to get them to grow to their best, takes infinite pains to keep them little. His purpose is to grow dwarfs, not giant trees. From the time of their planting they are repressed, starved, crippled, stunted. When buds appear, they are nipped off. So the tree remains only a dwarf all its life.

Some Christian people seem to do the same thing with their lives. They do not allow themselves to grow. They rob themselves of spiritual nourishment, restrain the noble impulses of their nature, shut out of their hearts the power of the Holy Spirit, and are only dwarf Christians when they might be strong in Christ Jesus with the abundant life which the Master wants all his followers to have.

Whatever is out there that stunts your growth, get rid of it! God is after towering oak trees, not little bonsai babies.

JUDGES 1; ACTS 5; JEREMIAH 14; MATTHEW 28

How to Miss God

And He said to her, "Daughter, your faith has made you well;
go in peace, and be healed of your affliction."
MARK 5:34, NASB

Have you ever wondered why some people receive from God and others don't? I believe one reason is that somtimes people just miss out on God. The woman described in today's text received a miracle. If she were alive today, she would agree that any of the following points would have prevented her from receiving that miracle.

Close your ears. If this woman had shut her ears to the news that Jesus was in town, a miracle would have never taken place.

Trust your own understanding. If you want to miss God, let your natural mind reason Him out of the picture. This woman, sick for 12 years and steadily growing worse, could easily have been discouraged. Her natural mind was probably saying, "You've spent all your money; you've seen all the doctors; what good is it to go to God?"

Listen to everyone else's opinion. I wonder what would have happened if she had asked a religious leader about Jesus. I'm sure they would have discouraged her from touching the Healer.

Do absolutely nothing. When you hear about the miracle-working power of Jesus—when you know He can heal you and change you—just sit there. Do absolutely nothing.

No Room for Pride

He brought me up also out of an horrible pit, out of the miry clay, and set my feet upon a rock, and established my goings.

PSALM 40:2

Hardly a week goes by when I don't meet an arrogant, prideful man. He struts around on the two legs God gave him, works with the hands God created, eats the food God has planted and breathes the air God has provided. Yet he acts as if it is all his doing. This is the epitome of ingratitude. It is poisonous pride and needs to be taken to the Cross and crucified. *Morning and Evening Devotions,* written by William Jay, has been daily nourishment for thousands over the years. Here's what he had to say about those who are proud.

> We are prone to think more highly of ourselves than we ought to think; but with the lowly is wisdom. God resists the proud, but gives grace unto the humble. Surely we have enough to hide pride from us, if we reflect properly. If we are now wise, we were once foolish: if we are now justified, we were once condemned; if we are now the sons of God, we were once the servants of sin. Let us look to the rock [of] which we were hewn, and to the hole of the pit [from] which we were dug.

It would do us all good to sit down and meditate on our humble beginnings. There was a time when someone nursed us, washed us, taught us to walk and how to talk. At one time, we were totally dependent on others. In reality, nothing's changed. If God pulled His Spirit from us, we wouldn't have enough sense to tie our shoes. My friend, there's no room for pride, only room for God.

JUDGES 3; ACTS 7; JEREMIAH 16; MARK 2

Our Way of Escape

Our soul has escaped as a bird out of the snare of the trapper;
the snare is broken and we have escaped.
Our help is in the name of the LORD, who made heaven and earth.
PSALM 124:7,8, NASB

In my own life, I have found that faith is only active when confronted with an impossible situation. Let me give you an example. If you want to buy a piece of land for a certain amount of money, and that amount exists in your present bank account, there is no need for faith. However, if the price of the piece of land far exceeds the funds available, it is time to reach out in faith believing God to provide spiritually for what cannot be obtained naturally.

The distinguished Scottish preacher and theologian, Robert Leighton, knew what faith was all about.

> When the soul is surrounded with enemies on all hands, so that there is no way of escape, faith flies above them. Faith carries up the soul to take refuge in Christ, and there finds safety. That is the power of faith; it sets a soul in Christ, and there, looks down upon all temptations. When the floods of temptation rise and gather, so great and so many, that the soul is even ready to be swallowed up, then, by faith, it says, "Lord Jesus, You are my strength. I look to You for deliverance, help me!" This is how we overcome.

My dear friend, perhaps today you are facing a mountain of adversity. Maybe, like Leighton describes, you are surrounded with enemies. It is at a time like this that faith rises to the occasion. Trust in God. He knows your present circumstances and He knows your way of escape.

JUDGES 4; ACTS 8; JEREMIAH 17; MARK 3

Embrace the World

Moreover as for me, God forbid that I should sin against the LORD in ceasing to pray for you: but I will teach you the good and the right way.
1 SAMUEL 12:23

Sadly, many Christians today are embracing the world in a negative way. They have embraced the world's immorality; they cling to the world's culture; they dine on the world's delicacies. They covet the world's comforts but spend little time embracing the world in prayer.

The Word of God commands us to pray. Today's text even calls the lack of prayer sin. Robert Murray McCheyne knew the value and necessity of serious prayer.

> Pray to be taught to pray. Do not be content with old forms that flow from the lips only. Most Christians need to cast their formal prayers away, to be taught to cry, "Abba."
>
> Arrange beforehand what you have to pray for. Don't forget confession of sin, nor thanksgiving. Pray to get your closed lips opened in intercession; embrace the whole world, and carry it within the veil. Keep a small book where you mark down objects to be prayed for. I pray God to make you very useful in the church and in the world. Live for eternity. A few days more, and our journey is done. Oh! Fight hard against sin and the devil. The devil never sleeps. Be active doing what is good, and pray for the dead churches around you.

Yes, we should embrace the world. We should reach out with our arms of prayer to grasp the world and take it before the Lord. God forbid that we should sin against the Lord by refusing to pray.

JUDGES 5; ACTS 9; JEREMIAH 18; MARK 4

Satan's Ally

Why is it that you have conceived this deed in your heart?
You have not lied to men, but to God.
ACTS 5:4, NASB

Some may wonder why God chose to strike down Ananias and his wife in church. Perhaps it was to show the church and the world how serious they should be in serving Him. Many had heard of the love of God, but this reminded them of His judgment and wrath toward those with a divided loyalty.

I have learned an important truth. When genuine revival breaks out, you can be certain that Satan will be close by. It's easy to understand why. The Early Church had just been ignited by the fire of revival. Thousands had been saved on the Day of Pentecost. Teaching and discipleship was spreading. Thousands more were being added as God's power was witnessed. These new believers were not only denying themselves, but they were loving, sharing and praying for one another.

Where God is moving, Satan will be also. Peter asked the question, "Why hath Satan filled your heart to lie against the Holy Ghost?" (Acts 5:3). The answer is clear. Ananias and Sapphira were guilty of hypocrisy, deceit and greed—sins of which Satan is an expert. It wasn't the money for the land that had been divided, it was the couple's hearts. A divided heart is Satan's ally.

Ananias and Sapphira fell under the power of God. They were literally slain by God. This should be a warning to all of us to stay pure and holy in the midst of Holy Ghost revival.

JUDGES 6; ACTS 10; JEREMIAH 19; MARK 5

An Evil Conscience

And herein do I exercise myself, to have always a conscience void of offence toward God, and toward men.

ACTS 24:16

I can vividly remember the state of my conscience before meeting Jesus Christ. For many years I lived the life of a rebellious, sinful, godless young man. I did whatever was right in my own sight with no regard for others. Evil controlled me.

I remember being instructed as a child by faithful Lutheran Sunday School teachers. I learned about Martin Luther and his strong stand for biblical principles. He believed the gospel was meant to stir up the complacent, and that Jesus came not only to bring peace but a sword. Luther understood sin and how it would destroy a good man's character. Listen to his description of an evil conscience.

> The voice of an evil conscience is not one evil in particular, but a multitude of evils. It is like a barking hell-hound, a monster vomiting fire, a raging fury, a tormenting devil. It is the nature and quality of a guilty conscience to flee and be terrified, even when all is well.

My conscience had become exactly like Luther described. I was guilty of violating every biblical principle I had been taught. My conscience was a raging fury. Deliverance from that evil conscience came the moment I surrendered my life to Jesus Christ. When I stopped living in sin, there was no more fuel for that "raging fury." Is your conscience clear before God today? Silence the torment, friend. Your freedom is only a prayer away.

JUDGES 7; ACTS 11; JEREMIAH 20; MARK 6

Selecting Companions

Do not be deceived: "Bad company corrupts good morals."
1 CORINTHIANS 15:33, NASB

What could be more clear than this scripture, "Bad company corrupts good morals"? How many times have God-fearing parents raised their children up in the admonition of the Lord, only to send them off to college to be corrupted by the ungodly? How many on-fire young people have been sent off to Bible school only to be quenched by the lukewarmness of a cold-hearted professor? I could go on and on, and I'm sure you could too, relating stories of loved ones and friends who have been polluted by bad company.

I love the way George Swinnock attacks this issue in his writings.

> Waters vary their savor according to the veins of the soil through which they slide. Animals alter their natures answerable to the climates in which they live. Men are apt to be changed for the better or worse, according to the conditions of them with whom they daily converse. The election, therefore, of our companions is one of the weightiest actions of our lives. Our future good or hurt depends so much upon it.

Rev. Swinnock calls our selection of friends one of the weightiest actions of our lives. Today I would encourage you to take a quick examination of the people who influence you the most. Make sure they influence you toward God, rather than away from Him. If, in your friends, you see more of the world than you do the Word, perhaps it would be best to reevaluate those friendships.

Made One with Him

But he who unites himself with the Lord is one with him in spirit.
1 CORINTHIANS 6:17, NIV

I have met many believers who love the Lord and want to serve Him, but for some reason or other they are holding back. Interestingly enough, this is found in the Bible in the life of the disciples. Hannah Whitall Smith unfolds to us what the disciples went through, and what many believers today experience.

> The usual course of Christian experience is pictured in the history of the disciples. First they were awakened to see their condition and their need. They then came to Christ and gave their allegiance to Him. They followed Him, worked for Him and believed in Him. And yet how unlike Him! They sought to be set up one above the other; they ran away from the Cross, misunderstanding His mission and His words. They forsook their Lord in time of danger. Yet they were still sent out to preach, recognized by Him as His disciples, possessing power to work for Him.
>
> Then came Pentecost, and these same disciples came to know Him as one with them in actual union. Henceforth He was to them Christ within, working in them to will and to do of His good pleasure. No longer was there a war of wills and a clashing of interests. One will alone animated them, and that was His will. One interest alone was dear to them, and that was His. They were made one with Him.

There should come a time in every Christian's life when he or she totally yields to the lordship of Jesus Christ.

How then shall they call on him in whom they have not believed? and how shall they believe in him of whom they have not heard? and how shall they hear without a preacher?

ROMANS 10:14

The other night, while my wife and I were coming home from a revival service, a carload of young people pulled up beside us. They began screaming at the top of their lungs, "We've been out evangelizing! We've been witnessing!" Their shouts were filled with praise. It had obviously been a great night.

I am so proud of those who boldly share the gospel. Often there is a moving of the Spirit and people are saved. At other times, there is rejection and persecution. Regardless of the outcome, don't stop sharing the gospel. And remember these three points:

You are not alone. The Father, the Son and the Holy Ghost are on your side. A cord of three strands is not easily broken (see Ecclesiastes 4:12).

You shall reap if you don't give up. The Bible says that we shall reap a harvest if we don't give up. This is a promise from God's Word. Perhaps you might be planting seed, or maybe you're watering. Remember, the results are in God's hands.

You are right. That's the bottom line, no matter how much they argue and no matter if they cuss you out and call you a fool. They can say that your message is archaic and that God is dead, but the bottom line is, they are wrong and you are right. One day, they will bow before Jesus and confess that He is Lord!

In this you greatly rejoice, even though now for a little while,
if necessary, you have been distressed by various trials, that the proof of
your faith, being more precious than gold which is perishable,
even though tested by fire, may be found to result in praise and glory
and honor at the revelation of Jesus Christ.
1 PETER 1:6,7, NASB

Everybody wants a testimony, but nobody wants a test. Everybody wants victory but nobody wants to fight in the battle. Everybody wants to experience the "fourth man in the furnace," but nobody wants to be thrown in the fire. Everybody wants to share how they were delivered from lions, but nobody wants to be thrown into the den. I like the way Charles Spurgeon expressed this idea.

> We don't grow strong in faith on sunshiny days. It is only in strong weather that a man gets faith. Faith is not given to us like the gentle dew from heaven; it generally comes in the whirlwind and the storm. Look at the old oaks. How is it that they have become so deeply rooted in the earth? Ask the March winds and they will tell you. It was not the April shower that did it, or the sweet May sunshine, but it was March's rough wind, the blustering and shaking of the tree back and forth, causing its roots to bind themselves around the rocks. So it must be with us. We don't make great soldiers in the barracks at home; they must be made amidst flying shots and thundering battle. We can't expect to make good sailors in a small rowboat; they must be made far away on the deep sea, where the wild winds howl, and the thunders roll. Storms and tempests are the things that make men tough and hardy mariners. They see the works of the Lord and His wonders in the deep. So it is with Christians. Great faith must have great trials.

JUDGES 11:12-40; ACTS 15; JEREMIAH 24; MARK 10

Salvation to the Uttermost

Much more then, being now justified by his blood,
we shall be saved from wrath through him.
ROMANS 5:9

I have had the privilege of working in the ministry for many years. My ministerial experience covers just about every aspect of Christian work. From church planting on foreign soil to jail ministry in the United States; from performing marriage ceremonies to burying the deceased; from praying for the sick to be healed to casting out devils; the list goes on and on. Over the years, there stands one thing, and one alone, that causes my spirit to soar and my heart to rejoice. It's when a lost sinner repents and pleads forgiveness and is saved by the Blood of Jesus. I marvel at the power in the Blood.

Robert Hall saw the same thing 200 years ago that I see today.

The Blood of Jesus Christ is a deluge that drowns all the mountains of transgression. That pure ocean washes away all stains of guilt. It is a sacrifice whose odor fills all worlds! A satisfaction that extends to all the principles of the divine government.

Some may think they have wandered too long in ways of sin, stifled too many successive convictions, and sinned away the virtue of Christ's Blood. However long you may have sinned, if you will now repent, though at the eleventh hour, you shall be saved.

My friend, let this be an encouragement to you and your unsaved friends and loved ones. Jesus saves to the uttermost.

JUDGES 12; ACTS 16; JEREMIAH 25; MARK 11

How can a young man keep his way pure? By keeping it according to Thy word.
PSALM 119:9, NASB

People often ask me why I read the Bible. That, my friend, is a loaded question. It's like finding rich treasure every day. In its words you will find direction for life, assurance of your salvation, wisdom in decision making and comfort in times of need. There is an old proverb that says, "Beware of a man of one book." I would agree, unless that one book is the Holy Bible. In the Word, we find everything needed to exist.

I find great pleasure in reading the writings of history's great men and women of God. They were saturated with the Word, like William S. Plumer.

If God's Word is to give us hope and comfort, we must know it. If we would know it, we should hear it, read it, hide it in our hearts, not forget it, nor slight it, nor lightly esteem it. Think of it, muse on it, talk of it, study it, lay fast hold of all its truths. Earnestly seek to find out the meaning of all God has said. Seek the guidance of the Holy Spirit. He can make the darkest things plain. He pours floods of light on the sacred page and teaches us the mind of God so as no man or angel can do.

I trust you have been faithfully following the Bible reading guide at the bottom of each page. The year only has five months left. Read as much of the Word as you can in the days ahead. The Word is an anchor for your soul.

Keep Your Nose to Yourself

You hypocrite, first take the log out of your own eye, and then you will see clearly to take the speck out of your brother's eye.

MATTHEW 7:5, NASB

Have you ever found yourself sniffing around in other people's business? Have you ever been guilty of plowing into someone else's life, hoping to uncover some sleazy sin or dark secret? Have you ever wondered why so many millions of people are interested in the affairs of political leaders and famous celebrities?

Jeremy Taylor, the writer of the classic *Holy Living and Holy Dying,* counsels us on keeping our noses clean.

> Let us not probe into the affairs of others that do not concern us, but be busy within ourselves and our own lives. Remembering that to pry into the actions or interests of others, not under our charge, may lead to pride, to cruelty, or to trouble unless duty or intentions of kindness and friendship do warrant it.

We should take heed to Reverend Taylor's counsel. Just taking care of our own affairs is a full-time job, often requiring overtime. While our nose is sniffing around in someone else's garden, our garden is being overrun with weeds. As our ears are tuned in to someone else's problems, our own problems are spreading like an uncontrollable cancer. While our feet take us into the lives of others, often racing to judgment, our own lives are in desperate need of mercy and forgiveness.

I Have Sinned

And David said unto Nathan, "I have sinned against the LORD."
2 SAMUEL 12:13

In true revival, just like in the Bible, when sinners are convicted, they are often found making the following statement: "I have sinned." In order to experience true repentance, we must understand just what this statement means.

First of all, "I have sinned" is a *personal statement.* "I" is a personal pronoun. It doesn't mean he, she or they. It refers solely to the person making the confession. In the Garden of Eden, when God confronted Adam about his sin, Adam blamed the woman, and even blamed God for having given him the woman. Similarly, Eve blamed the serpent. Unfortunately, they both failed to realize they were each personally responsible for their own actions.

"I have sinned" is also a *positive statement.* The word "have" used alone is different from *might* have, *could* have, or *I think* I have. When you say "have," it is past tense—no doubt about it...it's over and done with. There is no way to go back in time and erase the fact that sin has been committed. The word "have" denotes ownership. The sinner claims responsibility for his sin.

Further, "I have sinned," is a *pointed statement.* The texts do not read, "I have made a mistake," or "I have done a really stupid thing," or "I have blown it." The statement "I have sinned," doesn't dodge the issue. It points to the bottom line: sin. Mistakes and blunders can be fixed by man. Sin, however, is transgressing God's law and can only be pardoned by the Blood of the Lamb.

Silent Waiting

My soul waits in silence for God only; from Him is my salvation.
PSALM 62:1, NASB

You have made a very wise decision by taking time for daily devotions. The fact that you are reading *Daily Awakenings* and have involved yourself in the Bible guide indicates your desire to wait upon God. I find it so sad that people have time for everything but Jesus. We spend more time getting ready to meet man than we spend getting before God. The great writer, F. B. Meyer, was concerned over the inattention paid to waiting on God.

> Life is so hurried. You do not take time enough for meditation and prayer. The Spirit of God within you and the Presence of God without you cannot be discerned while the senses are occupied with pleasures, or the brain is filled with the tread of many hurrying thoughts. It is when water stands that it becomes transparent and reveals the pebbly beach below. Be still, and know that God is within you and all around! In the hush of the soul the unseen becomes visible and the eternal real. The eye dazzled by the sun cannot detect the beauties of its pavilion till it has had time to rid itself of the glare. Let no day pass without its season of silent waiting before God.

It's never too late to begin going after God. As long as we have breath in our nostrils, there is hope for our souls. If you have allowed the swirl of life to sling off your quiet time with God, then determine now to stop the ride, get off and go after God. He is waiting for you in silence.

JUDGES 16; ACTS 20; JEREMIAH 29; MARK 15

Dying to Self (I)

I am crucified with Christ: nevertheless I live; yet not I, but Christ liveth in me: and the life which I now live in the flesh I live by the faith of the Son of God, who loved me, and gave himself for me.

GALATIANS 2:20

Early on in my Christian life, I learned the biblical principle of dying to self. I learned that my life was not my own. I began to understand that my way of thinking, my will and my desires, had to be taken to the Cross and crucified. I now belonged to Jesus. Whoever wrote the following article on dying to self refused to put his or her name as the author. It serves as a clear example of what the Christian life should be.

When you are forgotten, or neglected, or purposely set at naught, and you don't sting and hurt with the insult or the oversight, but your heart is happy, being counted worthy to suffer for Christ, that is dying to self.

When your good is evil spoken of, when your wishes are crossed, your advice disregarded, your opinions ridiculed, and you refuse to let anger rise in your heart, or even defend yourself, but take it all in patient loving silence, that is dying to self.

When you lovingly and patiently bear any disorder, any irregularity, any impunctuality, or any annoyance; when you can stand face-to-face with waste, folly, extravagance, spiritual insensibility...and endure it as Jesus endured it, that is dying to self.

When you are content with any food, any offering, any raiment, any climate, any society, any solitude, any interruption by the will of God, that is dying to self.

JUDGES 17; ACTS 21; JEREMIAH 30—31; MARK 16

I protest by your rejoicing which I have in Christ Jesus our Lord, I die daily.
1 CORINTHIANS 15:31

My friend, it is so true that everyone wants the benefit of the Cross, but no one wants to be crucified. Everyone wants to go to heaven, but nobody wants to die. Everyone wants Jesus to change them, but no one wants to die to self. "And being found in fashion as a man, he humbled himself, and became obedient unto death, even the death of the cross" (Philippians 2:8).

> When you never care to refer to yourself in conversation, or to record your own good works, or itch after commendation, when you can truly love to be unknown, that is dying to self.
>
> When you can see your brother prosper and have his needs met, and can honestly rejoice with him in spirit and feel no envy nor question God, while your own needs are far greater and in desperate circumstances, that is dying to self.
>
> When you can receive correction and reproof from one of less stature than yourself, and can humbly submit inwardly as well as outwardly, finding no rebellion or resentment rising up with your heart, that is dying to self.
>
> Are you dead yet? In these last days the Spirit would bring us to the Cross. "That I may know Him...being made conformable to His death."

Philippians 2:8 tells us, "And being found in fashion as a man, he humbled himself, and became obedient unto death, even the death of the cross." If you're going to be a Christian, you must be willing to lay down your life. If you want to wear a crown, you must first carry a cross. If you want Jesus to live through you, you must begin dying to self.

Leap in the Dark

Have not I commanded thee? Be strong and of a good courage;
be not afraid, neither be thou dismayed: for the LORD thy God is with
thee whithersoever thou goest.
JOSHUA 1:9

I read a great story by Hannah Whitall Smith that illustrates what it means to step out by faith.

A man was obliged to descend into a deep well by sliding down a fixed rope which was supposed to be of ample length. But to his dismay he came to the end of it before his feet had touched the bottom. He had not the strength to climb up again, and to let go and drop seemed to him but to be dashed to pieces in the depths below. He held on until his strength was utterly exhausted, and then dropped, as he thought, to his death. He fell—just three inches—and found himself safe on the rock bottom.

Are you afraid to take this step? Does it seem too sudden, too much like a leap in the dark? Do you not know that the step of faith always "falls on the seeming void, but finds the rock beneath?" If ever you are to enter this glorious land, flowing with milk and honey, you must sooner or later step into the brimming waters, for there is no other path; and to do it now may save you months and even years of disappointment and grief.

Many people are afraid to follow Jesus. They fear the unknown. They want to know, ahead of time, what's in the future. But God isn't like that. He wants us to step out in faith. The apostle Peter would never have walked on water if he had not first stepped out of the boat.

JUDGES 19; ACTS 23; JEREMIAH 33; PSALMS 3—4

Out-and-Out Christians

*But thanks be to God, who always leads us in triumphal procession in Christ
and through us spreads everywhere the fragrance of the knowledge of him.*
2 CORINTHIANS 2:14, NIV

One of the greatest men of faith who ever lived was George Müller.
He dedicated his life to helping orphan children, and was well known
for his adamant belief that God would provide everything that was
needed for his orphanage. He never asked man for a thing, yet miraculously God met his every need. Reverend Müller wrote this about the
Christian life:

> If the world only knew the blessedness of thus having God as
> our refuge, I think the whole world would seek at once after
> the Lord. It is only because they think it is something miser-
> able to be a Christian, and do not know that it is infinitely
> more precious to be a Christian than to be without God, that
> they are content to remain unsaved.
>
> This is one great reason why they do not seek to enjoy the
> things of God. And it is just the reason why you and I should
> make it our business to be out-and-out Christians. We must
> show the world what it is to be truly happy Christians. There
> must not be a seeking to hold fast the things of the world, and
> yet seeking to get to heaven at the same time. If this be the
> case with us, we shall have just enough Christianity to make
> us miserable, and too little to make us happy.

We would do well to meditate on the words of Müller. We must
give ourselves totally to Jesus Christ, not holding anything back.

Résumé of the Righteous

For I have given you an example, that ye should do as I have done to you. Verily, verily, I say unto you, The servant is not greater than his lord; neither he that is sent greater than he that sent him.

JOHN 13:15,16

A résumé is a list of accomplishments. It is a compilation of successes in one's life used to secure the favor of another in order to obtain a desired position of employment. When it comes to Christianity, I have noticed a pattern in the Word. There are several steps found in the lives of the disciples that should be in our own lives. This can be called the "Résumé of the Righteous."

First of all, the followers of Jesus were His servants, and He their Master (see John 13:16). When you first become a Christian, you come as a humble servant.

Second, they became His disciples and He their Teacher (see John 15:8). A disciple is a loyal, learning follower. As you begin to listen to His teachings, incorporating them into your own life, you begin to bear forth fruit.

Third, they became friends (see John 15:13). Once you have solidified the servant factor and are convinced that He is the Teacher and you are the student, then you move into the area of friendship.

Fourth, He called them His family (see Matthew 12:49,50). Once your loyalty has won the Lord's heart, as you continue in His will, He calls you brethren.

And finally, we are incorporated into Him and made partakers of His glory. We become heirs of Christ (see Romans 8:17).

This is the blessed résumé of the righteous.

Sincerely Obedient

His mother saith unto the servants, Whatsoever he saith unto you, do it.
JOHN 2:5

This one statement by the mother of Jesus ushered in the very first miracle of our Lord. I find it interesting that it came from the lips of a family member, someone who knew Jesus from birth. Mary was certain that Jesus was about to perform a miracle. This certainty expressed itself in a mandate to those around her. What faith! What obedience! What a miracle!

Thomas Brooks takes a look at this miracle and extracts the most important ingredient—sincere obedience.

> A soul sincerely obedient will not pick and choose what commands to obey and what to reject, as hypocrites do. An obedient soul is like a crystal glass, with a light in the midst which shines forth through every part thereof. A man sincerely obedient lays such a charge upon his whole man, as Mary did upon the servants at the feast (John 2:5). Eyes, ears, hands, heart, lips, legs, body and soul. You need to seriously and affectionately observe whatever Jesus Christ says unto you and do it.

We must be ready, at all times, to obey and follow the Lord in everything He asks us to do. Could you imagine the forward strides Christianity could make if everyone who calls himself a Christian would obey the Lord with all their heart, soul and strength? On a more personal note, you will make a quantum leap forward when you follow Jesus with total abandonment. Don't be concerned about His part, just follow Him in sincere obedience.

RUTH 1; ACTS 26; JEREMIAH 36,45; PSALM 9

Mending Our Manners

The one who practices sin is of the devil; for the devil has sinned from the beginning. The Son of God appeared for this purpose, that He might destroy the works of the devil.

1 JOHN 3:8, NASB

Jesus was constantly criticized for hanging out with sinners. One of my favorite scriptures in the Bible is found in Luke 15:2 (*NASB*), when the Pharisees and Scribes murmured, saying, "This man receives sinners and eats with them." My friend, the very fact that we are sinners is what draws Jesus to our side. Trying to cover up our sin by denial, good works or religious actions only serves to repel Him. Charles Finney put it this way:

> Sinners often think if they were pious and good, the Lord might love them. So they try to win His love by doing some good things. They try in every such way to make God love them, and especially by mending their manners rather than their hearts. Alas, they seem not to know that the very fact of their being sunk so low in sin is moving God's heart to its very foundations!
>
> So the sinner's great degradation moves the compassions of his divine Father to their very depths. Sinners should remember that the very fact of their being sinners is the thing that moves God's compassion and pity. Christ died for us that He might save us, not in, but from our sins.

It is a futile task to try and mend our manners in order to please the Lord. Remember, Jesus came to heal sickness, both spiritual and physical. We must come to Him as a sinner in order for Him to come to us as a Savior.

Help Each Other Grow

Let the word of Christ dwell in you richly in all wisdom; teaching and admonishing one another in psalms and hymns and spiritual songs, singing with grace in your hearts to the Lord.

COLOSSIANS 3:16

What would we do without each other? How could we exist without fellowship one with the other? Where would we be without the prayers of our brothers and sisters in Christ?

I have grown to appreciate the family of God. Yes, we are all like little stones with rough, jagged edges. The Church is the tumbler. God is the stone polisher. He tosses us all in, pours in the oil of the Holy Spirit and begins to turn the crank. We bang against each other, knocking off rough edges, until the final product is produced.

No one puts it more eloquently than the writer of *The Pilgrim's Progress*, John Bunyan. He likens the church to a garden, and the gospel message as gentle dew.

> The Gospel is like the dew and the small rain that rests upon the tender grass, ensuring that it will flourish, and is kept green. Christians are like the several flowers in a garden that have upon each of them the dew of heaven, which being shaken with the wind, they let fall their dew at each other's roots, whereby they are jointly nourished and become nourishers of one another. For Christians to commune of God's matters with one another is as if they opened boxes of perfume to each other's nostrils.

Like it or not, we help each other grow. No matter how you describe it, we absolutely need each other.

RUTH 3—4; ACTS 28; JEREMIAH 38; PSALMS 11—12

For as high as the heavens are above the earth, so great is His
lovingkindness toward those who fear Him.
PSALM 103:11, NASB

There's nothing like fatherhood. I have the privilege of being the father of three wonderful children, whom I cherish with all my heart. My love for them is boundless. There is absolutely nothing I wouldn't do for my kids. Yet as great as my love is for them, it is still imperfect. At times I fail. There are moments when they need me and I'm not there. There are situations where they need direction, and I feel so inadequate. My best, sometimes, just doesn't seem good enough. But God is not like that. He is the perfect Father. Timothy Dwight captured the perfect love of the Father in these few words:

> He will in no wise cast you out. He will never leave you or forsake you. His eye, before which the night shines as the day, will watch over you with unceasing care. His hand, which nothing can resist or escape, will guard you with infinite tenderness. In every sorrow He will comfort; in every danger He will deliver. The bed of death He will spread with down, the passage into eternity He will illumine with the light of His own countenance. In the judgment He will acquit you of all your guilt, and in His own house, the mansion of eternal light and peace and joy, He will present you to His Father as trophies of His cross and monuments of His boundless love.

Yes, God's love is perfect. He watches over you with eyes of compassion. He will never leave you. He will never forsake you. Think about this truth throughout your day and rest in the fact that He will guide you safely to heaven's harbor.

1 SAMUEL 1; ROMANS 1; JEREMIAH 39; PSALMS 13—14

Worse Than the First

Afterward Jesus findeth him in the temple, and said unto him, Behold,
thou art made whole: sin no more, lest a worse thing come unto thee.
JOHN 5:14

Many of us have, at one time, received full pardon for our sin.
Noah Webster, in his 1845 dictionary, defined pardon as "release from
liability to suffer punishment." By His sacrifice, Jesus released us from
our liability to suffer the punishment of eternal damnation. Jesus, who
knew no sin, took upon Himself the punishment each of us deserved.

The Word of God warns us that once a man is forgiven—washed
and cleansed—and falls back, his spiritual state becomes worse than if
he had never been forgiven. Why? One of the reasons is that in man's
limited understanding, he can't imagine the Lord forgiving him. He's
tasted of the Lord, yet knowingly turned from Him, and now he feels
guilty. Others have seen him live for God, and now he feels ashamed.
His life now is worse than before he first met the Lord.

Often, the backslider wants God to make life easier. He may be a
believer in the teachings of Jesus, but he's not a true disciple. A disciple is a loyal, learning follower of Jesus. It is the responsibility of every
Christian to maintain a personal fire and zeal for his Savior.

Good news! God is willing to forgive...again! Peter is a supreme
example of someone who received a second chance. He completely
denied knowing the Lord, even to the point of cursing. Yet his ears
were open to hear Jesus speak into his life. He received full pardon and
followed after the Lord.

Be Sober and Vigilant

Be sober, be vigilant; because your adversary the devil, as a roaring lion, walketh about, seeking whom he may devour.
1 PETER 5:8

In the United States of America, tens of thousands of people die yearly—suddenly and unexpectedly. From car accidents to high school killings, people are ushered into the presence and judgment of God. The Lord gave me a message concerning the reality of sudden death and the importance of living ready. I titled it *Die Right*. The altars, when I preached this message, were jammed with hundreds of people going after God. They wanted to be ready.

One of John Wesley's friends, Phillip Doddridge, consistently preached on the importance of living sober.

Since we continually see so many around us suddenly surprised into the eternal world, and fixed in that state in which judgment will find them, let us be very careful that the day of the Lord may not overtake us as a thief. We must maintain a continual watch. How many are at this hour speaking peace and safety to themselves, over whose heads instantaneous destruction is hovering.

Let us endeavor to awaken ourselves and each other. Let us rouse ourselves, and be on guard against the most sudden attacks from our spiritual enemies.

Do not allow the enemy to lull you away from your post. He longs to destroy you, even if by default. He will tell you all is well when all is hell. But victory will come to those who remain sober and vigilant, on guard against the enemy of our souls.

1 SAMUEL 3; ROMANS 3; JEREMIAH 41; PSALM 17

You Are My Desire

Whom have I in heaven but thee? and there is none upon earth that I desire beside thee. My flesh and my heart faileth: but God is the strength of my heart, and my portion for ever.

PSALM 73:25,26

People say they want to know God, but they're unwilling to take the time to develop a relationship with Him. To hunger after God is to desire Him with all that is within you. Your thoughts are consumed with Him. You wake up in the morning with Jesus on your heart, and you go to sleep at night thinking of Him.

Andrew Murray was a man who hungered after God and spent his life leading others in their quest for Him. He believed that a person who had faith in God would automatically seek after God.

> Faith seeks for God; it believes that He is; it keeps the heart open towards Him; it bows in humility and hope for Him to make Himself known. To know God, to see God in everything and everywhere in our daily life, to be conscious of His presence so that we always walk with Him—this is the true nobility of man. This is the life that faith lives. This is the blessedness Jesus has now fully revealed in the rending of the veil.
>
> Faith can walk with God. He that cometh to God must believe that He is and that He is a rewarder of them that seek after Him. Faith believes that God can be found; that He can and will make Himself known; that He cares for everyone who truly longs for Him; that He has a divine reward for those who seek Him.

My friend, a hungry man seeks food, a spiritually hungry man seeks God.

1 SAMUEL 4; ROMANS 4; JEREMIAH 42; PSALM 18

Curse of an Achan Heart

There are things under the ban in your midst, O Israel.
You cannot stand before your enemies until you have removed the things
under the ban from your midst.
JOSHUA 7:13, NASB

In Joshua 7, we read how disobedience to God's command brings unavoidable consequences. God intended to destroy the city of Jericho. It was to be an awesome victory. But a man named Achan was greedy. We read later that the consequences of disobedience were far too severe for the sin to be worth committing.

We also learn in this story that brokenness and prayer to God, without dealing with the sin issue, is a waste of time. Joshua was seeking God, but to no avail. There was sin in the camp! Lesson: God sees what we think is hidden from view. Be sure your sin will find you out. There are always three witnesses—the Father, the Son and the Holy Ghost. Joshua was crying out to God after losing a battle, but my friend, sorrow and grief won't get the sin out, repentance will.

There are so many lessons in this story, such as, the consequences for personal sin also affect the innocent. As a result of Achan's sin, 36 men lost their lives in battle. Achan was stoned to death and burned for his sin, but he was not alone; his innocent sons and daughters and all he owned suffered the same consequences.

Joshua and the children of Israel wasted no time getting the sin out of the camp. They knew they could not stand against their enemies otherwise. We, too, when convicted of sin, must repent and get out from underneath the curse of an Achan heart.

1 SAMUEL 5—6; ROMANS 5; JEREMIAH 43; PSALM 19

Daring Damnation

As a dog returneth to his vomit, so a fool returneth to his folly.
PROVERBS 26:11

Today's text and devotional thought may seem a little harsh, but it contains as much truth as any other page in this book. We are all stunned as we scan the headlines or watch the evening news and are abruptly confronted by the atrocities committed at the hand of sinful man. We wonder how anyone could stoop so low. How could a member of the human race be so vile, so lewd, so unfeeling toward his fellow man? "How bad can it get?" we ask. John Newton, the author of the hymn *Amazing Grace*, knew what it was like to be a wretched sinner.

There is no fool like the sinner, who prefers the toys of earth to the happiness of heaven. He is held in bondage by the foolish customs of the world, more afraid of the breath of man than of the wrath of God.

Again, man in his natural state is a beast. He looks no higher than to sensual gratifications. What shall we say of mothers destroying their children with their own hands, or of the horrid act of self murder! Men are worse than beasts, likewise in their obstinacy; they will not be warned. If a beast escapes from a trap, he will be cautious how he goes near it again. But man, though he be often reproved, hardens his neck; he rushes upon his ruin with his eyes open and can defy God to His face and dare damnation.

The only hope for fallen man is to come in contact with the risen Savior.

1 SAMUEL 7—8; ROMANS 6; JEREMIAH 44; PSALMS 20—21

In Holy Expectation

And all things, whatsoever ye shall ask in prayer, believing, ye shall receive.
MATTHEW 21:22

I've learned a secret concerning answered prayer. I remember stopping for a moment one day and looking over my prayer list only to discover that over half of my prayers had already been answered. People had been saved, the sick had been healed and financial needs had been met. It seems I had been so busy praying that I had taken little time to notice the results.

William Gurnall taught about this back in the 1600s, speaking about an expectant, believing heart.

An unbelieving heart in prayer is like one who shoots an arrow at random, without paying attention to where it falls. He doesn't follow the outcome of his praying.

Failing to look up may cause many a prayer to be lost. If you do not believe, why do you pray? And if you believe, why do you not expect? By praying, you seem to depend on God; but by not expecting, you again renounce your confidence. What is this, but to take His name in vain? O Christian, stand on your prayer in a holy expectation of what you have prayed for. Mordecai, no doubt, had put up many prayers for Esther, and therefore waited at the King's gate, looking for what answer God would give. You do likewise.

Take time today to think over your prayer list. Have you failed to recognize answers to some of your prayers?

From the end of the earth will I cry unto thee, when my heart is
overwhelmed: lead me to the rock that is higher than I.
PSALM 61:2

As a father, I can tell the difference when my children are crying out of sincere pain or when they're crying for mere attention. There is a heart-gripping tone in their voices when something is truly wrong and they urgently need me to come. Oh, that God would begin to hear from His children this heart-gripping tone! Something is desperately wrong with our country; He needs to hear our cry. Our loved ones are away from God; He needs to hear our cry.

Writers throughout the centuries have agreed on the importance of crying out to God. William Jay shared his views on this crucial subject, using David's prayer as an example.

We may here learn much from the example of David. How would he pray? "I will cry unto thee." Crying is a substitute for speech; and also the expression of earnestness. A child can cry long before it can articulate; and its cries as much move the parent as any eloquence of words. A person in great danger, or want, or pain, not only utters, but cries out, and often aloud, according to the pressure of his feelings.

I may not be able to express my desires as some do; but, if I am deeply affected by them, and they spring from a broken heart and a contrite spirit, they shall not be despised.

Practice lifting up your voice to cry out to God like the psalmist. Let your heavenly Father feel the urgency of your requests.

Up on the Rooftop

For there is nothing covered, that shall not be revealed; neither hid, that shall not be known. Therefore whatsoever ye have spoken in darkness shall be heard in the light; and that which ye have spoken in the ear in closets shall be proclaimed upon the housetops.

LUKE 12:2,3

Could you imagine if everything you had done wrong was shouted openly to the public? Just the thought of this causes most people to cringe. But my friend, that's exactly what this scripture means. It is time we begin taking the Word of God at face value. The Lord does not mince words. If we really believe the Word, how different would our words and actions be? What else does the Bible say on this subject?

The Lord sees and hears everything we do. According to the Word of God, our deeds, whether they be good or bad, right or wrong, are being recorded. They are being written down. "[God] will render to every man according to his deeds" (Romans 2:6).

There is absolutely no way for us to cover our sins. "For by grace are ye saved through faith; and that not of yourselves: it is the gift of God: not of works, lest any man should boast" (Ephesians 2:8,9). All our good deeds, even if they are incredible in the eyes of man, won't cover one tiny sin in the eyes of God.

What I learned from these scriptures is this: If I don't want my sins shouted out up there, I need to repent and confess Jesus as Savior and Lord down here.

August 20

For the Master's Use

But he knoweth the way that I take:
when He hath tried me, I shall come forth as gold.
JOB 23:10

There is a purpose behind every trial. There is a reason for every difficulty we face. The Lord uses the temptations and struggles of life to make men and women of God fit for the Master's use.

Robert Murray McCheyne spent most of his life suffering from physical ailments that eventually took his life. He always referred to afflictions as sent from God to make him more like Jesus.

"When He hath tried me, I shall come forth as gold." This is precious comfort. There will be an end of your affliction. Christians must have "great tribulation" but they do come out of it. We must carry the cross; but only for a moment—then comes the crown. There is a set time for putting into the furnace, and a set time for taking out of the furnace. There is a time for pruning the branches of the vine, and there is a time when the husbandman lays aside the pruning hook. Let us wait His time; God's time is the best time.

But shall we come out the same as we went in? Ah! No, "we shall come out like gold." It is this that sweetens the bitterest cup; this brings a rainbow of promise over the darkest cloud. Affliction will *certainly* purify a believer. Oh that all the dross may be left behind in the furnace!

McCheyne indeed came forth as gold. Be encouraged by his words here, and press on in the hope that the dross be left behind and that you, too, shall emerge fit for the Master's use.

1 SAMUEL 12; ROMANS 10; JEREMIAH 49; PSALMS 26—27

AUGUST 21

All Your Affections

*And thou shalt love the LORD thy God with all thine heart,
and with all thy soul, and with all thy might.*
DEUTERONOMY 6:5

We are rapidly approaching the end of summer. Many Christians started the summer as holy, God-fearing warriors of the Word, but over the weeks and months they began to slip into lethargy and sin. God, at the beginning of summer, was first place in their lives. Now He has taken a backseat to friends and parties. Reverend J. G. Pike called that the greatest of sins.

> Has God had all your heart? Have all your affections been fixed on Him? Has He been loved with all your soul and mind; and thus stood highest in your esteem? If not, however fair and pleasing your outward conduct may be, you have been committing the greatest of sins; for you have lived breaking God's first and great commandment. If to love God above all things is the first and greatest commandment, to live negligent of Him must be one of the greatest of sins, and indeed a sin that opens the way to every other.

These words may be strong, but they are so true. We are dealing with the first commandment. God chose this particular commandment to lead all others. Without God reigning supreme in our affections and desires, we are open for all other idols to enter in. An idol is anything that takes the place of God. The reason people commit all the other dark sins, such as murder and adultery, is because they haven't fulfilled the first commandment.

August 22

Perpetual Love

For I am persuaded, that neither death, nor life, nor angels, nor principalities, nor powers, nor things present, nor things to come, nor height, nor depth, nor any other creature, shall be able to separate us from the love of God, which is in Christ Jesus our Lord.
ROMANS 8:38,39

Every man, woman and child knows what it's like to commit a sin and feel horrible about it. We are all well aware of the deep emotions of guilt, remorse and shame. But on the other side of sin is a Savior. On the other side of shame is His shoulder. On the other side of degrading guilt is an uplifting God. His love is greater and deeper than man can comprehend. He never stops loving us.

Stephen Charnock, author of *The Attributes of God*, spent his life sharing God's everlasting love.

This love is perpetual. [God] was in Christ reconciling the world; He will to the end of the world beseech men to be reconciled to Him. Love was the motive, the glory of His grace was the end; what was so from eternity will be so to eternity. His love is as strong as it was, for infinite receives no diminution; His glory is dear as it was, for to deny His glory is to deny Himself. How great will be the joy of those that accept it! How dismal the torment and sorrow of those that refuse it!

Today is the day to recognize that God is love. He does not want anyone to perish. He wants all to come to repentance. He is waiting, ready to forgive, ready to embrace, ready to love. It's impossible to fully understand, especially when we feel unworthy and undeserving. My friend, put your feelings aside and receive His perpetual love.

1 SAMUEL 14; ROMANS 12; JEREMIAH 51; PSALM 30

The God Seekers

This is the generation of those who seek Him, who seek Thy face.
PSALM 24:6, NASB

Are you willing to go after Jesus regardless of the cost? Throughout the Scriptures, we find people who were desperate for God and disregarded the scorn of the crowd.

Will you go after Jesus regardless of how painful the present circumstances may be? Perhaps you're like the woman with the issue of blood, described in Mark 5:25-34. Like her, you've exhausted all your resources. She was extremely sick, but she still went after God.

In the book of John, chapter nine, there is a story of a blind man who came to Jesus for healing. Jesus instructed him to go wash in the pool of Siloam. He did and received his sight. He had sought and found Jesus, but then had to follow His instructions.

Do you maintain an open heart, always ready to embrace new revelation from the Lord? Read the account of Apollos as written in Acts 18:24-28. Apollos already had a great following, but when confronted about receiving more from Jesus, he was hungry, not haughty. He was a God seeker, not a self-seeker. Therefore, he was open to receive new revelation from the Lord.

The Bible says this is the generation that seeks the Lord. For many years, Christians were seeking the hand of God—always wanting something from Him. But now they're seeking the face of God—wanting to be like Him.

Are you willing not only to go after Jesus but also to obey His words?

1 SAMUEL 15; ROMANS 13; JEREMIAH 52; PSALM 31

He Has Enough

Now the God of hope fill you with all joy and peace in believing, that ye may abound in hope, through the power of the Holy Ghost.

ROMANS 15:13

You can never exhaust God's resources. He has plenty of power to go around. He has healing virtue for the multitude. He owns all the gold this world contains. Every ounce that is unearthed today was already in God's ledgers from the beginning. Yes, His resources are limitless. What is it that you need from Him today? These words of Thomas Watson encourage us to not only cast all our burdens upon Him, but to also be content in His provision.

First, if God be our God, let us improve our interest in Him. We must cast all our burdens upon Him—the burden of our fears, our wants, our sins. Wicked men, who are a burden to God, have no right to cast their burden upon Him. But such as have God for their God are called upon to cast their burden upon Him. Where should the child ease all its cares but in the bosom of its parent? Christian, what troubles you? You have God to pardon your sins, to supply your wants—therefore roll your burden on the Lord.

Second, if God be our God, let us learn to be content. Contentment is a rare jewel; it is the cure of care. He who hath God hath enough. If a man be thirsty, bring him to a spring, and he is satisfied. In God there is enough to fill the heaven-born soul. Other things can no more fill the soul than a mariner's breath can fill the sails of a ship; but in God is an infinite fullness; He has enough to fill the angels, therefore enough to fill us.

Never Mind

But as many as received him, to them gave he power to become the sons of God, even to them that believe on his name.

JOHN 1:12

I learned, early on, that it was not necessary for me to understand everything. After all, I had not been chosen to sit on God's committee to run the universe. He did not have to consult me on His heavenly decisions. He wanted me to just plain trust Him. Charles Spurgeon knew a lot about faith, and saw the results of simple trust in God.

Faith believes that Christ will do what He has promised. Since He has promised to cast out none that come to Him, it is certain that He will not. Whatever Christ has promised to do He will do. We must believe this, if we are to receive pardon, justification, preservation and eternal glory from His hands.

The great matter is to believe on the Lord Jesus, using simple, childlike faith. Never mind definitions and deep dissertations. A hungry man eats though he does not understand the composition of his food, the anatomy of his mouth or the process of digestion. He lives because he eats. Another far more clever person understands thoroughly the science of nutrition; but if he does not eat he will die with all his knowledge. There are, no doubt, many at this hour in hell who understood the doctrine of faith but did not believe. On the other hand, not one who has trusted in the Lord Jesus has ever been cast out, though he may never have been able intelligently to define his faith.

How simple life becomes when we learn the importance of trusting God with childlike faith, never minding the rest.

1 SAMUEL 17; ROMANS 15; LAMENTATIONS 2; PSALM 33

Sleepyhead

Wherefore he saith, Awake thou that sleepest, and arise from the dead, and Christ shall give thee light. Redeeming the time, because the days are evil.
EPHESIANS 5:14,16

My friend, don't allow anything or anyone to cause you to fall back into spiritual slumber. Heed the words of Horatius Bonar:

It may have been long since the Holy Spirit awoke us from our sleep of death. Into that same deep sleep we know that we shall never fall again. He who awoke us will keep us awake until Jesus comes. In that sense, we shall sleep no more.

Still, much of our drowsiness remains. We are not wholly awake, and oftentimes much of our former sleep returns. Dwelling on the world's enchanted ground, our eyes close, our senses are bewildered, our conscience loses its sensitiveness and our faculties their energy. We often fall asleep even upon our watchtower, forgetful that the night is far spent and the day is at hand.

While thus asleep, or half-asleep, all goes wrong. Our movements are sluggish and lifeless. Our faith waxes feeble; our love is chilled; our zeal cools down. Our boldness has forsaken us. Our plans are carelessly devised and drowsily executed. The work of God is hindered by us instead of being helped forward. We are a drag upon it. We mar it.

But God will not have it so. Neither for His work's sake, nor for His saint's sake, can He suffer this to continue. We must be aroused at whatever the cost.

Refuge of Lies

You boast, "We have entered into a covenant with death, with the grave we have made an agreement. When an overwhelming scourge sweeps by, it cannot touch us, for we have made a lie our refuge and falsehood our hiding place."
ISAIAH 28:15, NIV

The Lord desires to bless us; His plan for our lives is perfect. However, many of us choose to distance ourselves from His presence. Fear of His demands or shame over our sin causes us to run and hide. But where do we take refuge?

The devil lies to us by inviting us to hide in the *refuge of running*. Adam, Eve, and especially Jonah can testify to the frailty of such a fortress. What foolishness to try to outrun God. This is not a feasible feat.

Others are hiding in the *refuge of relationships*. Running to friends before running to God is no answer. Whose companionship do you value more highly than the Savior's? Your friends and family can't stand beside you on Judgment Day. This hiding place is like a house of cards. When the wind of His Spirit blows, it comes crashing down.

Perhaps you are hiding in the *refuge of religion*. Religion is an adherence to a set of beliefs—it will never serve as payment for pardon. Our religious acts won't save us. A person can go to hell hiding behind a choir robe.

Many are hiding from the Lord in the *refuge of riches*. It is sad how countless people are caught up in creature comforts. Rather than running to God, many are found running from Him, indulging in selfish, sensual pleasures.

The Lord will destroy the refuge of lies. My counsel to everyone is this: If you're going to run, do it full speed into the arms of Jesus. He is the only refuge!

1 SAMUEL 19; 1 CORINTHIANS 1; LAMENTATIONS 4; PSALM 35

Where Are You Heading?

I am a companion of all them that fear thee, and of them that keep thy precepts.
PSALM 119:63

Jesus Christ changed my life over two decades ago. A few days after my conversion, I began to experience the blessedness of fellowship with other believers. What a joy it was to talk about God with those who believed just like I did! Of course, I was experiencing what had been going on for centuries. It's called the family of God, and I was a brand-new, adopted member. George Swinnock spoke of how the company we keep can declare our destiny.

> Birds of a feather will flock together.... The young partridges hatched under a hen go for a time along with her chickens. They keep them company, scraping in the earth together. However, when they are grown up, and their wings fit for the purpose, they mount up into the air.
>
> A Christian, before his conversion, is brought up under the prince of darkness, and walks in company with his cursed crew, according to the course of this world. But when the Spirit changes his disposition, he quickly changes his companions, and delights only in the saints that are on earth.
>
> Servants of the same Lord, if faithful, will join with their fellows, and not with the servants of His enemy. The company they delight in—whether those that walk in the "broad way" of the flesh, or those who walk in the "narrow way" of the Spirit—will declare whether they are going towards heaven or towards hell.

1 SAMUEL 20; 1 CORINTHIANS 2; LAMENTATIONS 5; PSALM 36

Varieties of Conscience

Pray for us. We are sure that we have a clear conscience and desire to live honorably in every way.

HEBREWS 13:18, NIV

The other day while scanning my library shelves, I came across the writings of Andrew Fuller. I was immediately drawn to a teaching on the five different kinds of consciences. I found these types so interesting, and so relevant to our lives.

First, an *ignorant conscience,* which neither sees nor says anything; neither beholds the sins in a soul, nor reproves them;

Second, the flattering conscience, whose speech is worse than silence itself, which though seeing sin, soothes men in the committing thereof.

Third, the seared conscience, which hath neither sight, speech, nor sense in men that are past feeling.

Fourth, the wounded conscience, frightened with sin. (By the way, this conscience is often found leading men to repentance.)

Fifth, the quiet and clear conscience, which is the best, pacified in Christ Jesus.

Our text today exhorts us to live with a clear conscience. Ever since becoming a Christian, I have endeavored to live with a pure heart between God and man. If there is anything between you and another brother, or you and God, confess it to God, or make it right with your brother, and determine in your heart to close this day with a clear conscience.

1 SAMUEL 21—22; 1 CORINTHIANS 3; EZEKIEL 1; PSALM 37

Christian Love

Love worketh no ill to his neighbour: therefore love is the fulfilling of the law.
ROMANS 13:10

It is not difficult to find a true Christian man in a crowd of sinners. He is the one shining like a star in the darkness of night. He is the one emanating the love of Jesus. Others can be cursing and reveling, controlled by a drunken spirit, but the Christian man is of clean speech, solid footing, and controlled by the Holy Spirit. The love of the Lord shines through him.

Pastor Rowland Hill, known for his straightforward sermons, shed some light on Christian love.

> If the sun shines on dull bricks or stones, they reflect none of its beams. There is nothing in them capable of reflection. Nor is there, in an ungodly man, any natural power of reflecting the light of God. But let the sun shine upon a diamond and see what rays of sparkling beauty it emits. It is similar in the Christian who has the graces of the Spirit. When God shines on his soul, beams of celestial loveliness are reflected by him on the world.
>
> Cultivate a spirit of love. Love is the diamond amongst the jewels of the believer's breastplate. The other graces shine like the precious stones of nature, with their own peculiar luster and various hues; but the diamond is the center of every grace and virtue.

The Bible testifies that the Church of the Lord Jesus Christ will be known by their love. Throughout this day, be a diamond, and shine forth the sparkling beauty of love.

1 SAMUEL 23; 1 CORINTHIANS 4; EZEKIEL 2; PSALM 38

Sword of Revival

*For the word of God is quick, and powerful, and sharper than any
twoedged sword, piercing even to the dividing asunder of soul and spirit,
and of the joints and marrow, and is a discerner of the thoughts and
intents of the heart.*

HEBREWS 4:12

There is a movement in the world today to water down the Word
of God. There is a humanistic, anti-God philosophy permeating our
society, that I liken to a cancer destroying the precious cells in a body.
This group of people believe the Bible to be archaic and untrustwor-
thy, but I feel sorry for them. They're dealing with unchangeable truth.
The very Book they're trying to destroy will come back and destroy
them.

Missionary Jonathan Goforth declared the Bible's case with great
clarity:

> The Author of the Bible is being greatly dishonored these days
> by the doubt cast upon His Word. It must, indeed, be a cause
> of intense grief to Him that the Book which alone testifies of
> the Lord Jesus should be so lightly esteemed by man. Unless
> the Bible is to us the Word of God, our prayers can be no more
> than sheer mockery. There never has been a revival except
> where there have been Christian men and women thoroughly
> believing in and wholeheartedly pleading the promises of
> God.
>
> The Sword of the Spirit, which is the Word of God, is the
> only weapon which has ever been mightily used in revival.
> Where it has been given for what it claims to be, the Word of
> God has always been like a sharp, two-edged sword, like fire,
> and like a hammer that breaks the rock in pieces.

---

1 SAMUEL 24; 1 CORINTHIANS 5; EZEKIEL 3; PSALM 39

The Heart of Revival

For God so loved the world, that he gave his only begotten Son, that whosoever believeth in him should not perish, but have everlasting life. For God sent not his Son into the world to condemn the world; but that the world through him might be saved.

JOHN 3:16,17

What is true revival? What is the heart of this moving, living organism called revival? Placed under the equivalent of a surgical microscope, diligent investigators who cut through and probe would soon find several key elements: holy, compassionate pastors who crave the salvation of lost humanity; devoted laborers willing to pray, and pay the price, for revival; evangelists who weep over the lost and preach the uncompromising Word of God.

Probing deeper, they would find that the evangelist and all the others are pointing in a particular direction—to an inner organ that reveals the pulsation of blood flowing freely. Yet there seems to be an obstruction that appears to be two shafts of lumber. One piece is straight up and down, the other perpendicular.

At the center of revival, at the heart of any move of God, is nothing more and nothing less than the splintered, Blood-stained Cross. The cross of Christ represents the epitome of suffering and the universality of salvation. Nothing but the Cross...nothing but the Blood...nothing but the salvation that was purchased. That alone is the heart of true Holy Ghost revival.

Partnership with God

And God is able to make all grace abound toward you; that ye, always having all sufficiency in all things, may abound to every good work.
2 CORINTHIANS 9:8

The great evangelist Dwight L. Moody was known for his simple stories to illustrate basic biblical truths. Over the years, they have served as a source of divine inspiration in my Christian life. I learned from Moody about not taking successes too seriously. He made the statement, "The devil is always waiting at the foot of the mountain." After reading that, I began to be more aware of satanic warfare following great, spiritual exploits.

I remember reading one of his classic statements, "If God be your partner, make your plans large." I was encouraged to tackle major church-planting projects in other countries because God was my partner. Read what else Moody said along these lines:

> I heard of a man who went into business out in the untamed west, where people said he was sure to fail; but he didn't. After he had been getting along very well for some years, and showing no signs of failing, it was discovered that the man had a brother. This brother lived in the East and was very rich. Anytime there was a need, the brother sent him the much needed help. Just so with you, sinner. You have a Brother who is very rich, and if you are joined in partnership with Him, He will help you to hold out. It is those who are not joined to Christ who fail, but they who are joined to Him have power and grace. They that trust the Lord shall not want any good thing.

When God is on your side, friend, you cannot fail. Acknowledge Him in all your ways and make your plans large!

1 SAMUEL 26; 1 CORINTHIANS 7; EZEKIEL 5; PSALMS 42—43

A Bona Fide Christian

Hereby know we that we dwell in him, and he in us, because he hath given us of his Spirit. Whosoever shall confess that Jesus is the Son of God, God dwelleth in him, and he in God.

1 JOHN 4:13,15

It's interesting to meet people who call themselves Christians but have absolutely no knowledge of what that means. To them, a Christian is simply a person who goes to church. To others, a person is automatically considered a Christian just by becoming a citizen of the United States of America. But friend, this is so far from the truth.

The following passage by William S. Plumer is actually one long sentence containing the characteristics of a bona fide Christian.

> But if Christ be found in us the hope of glory; if we have taken Him to be our prophet, priest and king; if His name is to us as ointment poured forth; if He is precious to our souls; if we esteem His reproach greater riches than the treasures of earth; if we had rather suffer than sin; if we rest the whole weight of our salvation on His righteousness; if we delight in His ordinances; if we esteem all His precepts concerning all things to be right; if we count His service a privilege; if we long for His grace and presence; if we hate all iniquity, even the thought of foolishness; if we strive to perfect holiness in the fear of God; if we weep over our shortcomings; if we greatly long to be made like Christ; *then* we are Christ's servants and friends, and we shall be finally and forever saved.

If you find yourself in this sentence, there's a good chance you're a true follower of Jesus Christ.

1 SAMUEL 27; 1 CORINTHIANS 8; EZEKIEL 6; PSALM 44

A Sure Sign

Hereby know ye the Spirit of God: Every spirit that confesseth that Jesus Christ is come in the flesh is of God: And every spirit that confesseth not that Jesus Christ is come in the flesh is not of God.

1 JOHN 4:2,3

During every great revival, there has always risen a fear of the counterfeit. While we should be aware of the abilities of Lucifer to deceive people, we should never be obsessed with the belief that he can actually thwart a true move of God. The Bible clearly states how to determine whether or not God's Holy Spirit is working. Jonathan Edwards, one of the most well-respected American revivalists of all time, confronted this issue in the following manner.

> We have the same rule given to distinguish the true Spirit from all counterfeits: "Wherefore I give you to understand, that no man speaking by the Spirit of God calleth Jesus accursed: and that no man can say that Jesus is the Lord, but by the Holy Ghost" (1 Corinthians 12:3). If the Spirit which is at work among a people is plainly observed to convince them of Christ, and lead them to Christ, it is a sure sign that it is the true and right Spirit. If the Spirit which is at work confirms their minds in the belief that He is the Son of God, and was sent of God to save sinners, and that He is the only Savior, it is a sure sign that it is the true and right Spirit. If the Spirit which is at work teaches that they stand in great need of Him, and instills in them higher thoughts of Him than they used to have, and inclines their affections more to Him—it is a sure sign that it is the true and right Spirit.

1 SAMUEL 28; 1 CORINTHIANS 9; EZEKIEL 7; PSALM 45

8,000 Minus 2

And Ananias hearing these words fell down, and gave up the ghost: and great fear came on all them that heard these things. Then fell [Sapphira] down straightway at his feet, and yielded up the ghost: and the young men came in, and found her dead, and, carrying her forth, buried her by her husband.

ACTS 5:5,10

Remember Hezekiah? On his sickbed, Hezekiah prayed for healing, and the Lord added fifteen years to his life (see 2 Kings 20:6). Matthew recorded Jesus saying that all the things we need will be *added* to us, if we seek first the kingdom of God and His righteousness (see Matthew 6:33). We all like God's addition.

However, we find that God is excellent at subtraction, too. God will often take away in order to multiply. He will often pluck up in order to replant. God will cut down an unfruitful tree in order to make room for a fruit-bearing tree (see Luke 13:6-9). Likewise, He will prune His Church in order to bring new growth.

Just as the Early Church was about to spring forth and multiply in great number (already the church numbered around 8,000), there arose two greedy hypocrites. Simply put, God killed them both—in church! You don't lie to God and get away with it. Yet, this sudden subtraction made way for multiplication. Holy fear swept the land as hundreds believed in the power of a holy God. The graves of Ananias and Sapphira served as part of the fearful foundation of the early Church.

Many say they want to see the manifestations of God's presence today. How about the "lie-to-God-and-die" manifestation? I don't think it would take too many times before a holy fear of God gripped the hearts of the nation once again. With a holy revival sweeping the land, be sure you are on the addition and not the subtraction side of God's mathematical table.

Prevailing in Prayer

Pray without ceasing.
1 THESSALONIANS 5:17

As Charles Finney explains, "If you would pray in faith, be sure to walk every day with God. If you do, He will tell you what to pray for. Be filled with His Spirit, and He will give you objects enough to pray for. He will give you as much of the spirit of prayer as you have strength of body to bear." Finney's story here is a good example.

> A good man once said to me, "Oh, I am dying for the want of strength to pray. My body is crushed, the world is on me, and how can I forbear prayer!"
>
> I have known that man to go to bed absolutely sick for weakness and faintness, under the pressure. And I have known him to pray as if he would do violence to heaven. I've seen the blessing come in answer to his prayer.
>
> Shall I tell you how he died? He prayed more and more. He used to take the map of the world before him and pray. He'd look over the different countries and pray for them, till he absolutely expired in his room, praying. Blessed man! He was the reproach of the ungodly and of carnal, unbelieving educators, but he was the favorite of heaven, and a prevailing prince in prayer.

What a way to go! Ushered into the presence of God while going after God on your knees. What a legacy!

You, too, can be a favorite in heaven. You too, can be a prevailing prince or princess in prayer.

---

1 SAMUEL 31; 1 CORINTHIANS 11; EZEKIEL 9; PSALM 48

Deep and Pure

Jesus answered and said unto them, This is the work of God, that ye believe on him whom he hath sent.

JOHN 6:29

There is a longing in my soul to see a move of God in this country. I want this nation shaken from the White House to the schoolhouse, from the stock market to the stockyard, from the interstate highways to the airline skyways, from the country clubs to the city pubs. I want to see revival.

This same desire was on the lips of Robert Murray McCheyne when he spoke these awesome words:

> Everything I meet with, and every day I study my Bible, makes me pray more that God would begin and carry on a deep, pure, widespread and a permanent work of God in Scotland. If it be not deep and pure, it will only end in confusion and grieving away the Holy Spirit of God by irregularities and inconsistencies. Christ will not get glory, and the country generally will be hardened and have their mouths filled with reproaches. If it be not widespread, our God will not get a large crown out of this generation. If it be not permanent, that will prove its impurity and will turn all our hopes into shame.
>
> I am also deepened in my conviction that if we are to be instruments in such a work, we must be purified from all filthiness of the flesh and spirit. Oh, cry for personal holiness, constant nearness to God by the Blood of the Lamb! Bask in His beams—lie back in the arms of love—be filled with His Spirit; or all success in the ministry will only be to your own everlasting confusion.

Choking on Steak

*Like newborn babies, crave pure spiritual milk, so that by it you may grow
up in your salvation, now that you have tasted that the Lord is good.*
1 PETER 2:2,3, NIV

There is a reason I do not preach theologically complex messages.
I leave that to teachers and ministers who are involved day in and day
out with their congregations. I am an evangelist. As such, I learned a
long time ago that my duty is to preach the simplicity of the Cross.
That is my job. When I step away from that job and begin trying to
impress people with lofty oratorical skills, I miss God. It is the simplicity of the Cross that gets people saved.

Remember, when reaching the lost, you may be speaking to someone who appears to have everything under control and everything
going for him, but inside he is starving to death. As you begin to pour
out the simple truths of the gospel for him, suddenly you see tears
streaming down his face. Be assured friend, you *are* feeding him what
he needs. He didn't need a steak. In his state of being, he wouldn't be
able to chew or digest a theological steak.

He's like a man lost in the desert, dying as he crawls across the
merciless sands of his empty life. Buzzards circling overhead declare
his hopeless state of starvation. Someone in that condition should
never stumble away from a revival meeting choking to death on "spiritual steak." He can't even be handed a full canteen of water. He needs
the pure truths from the Word. He can handle only a few drops on his
tongue. Immediately, thirst for the Word will develop. He will be
strengthened and he will be back for more.

2 SAMUEL 2; 1 CORINTHIANS 13; EZEKIEL 11; PSALM 50

Matters of the Soul

But God hath chosen the foolish things of the world to confound the wise; and God hath chosen the weak things of the world to confound the things which are mighty.

1 CORINTHIANS 1:27

Near the close of the millennium, a stream of violence swept through America's schools. Young children were more and more frequently gunned down by classmates, leaving an aftermath of devastation and unanswered questions. A flurry of secular commentaries immediately surfaced, trying to offer a quick fix. Though noble, their attempts were at best feeble and inadequate because the problem is not natural, but spiritual.

John Flavel, a master at writing about the heart (or soul), explained it well.

Men are prudent and skillful in secular and lower matters, yet ignorant and unskillful in the great and everlasting affairs of their souls! All their creativity, judgment, wit, and memory seem to be used for the service of the flesh. Some have piercing comprehension, solid judgments, and excellent articulation—but put them upon any spiritual supernatural matter, and they fall short. Even the weakest Christian, the babes in Christ, shall excel them in it, and give a far better account of regeneration, the work of grace, the life of faith than these can.

It is simple, friend, so simple that even a five-year-old can explain it. In the aftermath of such violence, God gave the *children* a voice—full of more wisdom than the loftiest professors' solutions. Whenever they got the chance, students stepped up to the microphone and simply said: "Man is away from God. He needs to repent of his sin and ask Jesus Christ into his heart."

2 SAMUEL 3; 1 CORINTHIANS 14; EZEKIEL 12; PSALM 51

How Much Can You Hold?

That you, being rooted and grounded in love, may be able to comprehend with all the saints what is the breadth and length and height and depth, and to know the love of Christ which surpasses knowledge, that you may be filled up to all the fulness of God.
EPHESIANS 3:17-19, NASB

Over 20 years ago, I heard a sermon that I'll never forget. The preacher was a young, dedicated, fervent follower of Jesus. He stood before the congregation, lifted up his head, opened his mouth wide and belted out, "God is big!" He would make a comparative statement about something big, such as the universe, the species of the world, the vast oceans, and then, raising both hands in the air, he would scream out, *"God is big!"* I remember feeling the impact of the enormity of God and His goodness. That simple, three-word statement was branded into my memory forever.

Several years later, while reading the works of Robert South, I came across this statement that would have fit well in this young man's message.

> We have a very lame and imperfect conception of our great God. And the reason is very clear. We are forced to understand that which is infinite, after a finite manner. Simply put: one thing receives another, not according to the full size of the object, but according to the scanty scope of its own capacity. If we let down a vessel into the sea, we shall bring up not what the sea can afford, but *what the vessel can hold*: and just so it is in our own understanding of God.

My friend, God is big, and for us to try to understand everything about Him is futile. His ways, His thoughts and His desires are so much greater than ours. People often say, "I want everything God has for me." My answer to them is, "How much can you hold?"

2 SAMUEL 4—5; 1 CORINTHIANS 15; EZEKIEL 13; PSALMS 52—54

How sweet are thy words unto my taste! yea, sweeter than honey to my mouth!
PSALM 119:103

Trying to describe the sweetness of the love of God to someone who has never known Him is like trying to explain what a strawberry tastes like to someone who has never tried one. You can hold it up before their eyes and say, "It's red...it's sweet...it's juicy..."

"Does it taste like a cherry?" they ask. "How about an apple? Is it sweet like an apple?"

"It is sweet, but it's different from an apple, and unlike a cherry." Out of frustration of failing to explain the taste, you finally offer a strawberry to taste. Once they've taken a bite of that sweet, juicy fruit, no more explanation is needed. They have experienced it for themselves.

It is the same with Jesus. You must experience Him for yourself. Thomas Watson illustrated the love of Jesus like this:

None can know how delicious and ravishing it is, but such as have felt it; as none can know how sweet honey is, but those who have tasted it. It puts a man in heaven before his time.

I have dedicated my life, and you should dedicate yours, to sharing the love of God with others. Though everyone might not love the taste of a strawberry, I am convinced that once a sinner tastes of the love and forgiveness of Jesus Christ, he will hasten to embrace Him as Lord and Savior.

Bright Closets

*But thou, when thou prayest, enter into thy closet, and when thou hast
shut thy door, pray to thy Father which is in secret; and thy Father which
seeth in secret shall reward thee openly.*

MATTHEW 6:6

Anyone who has attended our meetings has heard me say that the
true test of a man's soul is when he's alone with God. Friend, there is
absolutely nothing to compare with getting alone in God's presence.
Robert Murray McCheyne once said, "A calm hour with God is worth a
whole lifetime with man." How true this statement is. A personal word
from God in the quiet solitude of my study means more to me than
anything man can say. When I'm alone with Jesus, all my problems, all
the struggles, all the dark clouds seem to be so insignificant. My prayer
closet becomes the brightest place on earth. Horatius Bonar wrote,

> Our closets are the only places of light in a world which has
> now become doubly dark to us. All without and around is
> gloom. Clouds overshadow the whole region. Only the closet
> is bright and calm. We could spend our whole time in this
> happy island of light which God has provided for us in the
> midst of a stormy ocean. When compelled, at times, to leave
> it, how gladly do we return to it! What peaceful hours of soli-
> tude we have there, with God for our one companion! We can
> almost forget that the clouds of earth are still above us, and
> its tempests still rioting around us.

Thank God you have taken time to get alone with Jesus. An assur-
ing word from the lips of our Lord will mean more to you than any
counsel man can give. Spend as much time as you can in the brightest
place on earth—your prayer closet.

2 SAMUEL 7; 2 CORINTHIANS 1; EZEKIEL 15; PSALMS 56—57

Be a Worm

And immediately the angel of the Lord smote him, because he gave not God the glory: and he was eaten of worms, and gave up the ghost.

ACTS 12:23

God has chosen to use human beings as His vessels through which to flow. Through the ages, each one of God's choice men and women have had to deal with an area that has a tendency to rise up when any type of accomplishment is realized.

For example, when a miracle occurs in your church, in comes the army of inquisitive onlookers. They begin to interrogate everyone. "How did it happen? Who was the instrument?" Everyone points to the one whom God used. Maybe you're the one. At that moment, you have the sole responsibility of deflecting any honor and glory off yourself and onto the One who is the rightful recipient of the praise—Jesus Christ!

From today's text we should all learn a lesson. Herod relished the praise of man. He sought the honor of man above the honor of God, which brought deadly results. The worms of pride and conceit began their destructive work the moment he ceased to give God the glory.

Never forget, God is the one who gave you breath. If you sing magnificently it is because He gave you the ability. If someone pays you a compliment on your physical attractiveness, remember that it was God who knit you together in your mother's womb. If God uses you mightily in healings, remember that Jesus took the beatings. *He* was bruised; *He* was wounded; *He* was the one hurt for our healing.

Humble yourself with the knowledge that our great and mighty God chooses to *let* us participate in His plans and purposes. Now that's true "worm theology"!

2 SAMUEL 8—9; 2 CORINTHIANS 2; EZEKIEL 16; PSALMS 58—59

Father's at the Helm

And he arose, and rebuked the wind, and said unto the sea, Peace, be still.
And the wind ceased, and there was a great calm. And he said unto them,
Why are ye so fearful? how is it that ye have no faith?

MARK 4:39,40

We live in days of uncertainty. Paul defined this span of history as perilous times. I can personally feel the storm of life raging all around. Gone are the calm, peaceful days of smooth sailing. These are the days of violent spiritual warfare. The sea of life is raging and waves are crashing over the boat. At times, Christians feel that their very lives are in danger. But I've got good news, my friend. God has everything under control. J. G. Pike believed with all his heart that God is at the wheel.

The Christian often finds the path to heaven most secure when most beset with thorns; and the sea of life safest when most stormy. Afflictions to the children of God prove to be the best of mercies. The martyr's flames have often preceded the throne of heavenly joy, and the crown of thorns has been the forerunner of a crown of glory. It has been said that on board a ship, in the midst of a violent storm, when the mariners were in distress and alarm, one little boy remained composed, and being asked the cause of his composure, answered, "My father's at the helm." So may the Christian say in every trial, "My Father, my Almighty Father is at the helm; and He will steer me safe through every storm; or, when He pleases, say to the tempest, 'Peace, be still!' "

Regardless of your present struggle, there remains a constant. God is in control. Take a moment right now, and visualize your heavenly Father at the helm.

2 SAMUEL 10; 2 CORINTHIANS 3; EZEKIEL 17; PSALMS 60—61

Happy to Resemble

So God created man in His own image, in the image of God created He
him; male and female created He them.

GENESIS 1:27

I'm sure you've heard someone say, "You are the only Bible some
people will ever read." It is a fact that most people don't take the time
to read the Word, worship the Lord, and develop a relationship with
Jesus Christ. Therefore, they have no way of knowing what God is like.
Their only hope is in seeing Jesus through our lives.

As believers, we must daily occupy ourselves with becoming like
Jesus Christ. The popular adage, What would Jesus do? is exactly what
I'm talking about. William Jay takes it one step further.

We should keep His loving kindness before our eyes as the
Scripture calls upon us to be followers of God as children. We
are to be concerned to reverence Him, to be faithful as He is
faithful, to be holy as He is holy—to be patient, and forgiving,
and kind, like Him. Jesus instructs us, "Love your enemies,
bless them that curse you, do good to them that hate you, and
pray for them which despitefully use you, and persecute you;
that ye may be the children of your Father which is in heaven:
for he maketh his sun to rise on the evil and on the good, and
sendeth rain on the just and on the unjust" (Matthew
5:44,45). Therefore, be merciful, even as your Father which is
in heaven is merciful. God is love. We cannot equal Him, but
it is our happiness to resemble Him. He that dwells in love,
dwells in God, and God in him.

The Price of Revival

For which of you, intending to build a tower, sitteth not down first, and counteth the cost, whether he have sufficient to finish it?

LUKE 14:28

Charles Finney once said that revival should come as no surprise. It is certain, just as a crop of wheat will come after the farmer has tilled the land and sown the seed. When we seek the face of God and are willing to pay the price of revival, it will come. The words of the missionary statesman, Jonathan Goforth, shed new light on the price of revival.

Our reading of the Word of God makes it inconceivable to us that the Holy Spirit should be willing, even for a day, to delay His work. We may be sure that, where there is a lack of the fullness of God, it is ever due to man's lack of faith and obedience. If God the Holy Spirit is not glorifying Jesus Christ in the world today, as at Pentecost, it is we who are to blame. After all, what is revival but simply the Spirit of God fully controlling in the surrendered life? It must always be possible, then, when man yields. The sin of unyieldedness, alone, can keep us from revival.

But are we ready to receive Him? Do we value the giver and the gift sufficiently? Are we ready to pay the price of Holy Ghost revival? Take prayer for example. The history of revival shows plainly that all movements of the Spirit have started in prayer. Yet is it not right there that many of us wilt and falter at the cost?

"What is the secret of revival?" a great evangelist was once asked. "There is no secret," he replied. "Revival always comes in answer to prayer."

Fly to the Mercy Seat

For since He Himself was tempted in that which He has suffered, He is
able to come to the aid of those who are tempted.
HEBREWS 2:18, NASB

Mercy is undeserved forgiveness. I've had the privilege of working with the judicial system and have witnessed mercy firsthand. A criminal, standing before the judge on his third serious offense, is facing many years in the penitentiary. The criminal knows how serious it is. The judge has every right, under the law, to throw the book at him. Instead, to the guilty one's astonishment, the judge shows mercy. Every time this occurs, I am reminded of God's forgiveness. Evidently it was a subject dear to the heart of hymn writer Isaac Watts, as well.

Fly daily to the mercy-seat for divine aid. He [God] is exalted and authorized to take care of sinners who make Him their refuge. He is also compassionate, and ready to assist the tempted. There is cleaning virtue in the Blood of Christ to wash away the foulest guilt and to sprinkle the conscience of the humbly penitent with peace and pardon. There is all-sufficient power and grace with Him to subdue the most raging vices. Make haste to come to Him in humble faith and with most persistent prayer. Never rest until He has, by His providence and grace, delivered you from the dangerous temptation, or made you conqueror over the sin that easily besets you. There are countless souls in heaven who were once struggling here with the same impure temptations, but they gained the victory by the Blood and Spirit of Christ and are made more than conquerors through Him who loved them (see Romans 8:37).

2 SAMUEL 13; 2 CORINTHIANS 6; EZEKIEL 20; PSALMS 66—67

God's Water Walkers

And Peter answered him and said, Lord, if it be thou, bid me come unto thee on the water. And he said, Come. And when Peter was come down out of the ship, he walked on the water, to go to Jesus.
MATTHEW 14:28,29

There is so much to be learned from the story of Peter walking on water. Consider the circumstances surrounding Peter's historic act of faith. You may find that you are more ready to be a "water walker" than you think.

In Matthew 14, we see that this trial took place between two great seasons of miracles. The lesson is simple: We can go from a sunny day to a threatening storm in a matter of hours. You can have a great victory one day and a fierce battle the next. *Don't lose sight of the Lord's provision when you go from a victory into another trial. He is faithful.*

Another important point is that Jesus had compelled the disciples to get into the ship without Him. He knew then that there was a storm coming...and He knows about the storms in your life now. *At times, Jesus will pull away from us in order to test our faith and strengthen our walk with Him.*

Further, it wasn't until the darkest point of the trial that Jesus appeared on the scene. It was the fourth watch, the darkest time of the night. All hope was gone. *Sometimes, it is not until we are most desperate that we see the Lord's deliverance.*

Finally, consider that there is no way to practice walking on water. Peter had no prior experience, but he stepped out in faith. After all, Jesus was already out there! *There are times in life when we too must step out in "water-walking faith."*

2 SAMUEL 14; 2 CORINTHIANS 7; EZEKIEL 21; PSALM 68

Fixed on Jesus

The fear of the LORD is the beginning of wisdom:
and the knowledge of the holy is understanding.
PROVERBS 9:10

Have you ever had trouble concentrating? If you're like me, I'm sure you've struggled with this. Have you ever been in church with the full intention of worshiping Jesus, when out of the blue, your mind filled with a distracting thought? Suddenly you realized that a robbery has taken place in the spirit realm. Your desire was to focus on Jesus, but now you were thinking about yesterday's events or tomorrow's projects. It seems we spend our lives struggling to keep our hearts fixed on Jesus.

This struggle is nothing new. Robert Hall spoke of it years ago.

> The power of fixing the attention is most precious of the intellectual habits. Every man possesses it in some degree, and it will increase the more it is exerted. He who exercises no discipline over himself in this respect acquires such an instability of mind, such a roving imagination, as dooms him to be the sport of every mental vanity—it is impossible such a man should attain to true wisdom.

Although his words appear a little strong, they serve as good medicine for this condition. The Bible instructs us to take authority over every imagination and thought that exalts itself above the knowledge of Christ (see 2 Corinthians 10:5). The Bible doesn't say, "Try to cast down imaginations." It says to cast them down. If we are ever going to excel in our walk with God, we must learn to keep our hearts fixed on Jesus.

2 SAMUEL 15; 2 CORINTHIANS 8; EZEKIEL 22; PSALM 69

God Is Here

What? know ye not that your body is the temple of the Holy Ghost which is in you, which ye have of God, and ye are not your own?
1 CORINTHIANS 6:19

People often ask the question, Where is God? I quit asking that question almost 25 years ago. God is no longer a mysterious being who dwells in the realm of the unknown. Ever since I gave my life to Jesus, He now dwells in me, and can be found by others by my kind words and my good deeds. I agree with the words of Jeremy Taylor written hundreds of years ago.

> God is especially present in the hearts of His people, by His Holy Spirit. Indeed, the hearts of holy men are temples, and in type and shadow, they are heaven itself. For God reigns in the hearts of His servants—there is His kingdom. The power of grace has subdued all His enemies—there is His power. They serve Him night and day, and give Him thanks and praise—that is His glory.
>
> The temple itself is the heart of man; Christ is the high priest, who sends up the incense of prayers, and joins them to His own intercession, and presents all together to His Father. The Holy Ghost, by His dwelling there, has also consecrated it into a temple.
>
> As infancy is just short of manhood, and letters are portions of words, what is this short of heaven itself? It is the same state of life but not the same age. It is heaven in a looking glass, dark yet true, representing the beauties of the soul.

What a powerful truth. Christ in you, the hope of glory.

2 SAMUEL 16; 2 CORINTHIANS 9; EZEKIEL 23; PSALMS 70—71

Below the Surface

Deep calleth unto deep at the noise of thy waterspouts:
all thy waves and thy billows are gone over me.
PSALM 42:7

To God, it must be the most beautiful music, the sweetest incense. I speak of the sound of repentance. There is nothing like the roar of hundreds of people weeping and wailing over their lostness. One man said it sounded eerie. My response to him was, "You are listening to music that brings a smile to the face of God." It's the deepness of God calling to the deepness of man. It's the Spirit of God reaching down past the facade into the innermost recesses of our hearts.

Below the surface of every man, woman and child lies the true meaning of their existence. Just as the face of a clock can be exquisite, an incitement to the eye, an artistic masterpiece—the inside of the clock tells the true story. The sign outside may say "Fine Dining." The building may be gorgeous and the table set with sterling silver and expensive china, but it's the skill inside the kitchen that really matters. Likewise, the outside of man may appear beautiful, his countenance may declare a surety and confidence in life, but deep down, in the part no one sees, lies the truth. This is the place that God loves to go. The Spirit of God searches our hearts. He created us. He knows every secret place. He knows what's going on below the surface.

Always remember, Jesus Christ spends most of His time below the surface. Man sees the outward, but God sees the heart.

2 SAMUEL 17; 2 CORINTHIANS 10; EZEKIEL 24; PSALM 72

Give It All

And He said, "Truly I say to you, this poor widow put in more than all of them; for they all out of their surplus put into the offering; but she out of her poverty put in all that she had to live on."
LUKE 21:3,4, NASB

On the wall of the cardboard shack was a charcoal sketch of an impoverished family. I asked the poor woman about the people depicted in the crude drawing. She said, "Oh, brother Steve, these are the poor people in the Central American countries. We must pray for them; they have so little." Here I was, standing in the middle of a tiny cardboard shack in South America, with a family who lived with the barest necessities of life, and they were concerned about those who had even less. God spoke to my heart about the widow who gave all she had.

It is sad that these words of William Booth are still so true today:

It is easier to make a hundred poor men sacrifice their lives than it is to induce one rich man to sacrifice his fortune, or even a portion of it. I look over the roll of men and women who have given up friends, parents, home prospects, and everything they possess in order to walk bare-footed beneath a burning sun in distant India. They live on a handful of rice and die in the midst of heathen, for God and the Salvation Army. The Bible says, "From those to whom much is given much is expected." But alas, how little is realized! It is still the widow who casts her all into the Lord's treasury—while the wealthy deem it a preposterous suggestion when we speak of the Lord's tithe. They count it boredom when we ask only for the crumbs that fall from their tables.

If we could only stand back and see how this must look to the One who gave us all we have.

2 SAMUEL 18; 2 CORINTHIANS 11; EZEKIEL 25; PSALM 73

The Desertion of God

But Zion said, The LORD hath forsaken me, and my Lord hath forgotten me.
ISAIAH 49:14

Not long ago, during one of our baptism services, a man said, "I was in love with Jesus, but sin crept into my heart. When the sin came in, the presence of God left. I got angry at God because He was gone." The man was very thankful that when he got the sin out, he could once again feel the presence of the Lord. I believe he could well identify with what Robert M. McCheyne called "the bitterest of all kinds of desertion."

Desertion of God is when God withdraws from the soul of a believer, so that His absence is felt. The world knows nothing of this, and yet it is true. God has ways of revealing Himself to His own in another way than He does to the world: "The secret of the Lord is with them that fear Him, and He will show them His covenant." They feel His presence, they hear His words—their hearts burn within them. The Father is the refuge of His own. They feel His everlasting arms underneath them—they feel His eye watching over them—they feel His love pouring down upon them like streams of light from heaven. The Holy Spirit is within them. Oh! This is heaven upon earth—full, satisfying joy.

If you have found yourself in this most miserable of places, friend, stop everything. Take a close look at yourself. Ask the Lord to show you what may have caused His absence. Search for Him with all your heart. He promised that He will be found of you.

September 24

You Can't Have It

Behold, I come quickly: hold that fast which thou hast,
that no man take thy crown.
REVELATION 3:11

Today's text warns us that someone might try to take our crown. In order for someone to take our crown, we must first have one. Paul spoke of the crown of righteousness which is laid up for him in heaven (see 2 Timothy 4:8). That crown represented all he had done for Jesus' sake. My friend, if Paul was thinking about his crown, we should be thinking about ours.

Be assured, at the end of every life there's a time of reward or punishment. According to the Word of God, there exists a system of checks and balances, a judicial system, a standard by which we are expected to live. There is a Law Giver and there is a law. If the law is violated, there is punishment. If the law is followed, there is blessing. In order for you to have a crown up there, you must have first lived for Christ down here. To put on a crown up there, you must first be put on a cross down here.

The crown represents how you lived your life here on earth. Once you've earned a crown, this scripture teaches that it can be stolen from you. The devil can steal it from you, others can steal it from you, or you can freely give it up. The bottom line is this: The control of the crown is in your hands. Don't let anyone have it. When you stand before God, you will want a crown—a glorious crown!—to lay at His feet in worship.

Excessive Activity

*And whatsoever ye do in word or deed, do all in the name of the Lord
Jesus, giving thanks to God and the Father by him.*
COLOSSIANS 3:17

Have you ever heard the saying, When all is said and done, more is
said than done? This reminds me of the swirl of chatter taking place in
Christian circles. While we feverishly plan our days, promote our projects, discuss prayer and educate on evangelism, very little is actually
done. I wonder how this looks from heaven. I've got a feeling that God
would like to be consulted. He not only wants to be included in our
strategic sessions, but He would like to be in charge of every aspect.
Remember, His ways and plans are perfect. His wisdom far outweighs
our whims. Could you imagine what it would be like if every servant of
His consulted Him before moving on in a new venture? Charles
Spurgeon did, and he wrote this about it:

> It is necessary that we serve Him in the way of His appoint-
> ment. Could you imagine if a hired servant was continually
> running up and down stairs, roaming about every room, open-
> ing every closet, moving pieces of furniture, and generally keep-
> ing up a perpetual stir and worry? You would not call this serv-
> ice, but annoyance. All that is done contrary to orders is dis-
> obedience, not service; and if anything be done without orders,
> it may be excessive activity, but it certainly is not service.

We must ask Jesus for divine guidance. We must rid ourselves of
excessive activity, and fine-tune our lives to the dictates of our Lord.
Then, and only then, will we accomplish His purpose for our lives.

---

2 SAMUEL 21; GALATIANS 1; EZEKIEL 28; PSALM 77

Resting in His Arms

Surely I have behaved and quieted myself, as a child that is weaned of his
mother: my soul is even as a weaned child.
PSALM 131:2

There is a place that every believer must come to in the Christian life. Upon first receiving Christ, we desire to be pampered, nurtured, constantly cared for, just like a newborn baby. I remember those times as a new Christian. My life was fragile and God dealt with me in the most tender way. I was drinking the milk of the Word, and growing in spiritual strength and stature. Even members of my family commented on how I was growing and becoming a mature Christian. But you don't stay a baby or toddler forever. Crawling leads to walking; walking leads to running.

Jesus Christ was weaning me from the world and was now making a man of God. He's doing the same in your life. Every true believer must go through this process. John Gill spoke of this weaning in his writings on today's text:

> Weaned from the world: the riches, honors, pleasures, and profits of it. Weaned from nature: from self, from his own righteousness, and all dependence upon it. As a child that is weaned from the breast wholly depends on its mother for sustenance, so does a Christian wholly depend upon God. A child, while weaning, is usually discontent, fretful, and obstinate. But when he is weaned, he is quiet and easy in his mother's arms without the breast.

Perhaps God has taken you into a new dimension of His love. You've been weaned from the breast, and feel a little insecure. Relax. You're safe. You're resting in His arms.

2 SAMUEL 22; GALATIANS 2; EZEKIEL 29; PSALM 78:1-37

Without Reservation

So we, being many, are one body in Christ,
and every one members one of another.
ROMANS 12:5

Are you willing to do anything God wants you to do, anywhere He wants you to do it, for whomever He wants you to do it? That's what it means to serve Him without reservation, and that is the service He calls every believer to. Andrew Murray's writing on the subject gives an even clearer definition of God's calling.

Place yourself at Christ's disposal for service to your fellow Christians. Count yourself their servant. Selfishness may hesitate, the feeling of feebleness may discourage, sloth and ease may raise difficulties, but ask your Lord to reveal to you His will, and then give yourself up to it. Round about you there are Christians who are cold, worldly and wandering from their Lord. Begin to think what you can do for them. Pray for the Spirit of love. Begin somewhere. Do not continue hearing and thinking while you do nothing.

Let us believe in the power that works in us as sufficient for all we have to do. As I think of the thumb and finger holding the pen with which I write this, I ask, "How is it that during all these seventy years of my life they have always known just to do my will?" It was because the life of the head passed into and worked itself out in them. "He that believeth on Me," as his Head working in him, "the works that I do shall he do also." Faith in Christ, whose strength is made perfect in our weakness, will give the power for all we are called to do.

Are you serving the Lord without reservation? You can. His mind and His heart working in you will equip you to reach out and serve others as He did—without reservation. Start today. Somebody needs you.

---

2 SAMUEL 23; GALATIANS 3; EZEKIEL 30; PSALM 78:38-72

Love not the world, neither the things that are in the world. If any man love the world, the love of the Father is not in him.
1 JOHN 2:15

Most Christians will agree that the ways of the world have crept into the Church. Often, without even being aware of its presence, the culture of the world begins to infiltrate our lives. Before long we are in a backslidden condition, and are dumbfounded that we fell so low.

Allow me to list a few checkpoints to assess whether or not we love the world too much. We love the world too much when . . .

- for the sake of profit or pleasure, we willfully and deliberately do evil or transgress God's commandments;
- we work harder to obtain the luxuries of this life than we do for the kingdom of God;
- we are not content or patient when under awkward circumstances, particularly financial;
- we cannot part with anything that we possess to those who want it, who deserve it and who have a right to it;
- we envy the fortunes of others who are in the world;
- we notice people and esteem them higher just because of their financial standing, or we dislike others simply because everyone else looks down on them;
- worldly prosperity makes us feel proud, vain and superior.

It would be good to refer back to the list occasionally to see where you stand.

Keep the Sky Clear

I will be like the dew to Israel; He will blossom like the lily, and he will take root like the cedars of Lebanon. His shoots will sprout, and his beauty will be like the olive tree, and his fragrance like the cedars of Lebanon.
HOSEA 14:5,6, NASB

Hannah Whitall Smith beautifully portrays to us the secret of growing in God.

What we all need is to "consider the flowers of the field," and learn their secret. Grow, by all means, dear Christians; but grow...in God's way, which is the only effectual way. See to it that you are planted in grace, and then let the divine Husbandman cultivate you in His own way and by His own means. Put yourselves out in the sunshine of His presence, and let the dew of heaven come down upon you, and see the result. Leaves and flowers and fruit must surely come in their season; for your Husbandman is skillful, and He never fails in His harvesting.

Only see to it that you oppose no hindrance to the shining of the Sun of righteousness, or the falling of the dew from heaven. The thinnest covering may serve to keep off the sunshine and the dew, and the plant may wither, even where these are most abundant. And so also the slightest barrier between your soul and Christ may cause you to dwindle and fade, as a plant in a cellar or under a bushel. Keep the sky clear. Open wide every avenue of your being to receive the blessed influences your divine Husbandman may bring to bear upon you. Bask in the sunshine of His love. Drink of the waters of His goodness. Keep your face upturned to Him, as the flowers do to the sun. Look, and your soul shall live and grow.

And in the morning, rising up a great while before day, he went out, and departed into a solitary place, and there prayed.

MARK 1:35

As Christians, we often hear that the best time to pray is in the early morning hours. Sometimes, however, it's helpful to have a little more insight as to why. I believe you will be encouraged by these words of R. A. Torrey, a man noted for his deep understanding of prayer.

> Jesus chose the early morning hour for prayer. Many of the mightiest men of God have followed the Lord's example in this. In the morning hour the mind is fresh and at its very best. It is free from distraction. Absolute concentration upon God, which is essential to the most effective prayer, is most easily possible in the early morning hours. Furthermore, when the early hours are spent in prayer, the whole day is sanctified, and power is obtained for overcoming its temptations and for performing its duties.
>
> More can be accomplished in prayer in the first hours of the day than at any other time during the day. Every child of God who would make the most out of his life for Christ, should set apart the first part of the day to meeting God in the study of His Word and in prayer. The first thing we do each day should be to go alone with God and face the duties, the temptation, and the service of that day, and get strength from God for all. We should get victory before the hour of trial, temptation or service ever comes. The secret place of prayer is the place to fight our battles and gain our victories.

It's clear to see that the first thing we should do is the best thing we can do!

1 KINGS 2; GALATIANS 6; EZEKIEL 33; PSALMS 81—82

The True Pain of Calvary

*But Jesus turning unto them said, Daughters of Jerusalem, weep not for
me, but weep for yourselves, and for your children.*
LUKE 23:28

I am convinced that the greatest suffering Jesus experienced was
not temporary, physical pain, but rather eternal, spiritual pain. "Weep
not for me," He said, "but weep for yourselves." Nothing could have
hurt Jesus more than the inner pain He felt for mankind. When He
uttered the words, "Father, forgive them, for they know not what they
do," His true heart of compassion was revealed. In the midst of the
most agonizing physical suffering a man could endure, Jesus expressed
the true pain of Calvary.

I believe it came from the *apathy of mankind*. Apathy is a lack of
emotion or feeling; a lack of interest; total indifference. The world continues to pass by the Cross, looking up in empty response. "So what?"
they say. "Who cares? Eat, drink and be merry, for tomorrow we die."
In the words of Alexander McClaren, "There are none more monstrous
than the men who look, as some of us are doing, untouched on
Christ's sacrifice and listen unmoved to Christ's pleadings."

I also believe the true pain of Calvary is the *discontentment of
mankind*. Many are not satisfied with His suffering. They cry out to
God, "I know You sent Jesus to die for my sins, but God, You don't
seem to understand. I need more than this. You've got to make it easier. It's too hard to live for You." Not only did Jesus have to physically
endure torment for us, but now He must endure discontentment from
us. My friend, this should never be!

The Final Judge

But God is the judge: he putteth down one, and setteth up another.
PSALM 75:7

If only we would learn to live life through the eyes of eternity. That means we would live our lives as if we could die any moment and stand before Almighty God. How different our decisions would be. How much purer our motives. Even the way we treat others would be drastically affected.

I have had the opportunity to speak about eternity to thousands of lost sinners over the years. It comes as a shrill wake-up call to a sleepy soul. It serves as a reality check for those who are lost in the world of alcohol and drugs. It's like a slap in the face to the backslider. But I am not alone when it comes to warning people about eternity. God-fearing preachers and evangelists have been bellowing out this message for centuries. Listen to William Plumer:

> Have you counted the cost of the course you are now pursuing? If you are in sin, you are living at a dreadful cost. You are losing precious time, blessed opportunities. If you go on as you are now living, you will lose your poor soul, and will lose it for ever. Does your conscience say you are doing right? In your most solemn moments do you approve the choice you have made? What will you think of your present conduct when you come to die? Does God approve of your life? He is to be the final Judge.

These are hard, soul-stirring words that need to be heard. Time is slipping away. Even this year has but a few months left. We must live for eternity. We will one day face the final Judge.

1 KINGS 4—5; EPHESIANS 2; EZEKIEL 35; PSALM 85

And I will cleanse them from all their iniquity, whereby they have sinned against me; and I will pardon all their iniquities, whereby they have sinned, and whereby they have transgressed against me.

JEREMIAH 33:8

If we could only realize that the depth of God's mercy far exceeds the depth of our sin. Alexander McClaren summed it up well when he said, "You cannot believe too much in God's mercy." He continued:

> You cannot expect too much at His hands. He is "able to do exceeding abundantly above all that we ask or think." No sin is so great but that, coming clean from it, a repentant sinner may hope and believe that all God's love will be lavished upon him. Even if our transgression be aggravated by a previous life of godliness, and have given the enemies great occasion to blaspheme, as King David did, yet his penitence may in our souls lead on to his hope.
>
> Let no sin, however dark, however repeated, drive us to despair of ourselves, because it hides from us our loving Savior. Though beaten back again and again by the surge of our passions and sins, like some poor shipwrecked sailor sucked back with every retreating wave and tossed about in the angry surf, yet keep your face towards the beach where there is safety. You will struggle through it all, and though it were but on some floating boards and broken pieces of the ship, will come safe to land. He will uphold you with His Spirit, and take away the weight of sin that would sink you, by His forgiving mercy, and bring you out of all the weltering waste of waters to the solid shore.

Friend, we serve a forgiving God. His one desire is for you to make it safely to heaven's shore. Allow Him to help you in the journey.

1 KINGS 6; EPHESIANS 3; EZEKIEL 36; PSALM 86

Until the Answer Comes

*For this child I prayed; and the LORD hath given me
my petition which I asked of him.*

1 SAMUEL 1:27

There is much talk in Christian circles today about intercession. Over the years, I have known true intercessors. These are people who go after God, and God goes after them. Their cry to God is not based on prideful notoriety or on selfish pursuits, but rather motivated by a sincere burden to see the will of God done.

Leonard Ravenhill, a man who not only wrote about prayer, but prayed, challenges us with these words.

What twisted ideas we get about prayer in our day. To many of us, prayer is just a shortcut to receiving a desired thing. Yet if the Lord tarry, we must wait for His answer. "If Hannah's prayer for a son had been answered at the time she set for herself," said W. E. Biederwolf, "the nation might never have known the mighty man of God that it found in Samuel."

Hannah's prayer is a classic because in it are revealed the true ingredients of intercessory prayer (the highest type of prayer known to believers). In many churches there are warriors in prayer, and these gather collectively to fight the good fight of faith; others just pray. But true intercessors "stand in the gap" until through them comes the answer.[1]

We need more prayer warriors. We need those who will unselfishly seek the Lord until the answer comes.

1. Leonard Ravenhill, *Revival Praying* (Minneapolis, Minn.: Bethany House Publishers, 1962), pp. 45-46.

1 KINGS 7; EPHESIANS 4; EZEKIEL 37; PSALMS 87—88

And I set my face unto the Lord God, to seek by prayer and supplications,
with fasting, and sackcloth, and ashes.

DANIEL 9:3

Prayer, coupled with fasting, has a way of clearing up the fog of unbelief and calling down the life-changing power of God. I don't fully understand how it works, but I've seen its effect throughout my Christian life. R. A. Torrey recognized this power and encouraged all believers to experience the benefit of this serious Christian exercise.

If we would pray with power, we should pray with fasting. This of course does not mean that we should fast every time we pray. There are times of emergency or special crisis when men of earnestness will withdraw themselves even from the gratification of natural appetites, that they may give themselves up wholly to prayer. There is a peculiar power in such prayer. Every great crisis in life and work should be met in that way. There is nothing pleasing to God in our giving up in a purely Pharisaic and legal way things which are pleasant. However, there is power in that determination to obtaining through prayer the things of which we sorely feel our need, that leads us to put away everything, even things in themselves most right and necessary, that we may set our faces to find God, and obtain blessings from Him.

Like you, I have had many difficult situations that appeared impossible to overcome. These problems seemed to stop me dead in my tracks. What was I to do? How could I remove this mountain? The answer is always fasting and prayer. There is a special anointing that hovers over the fasting saint.

Breaking the Power of Sin

The sting of death is sin, and the power of sin is the law; but thanks be to God, who gives us the victory through our Lord Jesus Christ.

1 CORINTHIANS 15:56,57, NASB

As a preacher of the gospel, I get so tired of hearing people say they "just can't stop sinning." It's as if they are serving some type of anemic, half-sufficient Redeemer. Keep in mind that I was delivered from years of drug abuse and crime. When the Lord saved my soul from hell, He also delivered me from sin. Sin no longer had a stronghold on me. I have a hard time when Christians preach any other gospel. So did Charles Finney.

> Many seem to have hardened their hearts against all expectation of this deliverance from sin. They have heard the doctrine preached. They have seen some profess to be in this state of salvation from sin, but they have also seen some in this class fall again, and now they deliberately reject the whole doctrine. But is this consistent with really embracing the Gospel? What is the Christ to the believer? What was His errand into the world? What is He doing and what is He trying to do?
>
> He has come to break the power of sin in the heart and to be the life of the believer. He is working in him a perpetual salvation from sin, aiming to bring him to heaven at last. What is faith? What but the actual giving of yourself up to Christ that He may do this work for you and in you? What are you to believe of Christ if not this, that He is to save His people from their sins? Can you tell of anything else? Does the Bible tell you to expect something different and less than this?

1 KINGS 9; EPHESIANS 6; EZEKIEL 39; PSALM 90

God's Holy Demands

And he that taketh not his cross, and followeth after me, is not worthy of me.
MATTHEW 10:38

Christians can be very demanding people. They want everything from perfect nursery workers to a top-notch song leader. They demand a clean church but won't take the time to pick up trash from the yard. They complain over the faulty church plumbing but won't drop an offering in the plate to put in new fixtures. The list goes on and on.

But what about God's demands? After all, He's the one who formed us in our mother's womb. He's the one who has given us life. God is the Master Potter and we are the earthen clay. He is the one we will give an account to. Therefore, it would be good to know what He demands of us.

First of all, God demands a total allegiance to His person. That means He wants no other idols in your life. An idol is anything that takes the place of God in our lives. It can be sports, fame or money. Jesus even spoke of loving God more than family. For many, that is a strong demand, but it must be obeyed.

God also demands total allegiance to His cause. That means He expects you to spend your life speaking about His kingdom, not yours.

He also demands total allegiance to holiness. "Without holiness," the Bible says, "no one will see the Lord" (Hebrews 12:14, *NIV*). It is not a suggestion that we be holy—it is a command.

So next time demands are being made to God, make sure His demands are being met first.

1 KINGS 10; PHILIPPIANS 1; EZEKIEL 40; PSALM 91

Will Ewe Submit?

Though he were a Son, yet learned he obedience by the things which he
suffered; and being made perfect, he became the author of
eternal salvation unto all them that obey him.
HEBREWS 5:8,9

Submission is a very easy thing to do as long as it's someone else doing it. The best way to illustrate this would be to analyze a typical church congregation. The pastor is the shepherd; the people are the sheep. When a particular sheep begins to wander into dangerous territory (sin), the pastor's job is to find the sheep and bring it back into line. His position, appointed by God, is to watch over the flock. That's fine, you might say, but what does that have to do with me? The problem arises when the sheep he is going after is you. As long as someone else has the problem, we praise the pastor. But when we're the one being scolded or reproved, we often take offense and rebel.

I often wonder how people who are so easily offended at man's loving correction submit to God's authority. When we submit ourselves to God, that means we are yielding ourselves to His will for our lives.

According to John Howe, submission is the soul's real and practical acknowledgment of God's supreme majesty. Submission is the soul's homage to its Maker. It is that by which the blessed soul becomes in its own sense a consecrated and devoted thing, sacred to God, having its very life and being referred and made over to Him.

Jesus totally submitted Himself to His Father's will, even to the point of death on the Cross. Compared with His suffering, how can we, as Christians, resist submitting to God?

1 KINGS 11; PHILIPPIANS 2; EZEKIEL 41; PSALMS 92—93

Growth Spurts

Now therefore arise, go out and speak kindly to your servants, for I swear by the LORD, if you do not go out, surely not a man will pass the night with you, and this will be worse for you than all the evil that has come upon you from your youth until now.

2 SAMUEL 19:7, NASB

Many of the great ministers I have included in this devotional are favorites of mine because they were men and women who spoke the truth. And they were not concerned with whether or not people were happy after they heard it. John Owen is a good example. Severe trials are usually unavoidable, but Owen's writing here reminds us to make the most of those times for our personal growth.

Labor to grow better under all your afflictions, lest your afflictions grow worse. As Joab said to David, if he would not cease his lamentation over the death of Absalom, all the people would leave him, and then he should find himself in a far worse condition than that which he mourned. The same may be said to persons under their afflictions. If they are not improved in due season, that which is worse may befall them. Whenever God chooses this way, and engages in afflicting, He commonly pursues His work until He has prevailed. Lay down, then, the weapons of warfare against Him. Give up yourselves to His will. Follow after that which He calls you unto; and you will find light arising unto you in the midst of darkness. Has He a cup of affliction in one hand? Lift up your eyes, and you will see a cup of consolation in the other. And if all stars withdraw their light while you are in the way of God, assure yourselves that the sun is ready to rise.

Be of good courage in the face of trials. If you handle them correctly, you will soon find it was only a growth spurt.

1 KINGS 12; PHILIPPIANS 3; EZEKIEL 42; PSALM 94

Soul Care

*Be of good courage, and he shall strengthen your heart,
all ye that hope in the LORD.*
PSALM 31:24

This devotional book took an enormous amount of time to prepare. Hours upon hours were spent perusing old manuscripts and books. Many of my personal sermons were abbreviated and put into a simple format. What kept me going throughout the process was to know that one day a disciple of Jesus would use *Daily Awakenings* as a personal guide to their individual growth in the Lord. Your relationship with Jesus is the most important part of your life. Robert Murray McCheyne often encouraged his congregation to realize that their own soul was their "first and greatest care."

You know a sound body alone can work with power; much more a healthy soul. Keep a clear conscience through the Blood of the Lamb. Keep close communion with God. Study likeness to Him in all things. Read the Bible for your own growth first, then for those around you. Expound much; it is through the truth itself that souls are to be sanctified, not through essays upon the truth. Be easy to access, inclined to teach, and the Lord will teach you and bless you in all you do and say. You will not find many companions. Be the more with God. The prayerful are praying for you. Be of good courage; there remains much of the land to be possessed. Be not dismayed, for Christ shall be with you to deliver you.

McCheyne's words are timeless reminders of how to take care of our own souls. Each day holds new trials and new mercies. Keep your soul healthy and ready!

1 KINGS 13; PHILIPPIANS 4; EZEKIEL 43; PSALMS 95—96

Highway of Holiness

And an highway shall be there, and a way, and it shall be called The way of holiness; the unclean shall not pass over it; but it shall be for those: the wayfaring men, though fools, shall not err therein.

ISAIAH 35:8

When I first read this scripture, my mind immediately drew a parallel between the highway of holiness and driving down America's highways. Here we go:

1. To get on the highway of holiness, you must first make the right turn. That is, whatever road you're going down now, you must catch the on-ramp. The only way onto this highway is through the Blood of Jesus Christ. The destination is heaven, and Jesus said, "I am the Way."
2. To make progress on this highway, you must keep your foot on the accelerator. That is, you must continually move forward. There is no turning back. You will encounter numerous distracting billboards and demonic off-ramps. My friend, stay on the main highway.
3. To ensure your continual progress, you must stay between the lines. This has to do with holiness, and the Bible clearly marks the proper direction.
4. Be sure, on the highway of holiness, to keep your vehicle (soul) tuned up. Make sure you check the oil. The Master Mechanic (Holy Spirit) will keep your engine running smooth if you'll submit to His vehicle inspection.
5. You must stay on this highway until you reach your destination. Don't settle for Satan's substitutes. The devil's rest stops can turn into death stops. Take heed to these simple rules, and you'll be well on your way.

Doing Our Part

Now the God of peace, that brought again from the dead our Lord Jesus, that great shepherd of the sheep, through the blood of the everlasting covenant, make you perfect in every good work to do his will, working in you that which is well-pleasing in his sight, through Jesus Christ.
HEBREWS 13:20,21

Have you ever seen a tree grow? Well, probably not on a moment by moment basis, but you can certainly mark the growth difference from year to year. That tree, when it is just a sapling, doesn't spend time worrying if it will ever be more than just a sapling. "Saplinghood" is merely a phase in its maturity process.

A Christian goes through growth cycles as well. As Hannah Whitall Smith pointed out, God is doing the work. Our part is to trust Him to complete it.

> The maturity of a Christian experience cannot be reached in a moment. It is the result of the work of God's Holy Spirit, who, by His energizing and transforming power, causes us to grow up into Christ in all things. And we cannot hope to reach this maturity in any other way than by yielding ourselves up utterly and willingly, to His mighty working.
>
> The little babe may be all that a babe could be, or ought to be, and may therefore perfectly please its mother; and yet it is very far from being what that mother would wish it to be when the years of maturity shall come.
>
> God's works are perfect in every stage of their growth. By an act of faith we put ourselves into the hands of the Lord, for Him to work in us all the good pleasure of His will, and then, by a continuous exercise of faith, keep ourselves there. Our part is the trusting; it is His to accomplish the results.

Don't look at your life right now and declare, "I'll never be what God wants me to be." Chances are, you're on your way. He will make sure you get there if you do your part.

1 KINGS 15; COLOSSIANS 2; EZEKIEL 45; PSALMS 99—101

In My Name

*For where two or three are gathered together in my name,
there am I in the midst of them.*

MATTHEW 18:20

There is an army of Christian warriors rising up in the land. I can hear their marching footsteps. I can hear the battle cry of their Commander in Chief. There seems to be a strong unity developing among Christians of all denominations. This commotion of camaraderie is bringing great joy to the heart of God, and I'm sure, causing His ear to be attentive to our prayers. William Gurnall, who penned the classic *The Christian in Complete Armor,* knew all about the power of unity.

No doubt the prayers which the faithful put up to heaven from under their private roofs were very acceptable unto Him. If a saint's single voice in prayer be so sweet to God's ear, how much more the "church choir"—His saints' prayers in concert together. A father is glad to see any one of his children, and makes him welcome when he visits him, but much more when they come together. The greatest feast is when they all meet at his house.

There is a wonderful prevalency in the joint prayers of His people. When Peter was in prison, the church met and prayed him out of his enemies' hands. A prince will grant a petition brought by the hands of a whole city which he may not have granted if only brought at the request of a private subject, though he loves the individual no less. There is a specific promise to public prayer: "Where two or three are gathered together in my name, there am I in the midst of them."

1 KINGS 16; COLOSSIANS 3; EZEKIEL 46; PSALM 102

Sleeping Too Soundly

And as he lay and slept under a juniper tree, behold, then an angel touched him, and said unto him, Arise and eat.

1 KINGS 19:5

America has received many wake-up calls. The violence in our streets and the killings in our schools seem to stir her but not get her out of bed. Sadly, she reaches over and slaps the snooze button, then dozes back into a sound sleep. But God won't put up with our lazy streak. Horatius Bonar enlightens us with the stages of God's efforts to awaken us.

> In arousing us, God proceeds at first most gently. He touches us slightly, as the angel did Elijah, under the juniper tree, that He may awake us. He sends some slight visitation to shake us out of our security. He causes us to hear some distant noise; it may be the tumults of the nations, or it may be the tidings of famine, or war, or pestilence afar off. Perhaps this entirely fails and we slumber on as securely as ever. Our life is as listless and as useless as ever.
>
> Then He comes nearer and makes His voice to be heard in our own neighborhood, or within the circle of our family. This also fails. Then He comes nearer still—for the time is hurrying on—and the saint is still asleep. He speaks into our very ears. He smites upon some tender part, till every fiber of our frame quivers and every pulse throbs quicker. Our very soul is stricken through, as with a thousand arrows. Then we start up like one awakening out of a long sleep, and looking around us, and wonder how we could have slept so long.

Friend, if you've been slumbering soundly, repent. Go to God and ask Him to awaken your spirit. Seek to be one who rises at the first call of God. Be quick to go to prayer over the needs of those around you.

1 KINGS 17; COLOSSIANS 4; EZEKIEL 47; PSALM 103

Afflictions Lift the Soul

But the God of all grace, who hath called us unto his eternal glory
by Christ Jesus, after that ye have suffered a while, make you perfect,
stablish, strengthen, settle you.

1 PETER 5:10

Some of the greatest works of art have been painted during the darkest trials of the artist. Many of our most beloved hymns, such as, "It Is Well with My Soul," were composed while the writer was passing through a season of intense testing. Today's text relates suffering to our spiritual growth. Thomas Brooks penned some timeless words of encouragement on this subject.

God afflicts us for our profit, that we might be partakers of His holiness. Afflictions are the mother of virtue. God's house of correction is His school of instruction. All the stones that came about Stephen's ears did but knock him closer to Christ, the Corner-stone. The waves did but lift Noah's ark nearer to heaven. Afflictions lift the soul to more full enjoyments of God. "Behold, I will lead her into the wilderness, and speak comfortably unto her" (Hosea 2:14).

When was it that Stephen saw the heavens open, and Christ standing at the right hand of God, but when the stones were about his ears, and there was but a short step between him and eternity? And when did God appear in glory to Jacob, but in the day of his troubles, when the stones were his pillows, and the ground his bed, and hedges his curtains, and the heavens his canopy? Then he saw the angels of God ascending and descending in their glittering robes.

Dear saint of God, don't despise afflictions—they are lifting your soul to God.

Rejoice in the Lord always: and again I say, Rejoice.
I have no greater jo than to hear that my children walk in truth.
PHILIPPIANS 4:4; 3 JOHN 4

There is a word that I never used until after becoming a Christian. It appears over 150 times in the Word of God. It's a word that unbelievers will never understand.

I'm speaking of "joy." A word that basically means *gladness,* or better yet, *intense happiness.* Ever since meeting Jesus Christ, I have had the joy of the Lord bubbling up within me. I've often wondered why some Christians seem to constantly have gloom and doom written all over their faces, when the Lord speaks so strongly about having His blessed joy. You may ask, "Steve, where does this joy come from? Why are you so happy?"

I've got the joy of the Lord because my sins have been forgiven. The Bible says, "Blessed [happy] is he whose transgression is forgiven, whose sin is covered" (Psalm 32:1).

I've got the joy of the Lord because I'm now walking in fellowship with Jesus. I was once walking in darkness; now I'm walking in the light. I used to wake up with a hangover, but now I wake up with joy all over.

I've got the joy of the Lord because the best is yet to come. My eyes are focused on eternity, and I know that one day Jesus is coming back to take me home.

And finally, I've got the joy of the Lord because my spiritual children are living for Jesus. What a thrill to see so many people come out of darkness and walk in the light. There's no greater joy than to see my children walk in truth.

Friend, if you've been delivered—you've got a reason to be joyful. Even when everything else seems against you, stop and think about what He's done for you, and that joy will start bubbling up inside!

1 KINGS 19; 1 THESSALONIANS 2; DANIEL 1; PSALM 105

Whatcha Thinkin'?

The thoughts of the righteous are right:
but the counsels of the wicked are deceit.
PROVERBS 12:5

Probably the most difficult area of our lives to get under control is our thought life. I have seen drug addicts throw away their needles, alcoholics toss their bottles, prostitutes quit turning tricks and dishonest businessmen come clean...but this one obstacle—the thought life—blocked them from moving on with God. The book of James talks about how hard it is to tame the tongue, but my friend, the tongue is only going to speak what's already in the head. I believe that through saturating ourselves with the Word of God and protecting ourselves from the entrance of evil words and pictures, we can gain an incredible victory over our thought life.

One of my favorite devotional writers, William Jay, knew the danger of entertaining vain thoughts.

Vain thoughts are foolish thoughts, wandering thoughts, unbelieving thoughts, worldly thoughts, self-righteous thoughts, sinful thoughts. For observe that vain thoughts here do not mean empty ones, but evil ones; as when our Savior says, "that every idle word that men shall speak they shall give account thereof in the day of judgment." By "idle words" He does not mean merely frivolous, silly, and trifling words, but words of moral blame, and which will serve to condemn us in the last day.

The responsibility of our thought life remains solely in our hands. We must close the gate to anything that wants to enter and destroy the pure work of God in our lives.

1 KINGS 20; 1 THESSALONIANS 3; DANIEL 2; PSALM 106

Working for God

For God is my King of old, working salvation in the midst of the earth.
PSALM 74:12

Without the deep work of the Holy Spirit, there is absolutely no way a mere man can convince another man of his sinful state. It is God who is in the business of saving souls. Every true Christian is nothing more and nothing less than an employee of His business. Andrew Murray's words should inspire you to a greater appreciation of your Boss.

> The work of saving souls is God's own work. None but He can do it. The gift of His Son is the proof of how great and precious He counts the work, and how His heart is set upon it. His love never for one moment ceases working for the salvation of men. And when He calls His children to be partners in His work, He shares with them the joy and the glory of the work of saving and blessing men. He promises to work His work through them, inspiring and energizing them by His power working in them.

Every time I see someone weeping over their sinful condition, every time I see someone run to the altar for forgiveness, and every time I hear their victorious testimony of how God has set them free, I am reminded that this can only be done through the power of Jesus Christ. As an evangelist, I find myself overwhelmed at the incredible success of God's business.

I close with this bit of instruction from Andrew Murray; you might call it your "work ethic":

> Let every worker learn to say: *As the power that worked in Christ, let that power work no less in me.* There is no possible way of working God's work aright, but God working it in us.

---

1 KINGS 21; 1 THESSALONIANS 4; DANIEL 3; PSALM 107

The Wonder of His Works

For thou, LORD, hast made me glad through thy work:
I will triumph in the works of thy hands.
PSALM 92:4

We have a hummingbird feeder outside our home. I have often watched in amazement at how these little creatures can hover like a helicopter. It's as if they are suspended in midair by some imaginary thread. Upon closer observation, you can see the blur of their wings moving at a rate of up to 78 times per second. That's incredible! That is the wonder of His works. I stand in awe!

Let's slip into the prayer closet of Joseph Hall as he meditates and writes of the wonder of God.

The longer I live, O my God, the more do I wonder at all the works of Your hands. I see such admirable skill in the very least of all Your creatures. I am more and more astonished every day in my observations.

I do not have to look so far as heaven for something marvelous, while I have but a spider in my window, or a bee in my garden, or a worm under my foot. Every one of these overcomes me with a similar amazement—yet can I see no more than their outsides. Their inward form, which gives their being and operations, I cannot pierce into. The less I can know, O Lord, the more let me wonder; and the less I can satisfy myself with marveling at Your works, the more let me adore the majesty and omnipotence of You who created them.

I encourage you today to focus on the things you take for granted. Behold His creation, marvel at the detail, allow yourself to be carried away by the wonder of His works.

1 KINGS 22; 1 THESSALONIANS 5; DANIEL 4; PSALMS 108—109

None of Your Business

Peter seeing him saith to Jesus, Lord, and what shall this man do? Jesus saith unto him, If I will that he tarry till I come, what is that to thee? follow thou me.

JOHN 21:21,22

Church people are often caught up in the same whirlwind of worrisome antics as the world. They're so quick to make judgment calls and comparisons. They wonder why *he* is singing a solo when another person can carry a tune 10 times better. They question why *she* was hired as church secretary when they can type twice as fast. Why was *that person* chosen to lead the youth group...and the list goes on.

In today's text, Peter was probing Jesus about the future of another disciple. Jesus mildly rebuked Peter by saying, "What is that to thee?" There exists a powerful lesson in this text for all of us.

Many people spend their lives consumed with the affairs and business of others. This is a waste of time for anyone who wants to fulfill God's plan for their own lives.

It would be important for us to remember that we are not held accountable for what another man does. Of course, we should genuinely be concerned for our fellowman. Philippians 2:4 says, "Look not every man on his own things, but every man also on the things of others." This scripture doesn't mean that we should be preoccupied with God's plan for another man's life. Also, keep in mind that we are held accountable for our own salvation and our own walk with the Lord. The Bible clearly states in Philippians 2:12 that we should work our own salvation. What God is doing in the life of another is none of your business.

2 KINGS 1; 2 THESSALONIANS 1; DANIEL 5; PSALMS 110—111

For now we see through a glass, darkly; but then face to face: now I know
in part; but then shall I know even as also I am known.

1 CORINTHIANS 13:12

Have you ever been in the midst of a difficult trial and found it
hard to understand what good could come out of it? I am reminded of
the high school killings that took place in our country over the last
several years. Many Christian youth were martyred for their faith.
These were stormy times with little sunshine. However, looking back,
as a result of these martyrs, hundreds of people have given their lives
to Christ, and thousands of Christians have become bold with their
faith. F. B. Meyer offers a consoling word in times like these.

> There is a Divine and deeper meaning in the adversities of our
> lives. We have no excuse for despair in the face of crushing
> sorrow. Whether it comes from man or devil, all creatures are
> under the Divine control, holding to our lips cups which the
> Father's hand has mixed. He has no partnership with their
> evil, but they unconsciously perform His will. Even if you can-
> not see the Divine meaning, dare to believe that it is there.
>
> One day God will call us to His side in the clear light of
> eternity and will explain His meanings in life's most sorrow-
> ful experiences. Then we shall learn that we suffered, not for
> ourselves only, but for others.

Now we see through a glass darkly, but one day we will see clearly.
God takes dark, devastating circumstances and uses them for the
good. Our crushing sorrow brings forth pure gold.

2 KINGS 2; 2 THESSALONIANS 2; DANIEL 6; PSALMS 112–113

Holier Than Thou

For the eyes of the Lord are over the righteous, and his ears are open unto their prayers: but the face of the Lord is against them that do evil.

1 PETER 3:12

Have you ever been accused by someone of being too holy? Let me explain. Before becoming a Christian, I lived a life devoid of discipline. Whatever I wanted to do—cuss, cheat, steal, lie, drink, drugs—I did. I was by all means an unholy person. Then I got saved. As a result of my salvation, I no longer cussed, cheated, stole, lied, drank or did drugs. I became holy. To my astonishment, I thought everyone would be thrilled. But oh, to the contrary! I had people who were close to me actually verbally attack my cleanliness. Religious people, who still had a few sins tucked away, were offended by my pure walk with God and zeal for the Lord.

Today's scripture says that the eyes of the Lord are on the righteous, and that He hears their prayers. Try walking up to someone on the street and saying, "Hello there. I'm righteous. God hears my prayers and He answers them." Perhaps this person is drinking a beer and you say, "The face of the Lord is against those who do evil." My friend, the response would be something like this: "Who do you think you are? Holier than thou? Do you think you're better than me? Does God love you more than me?" Of course, we are no better than them, and God loves us both the same, but there is a bottom line. The Blood of Jesus has washed away our sins, and now we stand clean before Him. The difference is obvious to God. He divides everyone up into two categories: the righteous and the unrighteous.

Remember, being called "holier than thou" is not really an insult. However, be sure you are living a life worthy of the accusation.

2 KINGS 3; 2 THESSALONIANS 3; DANIEL 7; PSALMS 114—115

I'm Sorry

Repent, then, and turn to God, so that your sins may be wiped out, that times of refreshing may come from the Lord.
ACTS 3:19, NIV

We have a serious problem in this nation. An incredible epidemic of blame-shifting has infected people with the belief that man is not responsible for the things he does wrong. Even in the face of tragic events, everyone points the finger at someone else. Instead of railing accusations on television, what a difference it would make if someone were to genuinely say, "It's my fault, and I'm sorry. I have sinned, and I repent."

> Repentance and forgiveness are joined together in the experience of all believers. There has never been a person yet who genuinely repented of sin that was not forgiven. On the other hand, no one has ever been forgiven who had not repented of his sin. It is certain that in heaven there are no cases of sin being washed away, unless at the same time the heart was led to repentance and faith in Christ. Hatred of sin and a sense of pardon come together into the soul and abide together while we live. These two things act and react upon each other. The man who is forgiven, repents; and the man who repents is most assuredly forgiven. You will never value pardon unless you feel repentance; and you will never taste the deepest draught of repentance until you know that you are pardoned.

These words, which Charles Spurgeon penned years ago, are still true today. The Blood of Jesus has not lost, nor will it ever lose its power. But this most powerful of forces is only loosed when repentance comes forth.

Friend, be careful not to let the infections of society creep into your life. Be quick to say "I'm sorry." Be quick to take responsibility for your wrongdoing, and repent.

2 KINGS 4; 1 TIMOTHY 1; DANIEL 8; PSALM 116

The Christian Soldier

And let us not be weary in well doing:
for in due season we shall reap, if we faint not.
GALATIANS 6:9

If somehow Christians were afforded the opportunity to see the entire army of God assembled in one area, they would be astonished. Could you imagine over a half billion believers gathered together in full armor? What an encouragement this would be to the straggling soldier who feels as if he has lost the battle. What a blessing this would be for the warriors of the Lord in China to meet together with the sold-out saints in Nicaragua. What an honor to be a part of the greatest army in the world. Not only is it the greatest army in the world, but in the words of John Newton, it is assured of victory.

> The Lord has chosen, called and armed us for the fight; and shall we wish to be excused? Shall we not rather rejoice that we have the honor to appear in such a cause, under such a Captain, such a banner and in such company? A complete suit of armor is provided, weapons not to be resisted, and precious balm to heal us if we receive a wound, and precious ointment to revive us when we are close to fainting.
>
> Further, we are assured of the victory beforehand. And O what a crown is prepared for every conqueror. Jesus, the righteous Judge, the gracious Savior, shall place the crown upon every faithful head with His own hand! Then let us not be weary and faint, for in due season we shall reap.

So be encouraged, soldier. Today you carry your cross, tomorrow you wear your crown.

If ye walk in my statutes, and keep my commandments, and do them; then
I will give you rain in due season, and the land shall yield her increase,
and the trees of the field shall yield their fruit.
LEVITICUS 26:3,4

There are over 8,000 promises in the Word of God. Most every one of these promises exist with conditions. A condition is a provision upon which the carrying out of an agreement depends. Example: Conditions of employment might be that you must type 50 words per minute, must have a high-school diploma and must not have a criminal record. If you qualify in meeting these three requirements, there is a chance you could be employed by that company.

If you exercise and eat right, your body will last longer and work better. If you don't drink alcohol, you won't be arrested for drunk driving. If you bathe regularly and brush your teeth, you won't cause people to avoid you. These are all results of conditions being met.

God's promises are full of conditions. "If my people, which are called by my name, shall humble themselves, and pray, and seek my face, and turn from their wicked ways; then will I hear from heaven, and will forgive their sin, and will heal their land" (2 Chronicles 7:14).

Here are some conditions the Lord sets before us: I will allow you to find Me, if you will search for Me with all your heart (see Jeremiah 29:13,14); I will draw near to you if you draw near to Me (see James 4:8); I will save your soul if you will call out to Me (see Romans 10:13).

If you want to see more on God's conditional promises, read Deuteronomy 28. Throughout the Bible we find God saying, "I will if you will."

Sharpen My Eyes

*He that loveth his life shall lose it; and he that hateth his
life in this world shall keep it unto life eternal.*
JOHN 12:25

It was early one morning, while in my study, that I received an
urgent phone call from Leonard Ravenhill. "Stevie," he said, "This is
Len. I want you to make a sign for me to hang in my study. This is very
important. The sign only needs one word: Eternity." Without asking
any questions, I proceeded to make the small sign. The word "eternity" was suspended over a background of clouds. In just a few minutes
I was finished. He loved it!

Leonard introduced me to many of the classic Christian writers.
Joseph Hall was one who spoke often of eternity.

Eternity is that only thing which is worthy to take up the
thoughts of a wise man. When added to evil, thoughts of eternity make the evil infinitely more intolerable; and being
added to good, they make the good infinitely more desirable.
What soul is able to comprehend you? What strength of
understanding is able to conceive you? Be ever in my
thoughts, ever before mine eyes. Be the scope of all my
actions, of all my endeavors; and, in respect of you, let all this
visible world be to me as nothing. Further, since only the
things which are not seen by the eye of sense are eternal, Lord,
sharpen the eyes of my faith, that I may see those things invis-
ible; and may in that sight, enjoy Your blessed eternity.

I encourage you, dear reader, to begin to live each day focused on
eternity. Whatever circumstances you find yourself in will pale in comparison to that glorious reality.

2 KINGS 7; 1 TIMOTHY 4; DANIEL 11; PSALM 119:25-48

The wicked shall be turned into hell, and all the nations that forget God.
PSALM 9:17

I thank God that the writers of old were not afraid to speak out on the subject of Hell. Here is one example by Thomas Watson.

Why a hell? Because there must be a place for the execution of divine justice. Earthly monarchs have their prison for malefactors, should not God have His? Sinners are criminal persons, they have offended God, and it would not consist with God's holiness and justice to have His laws infringed and not appoint penalties for the sins.

And what about the dreadfulness of this place? If you could for one hour hear the groans and shrieks of the damned, it would confirm this truth that hell is a house of bondage. Besides the punishment of loss—which is the exclusion of the soul from the glorified sight of God—there will be punishment. In hell there will be a plurality of torments. Revelation predicts the lake of fire (other fire is but painted compared to this). The torments of hell abide for ever: "The smoke of their torment ascendeth up for ever and ever" (Revelation 14:11). Time cannot finish it, tears cannot quench it; the wicked live always in the fire of hell and are not consumed. After sinners have lain millions of years in hell, their punishment is as far from ending as it was at the beginning.

We speak so little of Hell for fear that people will be offended. But my friend, wouldn't you warn someone if you knew he or she was in grave danger? If someone's house was burning, wouldn't you do anything to free that person from potential harm? How much more then should we warn people about this place called Hell?

Found by God

Behold, God is my salvation, I will trust and not be afraid; for the
LORD GOD is my strength and song, and He has become my salvation.
ISAIAH 12:2, NASB

Above anything else in our lives, we must prioritize the building of
an intimate relationship with Jesus. I cannot explain with words what
it means to be in love with Jesus and to know that He loves me. The joy
of beginning a new day with praise on my lips and thanksgiving in my
heart is priceless to me.

I remember the darkness. On this day in 1975, a Lutheran minister led me to Jesus. The God who was so distant became personal. The
One in whom I really didn't believe became my very best friend.

I want to encourage you to become intimate with Jesus. He is all
you have on earth, and He is everything in heaven.

Whom have I in heaven but Him, or whom desire I in earth
besides Him? Oh the fairest among the children of men, the
light of the Gentiles, the glory of the Jews, the life of the dead,
the joy of angels and saints. My soul longs to be with You! I
will put my spirit into Your hands and You will not put it out
of Your presence. I will come unto You; for You cast none
away that come to You. You came to seek and save that which
was lost. You, seeking me, have found me. I desire to be with
You and do long for the fruition of Your blessed presence and
joy of Your countenance. You are the only good Shepherd.
You are full of grace and truth.

These words, penned by John Welch, should represent the heart-
beat of everyone who has been found by the Lord.

2 KINGS 9; 1 TIMOTHY 6; HOSEA 1; PSALM 119:73-96

A Taste for God

O taste and see that the LORD is good: blessed is the man that trusteth in him.
PSALM 34:8

The word "taste" means much more than our ability to savor food or drink. It encompasses the other four senses as well. It is the sensibility by which we recognize the beauty and deformity of nature, deriving pleasure from the one and suffering pain from the other.

Have you ever heard someone say, "That woman has a taste for the finer things in life"? This is an example of the involvement of all the senses.

A person can live their entire life without acquiring a taste for fresh fruits and vegetables if their parents only serve them junk food. As in the natural, so is the spiritual. If someone has never been offered Jesus, how can he acquire a taste for Him?

The Bible says we should taste and see that the Lord is good. That means that God has put in each and every one of us a spiritual sense of taste. Since childhood, we have the ability to taste God. We have ingrained in us the capability to derive pleasure from His presence. It's sad that a person can spend his entire life without acquiring a taste for God.

I've also learned that you can have a taste for God and lose it. Sin has a way of dulling our spiritual taste buds to the point where the things of God are no longer appetizing. But I've got good news. If you've lost your taste for God, you can acquire it again. Just as someone returns to eating healthy food after living on junk food, a backslider can return to God after living a life of sin.

2 KINGS 10—11; 2 TIMOTHY 1; HOSEA 2; PSALM 119:97-120

A Grasshopper Like Me

When I consider thy heavens, the work of thy fingers, the moon and the stars, which thou hast ordained; what is man, that thou art mindful of him? and the son of man, that thou visitest him?

PSALM 8:3,4

Every once in a while I'll meditate on the vastness of God and the littleness of man. I think of the One who knows every inhabitant of the earth by name, and has every hair numbered. He knows our beginning from our end. The more I think about Him, the smaller I become.

Then I think of His love; how the One who created every living thing, every species of every tree and every flower, was willing to leave His place of prominence to save a grasshopper like me. "Lift up your eyes to the heavens!" writes J. G. Pike (a fellow grasshopper). "Survey the countless glories of the starry firmament, all its fixed or moving worlds of light!" He continues:

> Let your thoughts rove from star to star! How great is He who formed them all, to whom they are but as a speck of flying dust! Yet He who hung out those brilliant fires stooped from His amazing heights of bliss and majesty to assume mortal flesh and appear a feeble infant and a suffering man.
>
> When you behold the midnight sky and mark the thousands of its glowing fires; then think that He who fixed them there once hung on Calvary for you. One day you will shine as a star in heaven, when all those stars shall shine no more. Think that He was once low and dishonored, stained with blood, and blue with blows, that you might have a treasure greater than a thousand worlds. Amazing Love!

Take time to look up. Think of how big He is and how small we are. What is man that He is mindful of us?

---

2 KINGS 12; 2 TIMOTHY 2; HOSEA 3—4; PSALM 119:121-144

Welcome Home

*In my Father's house are many mansions: if it were not so, I would have
told you. I go to prepare a place for you. And if I go and prepare a place
for you, I will come again, and receive you unto myself;
that where I am, there ye may be also.*
JOHN 14:2,3

The old adage is true: There's no place like home. This, of course,
only applies if you can relate to a good home life. I was raised by a good
father and mother. There was always food on the table and a warm bed
to sleep in. As a teenager I remember hitchhiking around the country,
often staying gone for months at a time. Then, homesickness would
set in. I started smelling Mom's cooking halfway across the country.
Sleeping in rescue missions and under bridges couldn't hold a candle
to the warm bed back home. Truly, there was no place like home.

If this truth relates to our earthly life, how much more our heavenly. We have a Father in heaven who is anticipating our arrival, and
Jesus, who has prepared a place for us.

Read how Samuel Rutherford, who spent much time in jail for his
walk with God, talked about his heavenly home.

I wonder how a child of God could ever have a sad heart, considering what the Lord is preparing for them. What a day when
we shall come home and enter into the possession of our
blessed Lord's fair kingdom. When our heads shall find the
weight of the eternal crown of glory. When we shall look back
to pains and sufferings, then we shall see life and sorrow to be
less than one step or stride from a prison to a glorious freedom. We shall see that our little inch of time spent suffering is
not worthy of our first night's welcome home to heaven.

2 KINGS 13; 2 TIMOTHY 3; HOSEA 5—6; PSALM 119:145-176

He's Everything to Me

Wherefore God also hath highly exalted him, and given him
a name which is above every name.
PHILIPPIANS 2:9

There is no better way to start out this month than to share how precious Jesus is to those who know Him.

To me, He's my Savior, my Redeemer, the Miracle Worker, the Healer of my body. He's Jehovah-Jireh, my provider. He's the Bishop; that is, the Shepherd of my soul. He's incomparable, invincible, unchangeable, unequaled, omnipotent, omnipresent, omniscient, full of love, truth and mercy. He's the Alpha and Omega. He's the Comforter to help me during my time of trouble. He's the Light, so I don't have to walk in darkness. He's the Teacher that answers all my questions. He's the Friend that sticks closer than a brother.

To the architect . . . He is the Chief Cornerstone.
To the banker . . . He is the Hidden Treasure.
To the baker . . . He is the Living Bread.
To the builder . . . He is the Sure Foundation.
To the carpenter . . . He is the Door.
To the astronomer . . . He is the Bright and Morning Star.
To the geologist . . . He is the Rock of Ages.
To the thirsty . . . He is the Fountain that never runs dry.
To the doctor . . . He is the Great Physician.
To the educator . . . He is the Great Teacher.
To the florist . . . He is the Lily of the Valley.
To the juror . . . He is the Faithful and True Witness.
To the jeweler . . . He is the Pearl of Great Price.
To the sinner . . . He is the Lamb of God that takes away the
    sin of the world.

Who is He to you?

Behold, to obey is better than sacrifice, and to hearken than the fat of rams.
1 SAMUEL 15:22

It is interesting to talk to people who once had the faith for God to save them, but now are lacking in faith for God to lead them. Like a child, weeping tears of repentance, they once humbly received Jesus Christ as Savior and rose in newness of life. Without faith, this would have been impossible. But now, years later, that same person who demonstrated saving faith in God is deficient in his *keeping* faith. I offer you the words of Charles Spurgeon on this matter.

Faith is the root of obedience, and this may be clearly seen in the affairs of life. When a captain trusts a pilot to steer his ship into the port, the pilot steers the vessel according to the captain's direction. When a traveler trusts a guide to lead him over a difficult pass, he follows the track that his guide points out. When a patient believes in a physician, he carefully follows his prescriptions and directions.

Faith that refuses to obey the commands of the Savior is a mere pretence, and will never save the soul. When we trust Jesus to save us, He gives us directions as to the way of salvation. We follow those directions and are saved. Never forget to trust Jesus, and prove your trust by doing whatever He asks of you.

My friend, the One who mightily saved you can also guide and direct you. If you have trusted Him with your life, is He not able to also care for it?

2 KINGS 15; TITUS 1; HOSEA 8; PSALMS 123—125

Behold, I stand at the door, and knock: if any man hear my voice, and open the door, I will come in to him, and will sup with him, and he with me.
REVELATION 3:20

This scripture is one of the most quoted texts from the Bible by those involved in evangelism. To the sinner, we will say, "Jesus is standing at the door of your heart. He is knocking and wants to come in. Won't you open the door and let Him fellowship with you?" In personal evangelism, I have used this passage over and over again. But there are also other ways that Jesus chooses to get our attention.

Andrew Bonar, probably the closest friend of Robert Murray McCheyne, was well aware of the methods Jesus will use to make us aware of His presence:

How does He knock? By His word; His warnings; His invitations. By providences; by trials; by comforts; by sorrows; by joys; by family troubles and national calamities; by wars at home or abroad; by the confusions and distresses of nations; by the changes of the year. By His Holy Spirit ever working, ever striving.

There's another crucial point that must be heeded, that I find rarely mentioned by teachers of the Word. The Bible says that Jesus is standing at the door, not sitting. To stand signifies quick mobility. It means He could turn away at any moment. He hasn't settled down and pitched a tent at our doorstep. He is knocking, patiently, but not forever. If you are involved in personal evangelism, please inform those who are away from God that Jesus' presence at the door does not mean He will remain there forever. We must respond now. We must open the door and let Him in.

The Savior's Serenade

The LORD hath appeared of old unto me, saying, Yea, I have loved thee
with an everlasting love: therefore with lovingkindness have I drawn thee.
JEREMIAH 31:3

The word "serenade" usually conjures up the image of a man standing outside a damsel's window at night, strumming a guitar, crooning out a melody of rapturous love. If that's what comes to your mind, then you're right on track with what I want you to see. Allow me now to spiritualize the act of serenading.

Since the beginning of your life, Jesus has been singing you a love song. He's been serenading outside your window from the very moment of your birth. He made the provision for basic needs like food and clothing to be given to you. He proved His love for your soul by offering Himself as the sacrifice for the greatest need of your life—salvation. What a beautiful song!

He continued His serenade even when He received no response to His love. Perhaps you felt His love at a Christmas cantata, but you refused to yield your heart. Or maybe someone spoke to you about Jesus. They had the love of God in their smile and on their lips, but once again you refused. Still, His serenade continues. All He wants is for you to stick your head out the window and open your heart to respond with reciprocal love. He is waiting for your response to His serenade.

Friend, don't take that tender song for granted. If you haven't yet responded to His wooing, beware. There is coming a day when the Savior's serenade will stop. Right now His song of love and mercy is loud and clear. But one day you'll wake up and hear nothing. Now is the time to respond.

2 KINGS 17; TITUS 3; HOSEA 10; PSALMS 129–131

But when He, the Spirit of truth, comes, He will guide you into all the truth; for He will not speak on His own initiative, but whatever He hears, He will speak; and He will disclose to you what is to come.

JOHN 16:13, NASB

Upon reading one of J. H. Jowett's excellent books, I found one of the finest writings on deception. I believe it will sharpen your senses, as it has mine.

> We are in peril when the wolf comes in sheep's clothing and when Satan mimics the angels of light. If temptation brought chains to bind us, we would steadily resist its approach; but if it brings garlands to crown us, we become the victims of its charms. We are dazzled by the brightness, not realizing that it is Satan who is decked out as an angel of light.
>
> And therefore have we need of fine eyes in order to see through the skins of things to their very hearts. Yes, it is imperative that we know the Tempter at his first approach. We must not offer him opportunity by our delay, or anytime give him the benefit of the doubt. We must know him as soon as he appears and begins to display his dazzling wares.
>
> Now, it is just this power of moral discernment which is the gift of the Holy Spirit. He is the Quickener of our powers, and He will so discipline and refine our moral sense as to enable us to pierce every deceptive guise and to expose the evil when it has borrowed the garments of the good. He is the Spirit of enlightenment, and in His gracious fellowship we shall not be led astray.

Reader, ask the Holy Spirit to give you wisdom and discernment. There will be a great falling away in the last days, but there is absolutely no reason you should be a part of it.

2 KINGS 18; PHILEMON 1; HOSEA 11; PSALMS 132—134

Living on Borrowed Time

But God said unto him, Thou fool, this night thy soul shall be required of thee: then whose shall those things be, which thou hast provided?
LUKE 12:20

We are living in dangerous, perilous times. We are at a place in this nation that I liken to the edge of a cliff. We have allowed ourselves so much freedom that we have loosed ourselves from any moral chains that bind. We have unshackled ourselves from family commitments and sacred values. We are like sheep that have gone astray. We've wandered, wallowed, wavered and worked our way up to the edge. We are teetering on the brink of judgment. By the grace of God, we haven't fallen headlong into the abyss.

If God has told you to do something, do it. I heard a story recently of a man who disobeyed God concerning an assignment. As this man was walking into a grocery store, he spotted a worker, high in the air, changing the advertisement on a billboard. The Lord said, "Tell that man I love him and that judgment is at the door." Perhaps thinking he had time, the man proceeded to shop for groceries. Upon leaving the store, he was alarmed to see red and blue lights flashing at the base of the sign. The man had fallen and broken his neck. He had died without ever hearing those timely words of warning.

My friend, please listen! Hundreds of people around you are living on borrowed time. If God has been speaking to you about issuing a warning, don't delay. What difference does it make if they choose to reject it? But what a difference it will make if they choose to respond.

The Fellowship of Worms

Above all, keep fervent in your love for one another, because love covers a multitude of sins. Be hospitable to one another without complaint.

1 PETER 4:8,9, NASB

Jonathan Edwards was used mightily of God to help usher in the first Great Awakening of the 1700s. Most Christians, upon hearing his name, immediately think of his sermon, "Sinners in the Hands of an Angry God." Not all of his sermons are so harsh, but I thank God that he did not hesitate to feed this nation the full gospel. Look at his handling on the subject of how Christians should treat one another:

> Christians, that are but fellow worms, ought at least to treat one another with as much humility and gentleness as Christ, who is infinitely above them, treats them. But how did Christ treat His disciples when they were so cold towards Him and so regardless of Him when His soul was exceeding sorrowful even unto death? He in a dismal agony was crying and sweating blood for them, and they would not watch with Him and allow Him the comfort of their company one hour in His great distress. One would think that was a proper time if ever to have reproved them for a devilish, hellish, cursed and damned slothfulness and deadness. But after what manner does Christ reprove them? Behold His astonishing gentleness! He says, "What, could ye not watch with me one hour? The spirit indeed is willing but the flesh is weak."

As you go through your day today, how humble, gentle and Christ-like will you be in the face of disappointment and irritation? A good tip: When we remember that we are *all* in the "fellowship of worms," it becomes much easier to maintain that necessary humility and gentleness.

2 KINGS 20; HEBREWS 2; HOSEA 13; PSALMS 137—138

Christ the Remedy

> *And as Moses lifted up the serpent in the wilderness,*
> *even so must the Son of man be lifted up: that whosoever believeth*
> *in him should not perish, but have eternal life.*
> JOHN 3:14,15

In Charles Finney, a born-again attorney, God raised up a man who shook this nation with the truth of the Word. He presented his case to the sinner with pinpoint accuracy. His listeners were riveted with conviction, and revival swept the land. This portion of one of his sermons elaborates the point made by today's text.

We may observe two points of analogy between the brazen serpent and Christ. First, Christ must be lifted up as the serpent was in the wilderness. And second, Christ must be held up as a remedy for sin, even as the brazen serpent was as a remedy for a poison. Whoever looked upon this serpent was healed. So Christ heals the soul and restores it to health. His power avails to cleanse and purify the soul.

Both Christ and the serpent were held up each as a remedy and—let it be specially noted—as a full and adequate remedy. The cure wrought then was immediate. It involved no delay. This serpent was God's appointed remedy. So is Christ, a remedy appointed of God, sent down from heaven for this express purpose. It was indeed very wonderful that God should appoint a brazen serpent for such a purpose—such a remedy for such a malady; and not less wonderful is it that Christ should be lifted up in agony and blood, as a remedy for both the punishment and the heart-power of sin.

Christ is evermore the only remedy for sin. Lift Him up before the lost and dying around you, knowing those who truly see Him through you will be immediately affected.

2 KINGS 21; HEBREWS 3; HOSEA 14; PSALM 139

Looking unto Jesus

And they that are Christ's have crucified the flesh with the affections and lusts. If we live in the Spirit, let us also walk in the Spirit.

GALATIANS 5:24,25

We live in a nation where the majority of the citizens believe that Jesus Christ is the Son of God. Some of the latest religion polls reveal startling statistics on what people actually adhere to when it comes to their beliefs. You might be surprised to know that the vast majority of North American adults believe that upon death they will stand before God and be held accountable for their sins. I've heard people say, "I want to be more like Jesus, but it's just so hard." My answer to them is simple: "If you really wanted to be like Jesus, then you would do everything possible to please Him. You would look to Him every day. You would crucify the flesh. You would do anything it takes to draw close to Him." I'll let Robert Murray McCheyne take it one step further:

> Some are saying, "Oh that the world were crucified to me, and I to the world! Oh that my heart were as dead to the world, and alive to Jesus!" Do you truly wish it? Look, then, to the Cross. Behold the amazing gift of love! Sit down and gaze upon a crucified Jesus and the world will become a dying thing.
> When you gaze upon the sun, it makes everything else dark. When you taste honey, it makes everything else tasteless. So, when your soul feeds on Jesus, it takes away the sweetness of all earthly things. Keep a continued gaze. Run, looking unto Jesus. Look, till the way of salvation by Jesus fills up the whole horizon, so glorious and peace-speaking. So will the world be crucified to you, and you unto the world.

Roots of Betrayal

Is it I?
MARK 14:19

To betray someone is to prove faithless, to violate a trust. Within every believer lurks a Judas. Let's take an honest look at the steps leading to the betrayal of our Lord, realizing that these same steps are evident when Christians betray one another.

Intimacy to a person or group of persons. You cannot betray someone without first being an intimate part of his or her life. Judas was a friend of Jesus and was listed as one of the Twelve.

Dissatisfaction. We become dissatisfied when our own preconceived dreams are not realized. All of the disciples experienced dissatisfaction. They wanted power; Jesus spoke of meekness. They wanted to attack and conquer; Jesus wanted to love.

Doubt and unbelief. When we begin to doubt the workings of God in our lives, the root of betrayal has begun to take hold. Mary anointed the Lord with costly perfume—a wonderful act of worship—yet Judas saw it as a waste.

Greed. Greed is defined as a selfish and grasping desire for possession. Judas began dipping into the money bag.

Counsel from the ungodly. The Bible says that Judas ran to the religious leaders, the enemies of Christ. The last step is so natural after the others have taken root. You will always find someone to agree with you, regardless of how wrong you are. Careful! Careful! The next step is the kiss on the cheek!

Every Man's Work

Every man's work shall be made manifest:
for the day shall declare it, because it shall be revealed by fire;
and the fire shall try every man's work of what sort it is.
1 CORINTHIANS 3:13

Today I offer you Joseph Parker's excellent analogy on how we must all work together.

All men cannot work in the same way. "There are diversities of operation." Upon the face of a watch you may see an illustration of my meaning. On that small space you have three workers: there is the second hand performing rapid evolutions; there is the minute hand going at a greatly reduced speed; and there is the hour hand, tardier still. Now, one unacquainted with the mechanism of a watch would conclude that the busy little second hand was doing all the work, clicking away at sixty times the speed of the minute hand; and as for the hour hand, that seems to be doing no work at all. You can see in a moment that the first is busy, and in a short time will see the second stir—but you must wait still longer to assure yourself of the motion of the third. So is it in the church. There are active men, who appear to be doing the work of the whole community, and others who are slower. But can we do without the minute and hour hand? The noisy second hand might go round its little circle forever without telling the world the true time. We should be thankful for all kinds of workers. The silent, steady hour hand need not envy its noisy little colleagues. Every man must fill the measure of his capacity. Your business is to do your allotted work so as to meet the approval of the Master.

2 KINGS 24; HEBREWS 6; JOEL 3; PSALM 143

The Next Level

But as it is written, Eye hath not seen, nor ear heard, neither have entered into the heart of man, the things which God hath prepared for them that love him.

1 CORINTHIANS 2:9

Many Christians are living far below God's intended plan for their lives. I want to encourage you today by saying that there is more of God than what you have. There is more of His power, presence, anointing, mercy, love, wisdom, grace and healing virtue. We could learn a lesson from the great inventors. Aren't you thankful that Thomas Edison wasn't satisfied with candlelight? He knew there must have been something better. He was also tired of shouting, which resulted in the invention of the telephone. Henry Ford was tired of riding in a horse-drawn buggy. He moved to the next level by building an automobile.

Allow me to list a few spiritual levels we can get stuck on:

Many spend their lives living on the *level of sinfulness*. They never seem to break away from their carnal, fleshly desires. They're stuck. If only they could move to the next level.

Many others are satisfied with the *level of salvation*. They've stepped from the level of sinfulness to being saved, but are not growing in God.

They must move to the *level of saturation;* that is, being continually filled with His Spirit.

After saturation, we will begin living on God's desired level—*the supernatural.*

My friend, keep moving on. There's more to God than what you have.

When God Withdraws

I opened to my beloved; but my beloved had withdrawn himself, and was gone.
SONG OF SOLOMON 5:6

I will never forget my graduation ceremony from Twin Oaks Academy in Texas. The graduating class was waiting for our leader and keynote speaker to deliver a challenging message. We sat in anticipation. Finally, David Wilkerson stood up and gave his sermon title: "Thou Shalt Have Spells." The entire message was focused on the difficult times we would all face. He drove home the fact that every Christian will experience seasons in their lives when they do not sense the presence of God.

Now, years later, I've found these words to be true. I've never met a Christian who hasn't, at one time or another, felt as if God had left them. These times are lonely and very difficult.

Solomon wrote about it in his Song of Songs. Centuries later, Thomas Watson experienced the absence of God and wrote these words:

> He who loves God, weeps bitterly over His absence. Mary comes weeping, "They have taken away the Lord" (John 20:2). One cries, my health is gone; another, my estate is gone; but he who is a lover of God, cries out, "My God is gone, I cannot enjoy Him whom I love! What can all worldly comforts do, when once God is absent?"

Dear Christian, you might not be able to feel His presence, but that does not mean He is gone. Unless sin has entered the picture, driving Him from you, then rest assured, He is close by, working out His perfect plan for your life.

1 CHRONICLES 1—2; HEBREWS 8; AMOS 2; PSALM 145

Beloved, now are we the sons of God, and it doth not yet appear what we shall be: but we know that, when he shall appear, we shall be like him; for we shall see him as he is.

1 JOHN 3:2

Every true Christian is part of the Bride of Christ. If you love Jesus, then one day your Groom will come, sweep you away and carry you across the threshold of heaven.

But something is troubling me. I find many people who claim to be born-again Christians, lovers of God, who spend the majority of their day thinking about everything but God. If we truly love Him, and can't wait to be with Him, then we should be like a young bride who is about to be married. I've never seen a sad bride. Any bride, prior to that great and wonderful wedding day, is consumed with thinking about her groom.

The relevance of J. H. Jowett's words on this subject should be heeded by every born-again believer.

They say that Samuel Rutherford used to fall asleep speaking of Christ, and that if during the hours of sleep his unconscious lips muttered anything it was found to be about his Lord. We need to practice ourselves in these things. The more we commune with the Lord, the more we will "love His appearing." The more time we spend with Him, the more we shall be charged with the consuming expectancy to see Him "as He is."

I'm afraid that many Christians are not ready to meet the Lord in the air. Are you? Are you consumed with Jesus, or are there other idols in your life? Is He your passion? Would you rather be with Him than anyone else on earth?

1 CHRONICLES 3—4; HEBREWS 9; AMOS 3; PSALMS 146—147

Beyond the Moon

And now, Lord, what wait I for? my hope is in thee.
PSALM 39:7

One evening, while speaking in a church, I called up a small child to use in an illustration. In one of my hands was a crisp 100-dollar bill, and in the other was a 10-cent lollipop. I told the child that he could have one or the other, but not both. Without hesitation, this innocent little one chose the lollipop. The congregation laughed, but the point was crystal-clear. If the child had known the value of the money, he would never have settled for the lesser item.

That's just how many Christians live while sojourning here on earth. We are pilgrims passing through, but I find many of God's people putting down deep roots, claiming out their earthly territory, and leaving the most precious item by the wayside.

The words of William Gurnall challenge us to look beyond this world.

Faith advances the soul to higher projects than to seek the things of this life. It discovers a world beyond the moon; and there lies faith's merchandise. As the psalmist David said of men, "Surely they are disquieted in vain: they heap up riches, and do not know who shall gather them" (Psalm 39:6). Let them that love the world, take the world; but, Lord, pay not my portion in gold or silver, but in pardon of sin: this I wait for.

We should set our sights higher. You don't find NASA talking too much these days about the moon. We landed there decades ago. The aeronautical engineers have their sights set much farther. As a Christian, you need to lift up your eyes toward heaven and look beyond the lollipops here on earth.

The Divided Mind

But his wife looked back from behind him, and she became a pillar of salt.

GENESIS 19:26

"Remember Lot's wife" (Luke 17:32). Jesus chose to use this woman's plight as a warning to future believers. I have studied what happened to Lot's wife, and would like to share with you some of the penalties we pay for having a divided mind.

First of all, we miss the joy that is the privilege of the decided. Our most wretched hours are generally the hours of indecision. To be unable to decide between two prizes is to experience the pain of missing both. Where did Lot's wife die? Neither in Sodom nor in the mountain heights. She died between two worlds. To find real joy in living, one must be wholehearted.

Secondly, a divided mind makes us unfit, because it robs us of our strength to go forward. You'll never travel swiftly toward heaven if you are constantly looking back toward Sodom.

Thirdly, a divided mind— indecision—usually ends in disaster. The tragedy of this story is not her physical death, but her spiritual. The crude figure of Lot's wife, frozen as a pillar of salt facing Sodom, gives us a photograph of the woman's soul. Death froze that backward-looking face, so that all the future centuries might see it. God had given her a chance to make a new start. She took that chance half-heartedly and you see the result.

To *almost* be a disciple is to miss knowing Jesus. To almost be saved is to be lost. Make up your mind today; are you going to be a pillar of salt, or the salt of the earth?

1 CHRONICLES 7—8; HEBREWS 11; AMOS 5; LUKE 1:1—38

Not Ashamed!

But whosoever shall deny me before men,
him will I also deny before my Father which is in heaven.
MATTHEW 10:33

There is a wave of Holy Ghost revival sweeping across the land. Christians who were once timid and shy are now lifting up their voices and speaking boldly about their Savior. Believers who were afraid to say the name "Jesus," and always found it "politically correct" to say "God," are now proclaiming their faith without hesitation. Jesus Christ is being lifted up, and men are being drawn to Him.

I read a story the other day of a challenge that came to a Christian soldier. Be encouraged by it.

A Christian soldier once said to his chaplain, "Last night, before going to bed, I knelt down and prayed. My companions raised a loud laugh and began to throw boots and clothes at me."

"Well," replied the chaplain, "suppose you defer your prayers till after you retire, and then silently lift up your heart to God." Meeting him soon after, the chaplain asked him if he had taken his advice.

"Sir," replied the God-fearing soldier, "I did take your advice for two or three evenings, but I began to think that it looked like denying my Savior; so I once more knelt down and prayed as at first."

"What followed?" asked the chaplain.

"Why sir, not one of them laughed at me anymore. The whole fifteen now kneel down, too, and I pray with them."

1 CHRONICLES 9—10; HEBREWS 12; AMOS 6; LUKE 1:39-80

Fear of Man

The fear of man bringeth a snare:
but whoso putteth his trust in the LORD shall be safe.
PROVERBS 29:25

Bishop Hugh Latimer (1485-1555) is noted in English history as a fearless preacher. This account of one of his sermons illustrates how much he feared God rather than man.

Bishop Hugh Latimer (1500s) once preached a sermon before King Henry VIII which greatly offended his royal highness by its plainness. In response, the king *ordered* Latimer to preach again the next Sunday, and to make public apology for his offense.

Accordingly, he ascended the pulpit the following Sunday, read his text, and began his sermon by speaking to himself. "Hugh Latimer, do you know before whom you are this day to speak? To the high and mighty monarch, the most noble and excellent majesty King Henry VIII...who can take away your life if you offend him. Therefore, take heed that you speak not a word that may displease. But then, consider well, preacher Latimer! Do you know from whom you come—who has sent you with this message? Even by the great and mighty God, who is all-present and beholds all your ways, and who is able to cast your soul into hell! Therefore, take care that you deliver your message faithfully."

And so beginning, Hugh Latimer preached over again, but with increased energy, the *exact same sermon* he had preached the week before! The fear of God swiftly delivered him from the fear of man!

If there is any fear of man left in you, contemplate these words of Leonard Ravenhill: "He who is intimate with God will never be intimidated by man."

1 CHRONICLES 11—12; HEBREWS 13; AMOS 7; LUKE 2

Bleeding Compassion

Say to them, "As I live!" declares the Lord GOD, "I take no pleasure in the death of the wicked, but rather that the wicked turn from his way and live. Turn back, turn back from your evil ways!"

EZEKIEL 33:11, NASB

Whatever you do, don't ever allow hard preaching against sin to cause calluses around your heart. Sin is the very thing that will damn countless sinners to a Christless eternity. Sin is the reason Jesus shed His Blood. Every minister of the Gospel has been chosen of God to preach His *whole* counsel; he is compelled to preach heaven sweet and hell hot. Mercy must be proclaimed as available, and judgment certain. It is so true that our loving Savior will one day be a severe Judge. Concerning hard preaching, Robert South said:

> Ministers should threaten death and destruction even to the very worst of men. They should preach in such a manner that it may appear to all their sober hearers that they do not desire, *but fear* that these dreadful things should come to pass. Let them declare God's wrath against the hardened and impenitent as I have seen a judge condemn a criminal with tears in his eyes. The true preacher of the Word should grieve with an inward bleeding compassion for the misery of those hardened sinners upon whom God is about to pronounce His judgment.

I live in a constant awareness of how insignificant our span of life appears in the sight of God. In just a moment we will all stand before the Judgment Seat. This is what motivates me to preach the truth regardless of how others may feel. Any good doctor will tell you what's wrong in order to bring about a healing. Any good preacher will talk about sin so that the hearers can be set free.

Got Salvation?

A new heart also will I give you, and a new spirit will I put within you:
and I will take away the stony heart out of your flesh, and I will give
you an heart of flesh. And I will put my spirit within you, and cause
you to walk in my statutes, and ye shall keep my judgments, and do them.

EZEKIEL 36:26,27

I had no idea what salvation really meant on the day I received
Jesus Christ as my personal Savior. I knew I was a sinner, and I knew
that sin had destroyed my life. But that was about as far as it went.
Later on, I learned what it really means to be saved.

Salvation is much more than escape from punishment. It is
deliverance from sin. Jesus Christ was sent to bless us "in
turning away every one of us from his iniquities." In believing
on Him we not only obtain pardon through His Blood, but
we become holy by the influence of His indwelling Spirit.
Though pardoned at once, we are not at once made perfect in
purity. This is an arduous, progressive work. Salvation in its
full sense implies conformity to Jesus as well as reliance upon
Him. It is a change of heart, a transformation of character, a
new life. It is the humbling of pride, the curbing of the passions, the destruction of self-will. It is the undoing the work
of all former years, the untwisting the coils which the devil
had long been winding round us, and the training us to new
habits of thought and action. It is not simply the avoiding sin,
but the abhorring it; not chiefly through fear of punishment,
but from love to the Redeemer. It is the heart which once
regarded its own pleasure as the highest good, now seeking as
its chief end and supreme delight the glory of its Maker.

If anyone could, I would say that Newman Hall captured the
essence of salvation in this passage. Don't limit God, friend. Be saved
to the uttermost.

1 CHRONICLES 15; JAMES 2; AMOS 9; LUKE 4

Then He Will Come

And then shall he send his angels, and shall gather together his elect from the four winds, from the uttermost part of the earth to the uttermost part of heaven.
MARK 13:27

Have you ever wondered why the Lord has not yet come back as He promised? After all, when is a good time? More and more people are being born every day. Thousands are being saved on a daily basis, but countless are backsliding on a daily basis. God sees it all, and has the balance in His hands. Robert Murray McCheyne shed some light on why God tarries.

> Sometimes, when I see some act of gross and open wickedness, my heart trembles within me. I think how the Lord sees all this wickedness committed over the whole world, yet He forbears. What a sight of forbearance and long-suffering compassion is here! This is the reason why He tarries, He has compassion for the vilest, and waits long before he comes.
>
> Christ is at this moment gathering a people from among the Gentiles. He is building up the great temple of the Lord, adding stone to stone. He cannot come till this is done. He told Paul to remain and preach at Corinth: "For I have much people in this city." For the same reason He makes His ministers remain and preach on; for He has much people still. There are, no doubt, many elect ones, many that were given Him by the Father before the foundation of the world, still in the sleep of nature. He waits till these are gathered. When the last of His elect are gathered, then He will come.

So friend, ours is not to question His judgment, but to anticipate His appearing.

The Cultured Christian

And be not conformed to this world: but be ye transformed by the renewing of your mind, that ye may prove what is that good, and acceptable, and perfect, will of God.

ROMANS 12:2

There is a demand on every believer to fit into society's mold. I've always been partial to J. B. Phillips's translation of this text: "Don't let the world around you squeeze you into its own mold." From the moment we become Christians, the battle begins with the world, the flesh and the devil. Jesus faced these temptations in the wilderness; you'll face these temptations in the world.

Society wants to dictate to you how to dress, what doctrine to believe, and how to make decisions. Let me ask you a question: Who are you following when it comes to fashion? How many young Christian girls are striving to look like some half-starved fashion model? They're choosing the world rather than the Word. The world will say, "You're too big, you're too small, you're pear-shaped, you're too skinny." God says, "You're just right."

A doctrine signifies what someone believes. There is a movement in America today to take the edge off the cutting Word of God. They want to flatten the point and dull the edge. Friend, don't let anyone dilute the Word. And about your decision making? Don't allow the ungodly to formulate your opinions. Let the Bible and other God-fearing Christians speak into your life.

Always keep in mind that the will of the world is in direct contrast to the will of God. Also, if you choose to yield yourself to this world's culture, you automatically bind yourself to this world's curse (see Deuteronomy 28).

Trust as a Child

> *Therefore take no thought, saying, What shall we eat? or, What shall we drink? or, Wherewithal shall we be clothed?...for your heavenly Father knoweth that ye have need of all these things.*
> MATTHEW 6:31,32

My wife and I have been blessed with three children. Each is unique, yet they all have one thing in common. Not one child rises in the morning with a concern of what he or she is going to eat, or if there's something to wear. They know that Mommy and Daddy will meet their every need. Rather than ask, "Is there any breakfast?" they say, "What's for breakfast?" They have a built-in trust that provision has been made for their growing stomachs. This serves as an inspiration to me. If my children trust me to take care of them, why can't I trust God to take care of me?

Hannah Whitall Smith had a similar enlightenment while visiting someone's home.

> I visited once in a wealthy home, where there was a little adopted child upon whom was lavished all the tender love and care that human hearts could bestow. The child ran in and out, free and light-hearted, without a care. I thought what a picture it was of our wonderful position as children in the house of our heavenly Father. And I said to myself, *Nothing would so grieve and wound the loving hearts around her as to see this little child beginning to be worried or anxious about herself in any way. How much more must the great, loving heart of our God and Father be grieved and wounded at seeing His children taking so much anxious care and thought!* And I understood why it was that our Lord had said to us so emphatically, "Take no thought for yourselves."

The Harder They Fall

*Put on the whole armour of God, that ye may be able to
stand against the wiles of the devil.*

EPHESIANS 6:11

This scripture in Ephesians should put the fear of God into everyone.
Some Christians act as if God has placed a protective coating around
them. They say that even being around sin does not affect them. Their
prideful attitude is an open door to Satan. Charles Spurgeon had
something to say about relying on our own strength.

> Watch out when you are in temptation. I have seen a tree in
> the forest that seemed to stand fast like a rock. I have stood
> beneath its wide-spreading branches and have tried to shake
> its trunk, to see if I could, but it stood immovable. The sun
> shone upon it, the rain fell, and many a winter's frost sprin-
> kled its boughs with snow, but it still stood fast and firm. But
> one night, there came a howling wind which swept through
> the forest, and the tree that seemed to stand so fast lay
> stretched along the ground. Its rigid arms, which once were
> lifted up to heaven, lay hopelessly broken, and the trunk was
> snapped in two. And so I have seen many a Christian, strong
> and mighty. Nothing seemed to move him. But the wind of
> persecution and temptation comes against him, and he creaks
> with murmuring, and at last breaks in apostasy. He ends up
> lying along the ground, a mournful specimen of what every
> man becomes who fails to make the Lord his strength, and
> who forgets to rely on the Most High.

God blesses humility, and true humility only grows on the grave
of pride.

1 CHRONICLES 19—20; 1 PETER 1; JONAH 3; LUKE 8

It Comes from the Lord

And the LORD was with Joseph, and he was a prosperous man; and he was in the house of his master the Egyptian.

GENESIS 39:2

This is an awesome story. If you've never taken the time to study the life of Joseph, it would be well worth your effort. Here was a man living in bondage, yet God was blessing him. I am reminded of how many Christians are working daily in secular businesses, yet God is mightily blessing them and using them for the promotion of His kingdom.

I wanted to share with you some excellent Christian truths that Rev. Joseph Parker gleaned from the life of Joseph.

The Lord was with Joseph, and yet Joseph was under Potiphar. Undoubtedly this is an abnormal state of life. Joseph was brought down to Egypt by his purchasers. He was bought, sold and exchanged like an article of merchandise; yet, he was a prosperous man!

Understand that there are difficulties which cannot impair prosperity, and that there is a prosperity which dominates over all external circumstances. It seems hardly correct to assert that Joseph was a prosperous man when he was to all intents and purposes in bondage. He was the property of another. Not one hour of his time belonged to himself. He was cut off from his father and from his brethren. Yet, it is distinctly stated that, notwithstanding these things, the Lord was with him and he was prosperous.

Friend, you never know the final outcome of the circumstances you may find yourself in, but God does! Like Joseph, if you remain faithful to God and trust fully in Him, you will not only realize your reward in the long run, you will learn to be happy in all circumstances along the way.

Glad to Help

How God anointed Jesus of Nazareth with the Holy Ghost and with power: who went about doing good, and healing all that were oppressed of the devil; for God was with him.

ACTS 10:38

The Lord has allowed me to be surrounded with true servants of God my entire Christian life. Those who have led me were always willing to do anything for Jesus, regardless of how menial the task. I saw true Christianity being lived out before my eyes.

The writer of the classic *The Complete Duty of Man*, put into words what every Christian should have in his heart. Don't just go through the words of Henry Venn, but let his words go through you.

This is the pattern for every Christian. He is a counterfeit one who does not strive to imitate it. The strength, the willingness, the joy of the soul is connected with this imitation. Christians are heavy and cast down, principally because they are idle and selfish. They often feel that the active, benevolent spirit of watching for opportunities to do essential service to our fellow-creatures is no more than menial. What good does it afford to merely believe in doctrines which are then put to no good purpose? Usefulness is the very excellency of life. No man, in the real church of Christ, lives unto himself. Every true Christian is a tree of righteousness, whose fruits are good and profitable unto men. He is glad to help and to comfort others. He is diligent and industrious. He speaks to edification; dwells in peace, gentleness and love. He reproves what is wrong by an excellent example, and recommends, by his own practice, what is pleasing to God.

In the Dark

My soul fainteth for thy salvation: but I hope in thy word.
PSALM 119:81

There have been times in my life when I felt as if the sky was falling in. Everything seemed to be going wrong. The enemy of my soul had risen up and was mounting a full-fledged attack. Even my closest friends seemed to be standing far off, waiting to see the outcome. Perhaps right now you are facing one of the darkest trials of your life.

Samuel Rutherford, a man of God who knew all about dark times, penned these words of encouragement.

> Believe under a cloud, and wait for Him when there is no moonlight nor starlight. Let faith live and breathe. Lay hold of the sure salvation of God when clouds and darkness are about you and appearance of rotting in the prison before you. Take heed of unbelieving hearts, which can father lies about Christ. Who dreams that a promise of God can fail, fall asleep or die? Who can make God sick, or His promises weak?
>
> Hold fast to Christ in the dark and surely you will see the salvation of God. Your adversaries are ripe and dry for the fire. Yet a little while and they shall go up in a flame; the breath of the Lord, like a river of brimstone, shall kindle about them.

It is during the raging battle that the soldier is tested. During these times, we must trust. It's called the making of a man or woman of God. I have found that God does much of His work in secret. He uses the dark, difficult trials of our lives to make us into vessels for His honor.

At the Door

And we know that all things work together for good to them that love God, to them who are the called according to his purpose.

ROMANS 8:28

One of the greatest shocks of my life occurred early on in my Christian walk. I had received Christ as Savior and was living, as best I could, for Him. The Lord had delivered me from the horrible pit of drug abuse and had placed my feet upon the solid rock. Then came the knock at the door. Late one evening, several policemen arrived at my home and arrested me for some old drug sales. I was handcuffed and taken to jail. As a new Christian, I was facing many years in the penitentiary. I couldn't understand why God allowed this to happen. On the wall of my cell was written this poem:

> *Dear Lord, I'm feeling kind of blue*
> *and things look awfully low.*
> *Nothing seems to be just right,*
> *but then, I guess you know.*
> *Dear Lord, I'm feeling all alone*
> *and don't know what to do.*
> *I'm just a foolish child, I guess,*
> *who always turns to you.*
> *It rained all day, skies are gray.*
> *Tomorrow let the sun shine bright.*
> *Dear Lord, watch over a restless child*
> *who is awfully blue tonight.*

Well, my friend, tomorrow came and the sun did shine bright. After a lengthy stay in jail, the Lord opened the door for me to enter a Christian program. The shocking knock at the door turned out to be a blessing from God. I learned the truth of today's text, that all things do work together for good.

1 CHRONICLES 24—25; 1 PETER 5; MICAH 3; LUKE 12

November 29

Get the Mail

All Scripture is inspired by God and profitable for teaching, for reproof, for correction, for training in righteousness; that the man of God may be adequate, equipped for every good work.
2 TIMOTHY 3:16,17, NASB

Have you ever heard someone say they had trouble "getting into" the Word of God? Perhaps it was because of their approach. Someone who is truly in love with the Lord soon comes to see the Bible as God's love letter to Christians. To that person, Abraham, Moses, Esther, Luke, John, Paul, Peter...all begin to feel like family. I like how Thomas Watson, a man devoted to the study of the Word, directs our thoughts about reading the Word.

> *Read the Bible with reverence.* Realize that in every line you read, God is speaking to you. The ark into which the law was placed was overlaid with pure gold, and was carried on bars, that the Levites might not touch it (see Exodus 25:14), and why was this, but to breed in the people reverence to the law?
> *Read with seriousness.* It is a matter of life and death; by this Word you must be tried. Conscience and Scripture are the jury God will proceed by in judging you.
> *Read the Word with affection.* Get your hearts quickened with the Word. Go to it to fetch fire. Labor that the Word may not only be a lamp to direct, but a fire to warm. Read the Scripture, not only as history, but as a love letter sent to you from God which may affect your heart.
> Pray that the same Spirit that wrote the Word may assist you in the reading of it.

Dear saint, have you checked your mail lately? There's a love letter waiting.

1 CHRONICLES 26—27; 2 PETER 1; MICAH 4; LUKE 13

That I may know him, and the power of his resurrection, and the fellow-
ship of his sufferings, being made conformable unto his death; if by any
means I might attain unto the resurrection of the dead.

PHILIPPIANS 3:10,11

There exists in my spirit a desire to break away and be free. I grow tired of being bound by flesh and blood. There are times, during worship, that I feel myself being lifted into a glorious realm with the Lord. The feeling is indescribable. Wonderful doesn't come close to revealing the freedom that comes in pure, unfiltered worship.

It is during those times that I moan with creation for it all to be over. I want to be with Jesus. I long for the labor, the fighting, the sickness, the pain, the misery to be ended. I know my feelings are shared by millions of other believers. This passage by John Welch echoes my sentiments:

> My desire to remain here is not great, knowing that so long as
> I am in this house of clay, I am absent from the Lord: and if it
> were dissolved, I look for a building not made with hands,
> eternal in the heavens.

There is coming a day, in the near future, when we will shed this house of clay. The boundaries will dissolve, the walls will come down, the limits will cease to be...we will be free. Until that time, we must fight for every moment to be with Jesus. We must tackle every trial, we must bring down every thought that lifts its head above the knowledge of Christ, and we must flee every temptation that seeks to dilute our relationship with the Lord.

My friend, as this year quickly comes to an end, determine in your heart to not allow anything to hold back your worship. Soon this clay house will crumble and we'll be free.

1 CHRONICLES 28; 2 PETER 2; MICAH 5; LUKE 14

Sure, I'm Sure!

Wherefore the rather, brethren, give diligence to make your calling and election sure: for if ye do these things, ye shall never fall.
2 PETER 1:10

A minister I had known for many years came up to me recently and said, "Steve, I'm not even sure whether I'm saved." This man was obviously being tormented by demonic thoughts. He was the recipient of constant, powerful jabs from Lucifer saying, "You're not saved; just look at yourself. You can't even control your thought life." My heart went out to my dear brother. There is no reason why he shouldn't be absolutely certain of his salvation.

"To be sure" means "to be resolved; to be certain; to be without doubt." Allow me to form an acrostic with this four-letter word to aid in your assurance of salvation.

Sin. First, admit that you are a sinner in desperate need of salvation. Unless we understand our sinful condition, we will never comprehend the need for the Cross.

Understanding. Realize that without Jesus, there's no way to be saved. He is the only solution to our sin problem.

Repentance. Thoroughly repent of all your sins. To repent literally means "to turn around." It signifies not only a sorrow for sin but a willingness to do something about it.

Eternity. Live every day of your life in the light of eternity. Once you receive Jesus as Savior, your lifestyle should be totally different. When temptation arises ask, "How will this affect eternity?" When you constantly think about your eternal life in heaven, it helps you to live holy in your temporal life on earth.

An Awful Weapon

But watch thou in all things, endure afflictions, do the work of an evangelist, make full proof of thy ministry.

2 TIMOTHY 4:5

As you know by now, one of my heroes of the faith is Robert Murray McCheyne. He made the following statement about those in ministry: "It is not great talents God blesses so much as great likeness to Jesus. A holy minister is an awful weapon in the hand of God."

This quote was used of God, early on, to shape my Christian character. I noticed that many people were depending on their talents and skills in spiritual warfare. That's the wrong thing to do. The simple truth is, when we live holy, allowing Jesus *full reign* in our lives, laying down our capabilities and picking up the Cross, *then* God has a weapon He can use against the enemy. McCheyne also noted:

Ministers are standard-bearers. Satan aims his fiery darts at them. If he can only make you a covetous minister, a lover of pleasure, a lover of praise, or a lover of good eating, then he has ruined your ministry forever. "Ah!" he says, "Let him preach on [for] fifty years, he will never do me any harm." Dear brother, cast yourself at the feet of Christ, implore His Spirit to make you a holy man. Take heed to yourself, and to your doctrine. Give yourself to prayer and to the ministry of the Word. If you do not pray, God will probably lay you aside from your ministry...to teach you to pray.

Oh friend, don't just read through this page. Let it soak in. Regardless of your ministerial position, you can be an awful weapon in God's hand. Dog-ear this page. Refer back to it often. Make it your aim to be a weapon He has formed!

No Cause to Be Jealous

For thou shalt worship no other god: for the LORD,
whose name is Jealous, is a jealous God.
EXODUS 34:14

The word "idolatry" conjures up images of exotic gods and tribal deities. But the scope of idolatry far surpasses these boundaries. An idol is anything that takes the place of Jesus in our lives. One night, a young man who received Christ was obviously struggling with a major stronghold in his life. Turns out, he was a hunter. His entire life revolved around hunting. He lived for the next open hunting season. Then he got saved, and the idol of hunting had to be destroyed. He realized that Jesus wanted first place in his life and he was willing to do anything to protect his newfound love for the Lord.

Thomas Watson has this to say on the subject:

Let us give God no just cause to be jealous. Let us avoid all sin, especially this sin of idolatry, or image worship. It is heinous, after we have entered into a marriage covenant with God, now to prostitute ourselves to an image. Idolatry is spiritual adultery, and God is a jealous God. He will avenge it!

Image worship makes God abhor a people: They "moved Him to jealousy with their graven images. When God heard this, he was wroth, and greatly abhorred Israel" (Psalm 78:58,59).

Is hunting, fishing, golf, other sports or obtaining wealth wrong? Of course not! But if they steal our precious time with Jesus, if they become more important than church attendance and worship, be warned! You have given God cause to be jealous.

December 4

The Gift

For by grace are ye saved through faith; and that not of yourselves: it is the gift of God: Not of works, lest any man should boast. For we are his workmanship, created in Christ Jesus unto good works, which God hath before ordained that we should walk in them.

EPHESIANS 2:8-10

When a person becomes a Christian, everything changes. I can speak of my own personal life better than any other. My thought life, my motives, my desires, my actions—everything changed after meeting Christ.

William Booth, in his book *In Darkest England*, based the whole plan of the Salvation Army upon such a change in the lives of the converted. He and his lieutenants saw men and women brought from darkness into light, from drunkenness, debauchery, and crime into sobriety, diligence and love.

> We go not forth in our own strength to this battle, our dependence is upon Him who can influence the heart of a man. There is no doubt that the most satisfactory method of raising a man must be to effect such a change in his views and feelings that he shall voluntarily abandon his evil ways, give himself to hard work and goodness in the midst of the very temptations and companionships that before led him astray. He then lives a Christian life, an example in himself of what can be done by the power of God in the very face of the most impossible circumstances.
>
> Multitudes of slaves of vice in every form have been delivered not only from these habits, but from the destitution and misery which they ever produce. Our experience, which has been almost world-wide, has ever shown that not only does the criminal become honest, the drunkard sober, the harlot chaste, but that poverty of the most abject and helpless type vanishes away.

Each of us is capable of presenting this magnificent, life-changing gift of God to those in need. Knowing the unlimited power and potential of this gift, how can any Christian be silent around a dying multitude? Who will you pass today—on your way to work or school or the grocery store—that needs this gift? In the light of eternity, what could be more important than sharing it?

2 CHRONICLES 3—4; 1 JOHN 3; NAHUM 2; LUKE 18

Judging Pleasure

Lovers of pleasures more than lovers of God.
2 TIMOTHY 3:4

Children, teenagers and even adults often find themselves in the situation of having to choose whether to go along with the "good" time their friends are having. Susannah Wesley gave her children a very good rule of thumb to follow regarding judging whether some bit of pleasure is okay or not.

> When judging the lawfulness or unlawfulness of pleasure, take this rule: Whatever weakens your reason, impairs the tenderness of your conscience, obscures your sense of God, or takes off the relish of spiritual things; in short, whatever increases the strength and authority of your body over your mind, that is sin to you, however innocent it may be in itself.

The Wesley family is known to this day as a most respected family. All of Susannah's 10 surviving children lived for God. I would expect that much of the reason could be traced back to her invaluable piece of advice on what is sin.

I have frequently had people come up to me, even in the midst of revival, and ask me why I don't spend more time fellowshiping, or golfing, or boating or things like that. The reason is simple. While none of those things are wrong in and of themselves, for me they are a distraction from my favorite things: my God, my wife and my family.

Relaxation, recreation and other things you find pleasurable may not be wrong in themselves. However, keep Susannah's words in mind. For "whatever increases the strength and authority of your body over your mind" can eventually destroy your relationship with God.

2 CHRONICLES 5—6:11; 1 JOHN 4; NAHUM 3; LUKE 19

The Evidence

Therefore if any man be in Christ, he is a new creature: old things are passed away; behold, all things are become new.

2 CORINTHIANS 5:17

In a criminal trial, the prosecuting attorney spends a large amount of time rounding up evidence to use against the accused. This attorney will search out both physical clues and character witnesses. His main objective is to state a convincing case before the judge and jury so as to produce a guilty verdict.

Just as a prosecuting attorney searches for evidence, we too should search for proof that we are absolutely guilty of being a Christian. See how many of the following points of evidence apply to your life.

1. Is there an inner witness that you are a child of God? (see 1 John 5:10).
2. Is there a new awareness of sin and sinful thoughts? (see 1 John 1:8,9).
3. Is there a new desire to read the Bible—God's love letter? (see Psalm 119:11).
4. Is there a desire to live holy and be like Jesus? (see Philippians 3:10).
5. Are you experiencing persecution and social pressure? (see 2 Timothy 3:12).
6. Is there a sense of urgency to share the gospel? (see Acts 4:20).
7. Do you have a new love for other Christians? (see 1 John 3:14).

If these points are evident in your life, congratulations! You must be guilty of being a Christian!

2 CHRONICLES 6:12-42; 1 JOHN 5; HABAKKUK 1; LUKE 20

God's Name in Vain

Thou shalt not take the name of the LORD thy God in vain; for the LORD will not hold him guiltless that taketh his name in vain.
EXODUS 20:7

Many of us have heard some form of this scripture since our childhood, but how many of us ever fully understood what it meant? I found Thomas Watson's interpretation to be eye-opening, and I believe you will, too.

We take God's name in vain when we speak slightly and irreverently of His name. We give earthly kings a title of honor such as "excellent majesty." We should all the more speak of God with such sacred reverence as is due to the Infinite Majesty of heaven. When we speak slightly of God or His works, God interprets it to be contempt.

When we profess God's name, but do not live answerably to it, that too is a taking His name in vain. "They profess to know God, but by their deeds they deny Him" (Titus 1:16, *NASB*). When under a mask of profession, men will lie and deceive and are unclean, these make use of God's name and abuse Him.

We take God's name in vain when we use it in idle conversation. God is not to be spoken of but with an holy awe upon our hearts.

We take God's name in vain when we worship Him with our lips but not our hearts. Isaiah 29:13 reads: "This people draw near me with their mouth, and with their lips do honor me, but have removed their heart far from me."

Be careful in your daily conversation, friend. There are many ways to take the Lord's name in vain. Be quick to repent and follow the commandment.

2 CHRONICLES 7; 2 JOHN 1; HABAKKUK 2; LUKE 21

Continual Virtue

How much more shall the blood of Christ, who through the eternal Spirit offered himself without spot to God, purge your conscience from dead works to serve the living God?

HEBREWS 9:14

There are several thousand books in my library. I have many of them categorized by subject and author. By far, my favorite section is the biography and autobiography shelf. Most of these books date back over 100 years, several of them even 200. They are so much fun to read. I am fascinated how a person's conversion two centuries ago can sound exactly like a person's conversion today. The way they talk about the Blood, their remarks on coming to Calvary and the tears poured out in repentance are as fresh today as they were back then. Even the old hymnals contain songs that are as relevant today as they were then. It's so true, the Blood will never lose its power. I love the way Robert Hall spoke about the freshness of the Lord's work on Calvary.

His Blood, so to speak, is just as warm and fresh as when it was first shed: it has an undecaying virtue. The Lamb forever appears as newly slain, though millions have been already saved, and millions more remain to be saved. No generation can arise that will not equally want this Savior, and none that will equally find Him sufficient; for all the fullness of God dwells in Him, and He ever lives to make intercession for us!

Should the Lord tarry His coming, I'll see my grandchildren washed in the same Blood that cleansed their granddad. Oh, the cleansing stream of continual virtue!

Power of the Word

The blood of Jesus Christ his Son cleanseth us from all sin.
1 JOHN 1:7

Charles Spurgeon paid a visit to Albert Hall where he was to preach on the coming Sabbath. In order to test out the hall with his voice, he mounted the platform and repeated the text, *"The blood of Jesus Christ his Son cleanseth us from all sin."* Not long afterward, he received word that the mere repetition of that text had born rich fruit. A painter, at work in some part of the great hall, was startled when he heard the voice of Spurgeon repeating that great sentence. The words so impressed him that he was converted and brought to Christ.

So often we fail to recognize the power in God's Word. Our earthly words fall to the ground and die after being spoken, but His Word endures forever. The Word of God is what pierces the sinner's heart, convinces him of his separation from God, and brings him to the altar. After all, how is someone going to know they have broken the law, unless you show them in the Book? Once they have been shown, it begins playing on their conscience. It's not the preacher that convicts, but rather the Holy Spirit bringing to light God's precious Word.

Spurgeon gave a warning that applies to every Christian when he said, "It will be our dull sermons that will haunt us on our dying beds." Why? Because only the Word of God endures. Nothing within us has the power to set a man free.

When you come in contact with the spiritually barren, the Word is the pure water they need. In the words of Paul, "Preach the word; be instant in season, out of season; reprove, rebuke, exhort with all long-suffering and doctrine" (2 Timothy 4:2).

2 CHRONICLES 9; JUDE 1; ZEPHANIAH 1; LUKE 23

Doesn't Anybody Care?

*I looked on my right hand, and beheld, but there was no man that would
know me: refuge failed me; no man cared for my soul.*

PSALM 142:4

When people have said to me, "Nobody knows what I'm going
through," I am always quick to respond, "You are not alone. Everyone
experiences troubles, and I care about you."

You see, my friend, I have seen victims of child abuse totally healed
and restored. I have witnessed firsthand the deliverance of alcoholics
and drug addicts. We can visit battered wives who are now married to
transformed, caring husbands. Those who were bound by lust,
pornography and life-controlling vices are now living in victory.
Thousands of backsliders who were living out of harmony with God
are now back in tune. All these changed lives, and hundreds of thousands more, are because someone cared.

Let me say that Jesus cares for your soul. The value of something
depends upon its intrinsic worth; that is, what it costs of time, labor,
sacrifice and means to secure it. Your soul cost Jesus His life. He shed
His precious Blood for you.

Let me also say that I care for your soul. That is one of the reasons
I've prepared this devotional. I want people to grow in God and receive
all He has for them.

The Church cares for your soul. Every night in our meetings there
are scores of intercessors praying that God would change lives. They
pray, not for money, but because they care. The children's ministry, the
youth, the ministry to the elderly are all there because the Church
cares for your soul.

Stirred to Compassion

*But whoever has the world's goods, and beholds his brother in need and
closes his heart against him, how does the love of God abide in him?*
1 JOHN 3:17, NASB

The word "compassion," in its original form, means "to suffer
together." That means, a person who is compassionate is willing to
take upon himself the burden of others, as if the burden were his own.

Our society often turns a cold shoulder to those in need. But Jesus
never did. He was the epitome of compassion. Bishop Gore compares
our unmoved hearts with the city culture that enables a pedestrian to
walk right past a dying man.

> The sight of a leprous man, or of a demon-distressed man,
> *moved* Him. The great multitudes huddling together after
> Him, so pathetically, like leaderless sheep—eager, hungry,
> tired—always stirred Him. And when He was so moved, He
> always did something. He clean forgot His own bodily needs,
> so absorbed did He become in the folks around Him.
>
> The healing touch was quickly given. The demonized
> man released from his sore bonds. The bread multiplied. The
> sight of suffering always stirred Him. The presence of a crowd
> seemed always to touch Him. He never learned that sort of
> city culture that can look unmoved upon suffering or upon a
> helpless crowd. The word "compassion," used of Him, is both
> deep and tender in its meaning.

We are the only Jesus most people will ever meet. Ask God to allow
you to demonstrate true compassion, the kind that drove Jesus to
come and save a dying world.

2 CHRONICLES 11—12; REVELATION 2; ZEPHANIAH 3; JOHN 1

And He said to them, "O foolish men and slow of heart to
believe in all that the prophets have spoken!"
LUKE 24:25, NASB

There was a pastor who preached on love one Sunday, to his congregation's delight. The next Sunday he preached again on love. And the next. And the next. Feeling the discontent of some fellow parishioners, a deacon confronted the pastor over his repetitive sermon subject. The pastor boldly replied, "I'm not going to stop preaching on love until you get it!"

Christians know that everything they need is found in Jesus. All their answers are in the Word, yet they struggle along like novices. Reverend Mason, in his book *Crumbs from the Master's Table*, expounded on this irony.

We faint when we should flee; crawl when we should run; halt when we should walk; turn back when we should press forward; and droop when we should rejoice. Why? Because we look down, look within, look back, or to the right or left, when we should look steadfastly up to Jesus our forerunner.

He has set an open door before us (Revelation 3:8). He ever lives to save unto the uttermost (Hebrews 7:25). He says, "I will receive you to myself, that where I am, there ye may be also" (John 14:3).

Now, after all this, may He not justly reprove each of us with, "Oh fools, and slow of heart to believe all that is written concerning Me!" (see Luke 24:25).

"Slow to believe" should be changed in each of our hearts to "quick to respond." That would bring joy to Jesus.

Therefore I say unto you, What things soever ye desire, when ye pray,
believe that ye receive them, and ye shall have them.
MARK 11:24

The Complete Duty of Man was likened to a textbook for every student in the school of God. I find it mentioned throughout the writings of some of the greatest men and women who ever lived. Here lies a portion of what Henry Venn wrote to the serious follower of Jesus.

> The sense of our own vileness must accompany our prayer. It is in opposition to Pharisaic self-conceit and is proof of our abiding consciousness that we can never be justified before God through our own works. But with this humiliation must be joined a commitment to God, and a holy boldness in approaching Him.
>
> When we ask, we must not fluctuate between hope and despondency, but assure ourselves that we will be as certainly helped. For instance, when we confess our sin with sorrow, shame, and humiliation, begging for mercy through the atonement, we must be fully persuaded that we do obtain mercy.
>
> When we pray for mastery over our natural corruptions, we must assure ourselves they shall be subdued.
>
> When in perplexity of mind and in great tribulation, we beg of God for deliverance. We must not entertain a fear that perhaps He will not hear us. We greatly dishonor Him by giving way to distrust by questioning whether He will perform the gracious promises which He has made.

God's "Silence"

These things hast thou done, and I kept silence; thou thoughtest that I was altogether such an one as thyself: but I will reprove thee, and set them in order before thine eyes.

PSALM 50:21

I've known people who felt they could do whatever they wanted and get away with it, because they weren't punished right away. "If what I am doing is so bad, why has God been quiet about it all these years?" they boast. Perhaps you know people like that as well. Ever wonder how to answer that question? Today's scripture is a very good place to begin.

You see, there are two very significant areas to remember about God's apparent silence.

The first has to do with what His silence *doesn't* mean. As stated in today's text, people have a tendency to believe that God is just like them. Therefore, God's silence—or His lack of instant judgment—must mean He is approving or winking at their ways. You see, man is very lenient toward himself, and therefore thinks God will also be tolerant of his sin. However, it is not like that at all. God's silence does not mean that He is thinking like us.

What His silence does mean is He is patient and long-suffering. According to this scripture, one might say He is quietly taking notes. One day, He will reprove the sinner and set his sins before his eyes. This military type of phrase means that on Judgment Day, the sinner's transgressions will march in unison toward him like a mighty army. There will be no one to spare him on that day.

Puts a little different light on things, doesn't it? His ways are not our ways. He does not think like we do. He is not lenient toward sin, considering the cost to deliver us from sin. Keep this in mind the next time you run into someone who thinks God's silence is a good thing.

To Die Is Gain

And they sing the song of Moses the servant of God, and the song of the
Lamb, saying, Great and marvellous are thy works, Lord God Almighty;
just and true are thy ways, thou King of saints.
REVELATION 15:3

It's so refreshing to find Christians once again talking about the
Rapture and heaven. It seems Christianity in America passed through
a season of unrestrained indulgence. No one wanted to talk or hear
about heaven. They were too happy lavishing upon themselves silly
creature comforts. But things have changed. Now believers are singing
and talking about eternity. And why not? It makes sense to be speaking about the place we will spend forever.

> I long to eat the fruit of that tree which is planted in the midst
> of the paradise of God. I long to drink of the pure river, clear
> as crystal, that runs through the streets of the new Jerusalem.
> I long to be refreshed in company with the souls of them
> that are under the altar, who were slain for the Word of God
> and the testimony which they held. To have the long white
> robe given me, that I may walk with those glorious saints who
> have washed their garments and made them white in the
> Blood of the Lamb. Why should I think it a strange thing to
> be removed from this place to that wherein is my hope, my
> joy, my crown? Wherein is my eldest Brother, my Head, my
> Father, my Comforter, and all the glorified saints; and where
> the song of Moses and of the Lamb is sung joyfully?

Can you agree with these words of John Welch? Or do they sound
foreign to you? It's time to start contemplating heaven. Soon we will
be standing before His throne.

2 CHRONICLES 17; REVELATION 6; ZECHARIAH 2; JOHN 5

Blessed Fruit of Affliction

O LORD of hosts, if thou wilt indeed look on the affliction of thine handmaid, and remember me, and not forget thine handmaid, but wilt give unto thine handmaid a man child, then I will give him unto the LORD all the days of his life, and there shall no razor come upon his head.

1 SAMUEL 1:11

Have you ever been overwhelmed with a burden to the point you didn't know what to do? This weight upon your shoulders was constantly with you throughout the day and into the night. It could have been an identifiable burden, such as the desire to see a family member saved or a friend healed. Or in many cases, it was an unexplainable weight that was only relieved when you spent time on your knees in prayer.

I remember sharing with Leonard Ravenhill during a particular time of heaviness, and I asked him to pray that God would lift it from me. His response was classic: "Why should I ask God to lift this from you, when I've been praying that He would put it on you?" He knew the burden was the very reason I was praying so much. If it was lifted from me, perhaps I would pray less. John Newton would have agreed with Leonard Ravenhill's views. "By affliction prayer is quickened, for our prayers are very apt to grow languid and formal in a time of ease."

So the next time you feel yourself collapsing under the load, maybe that's the exact place God wants you. Joseph Caryl once said, "According to the weight of the burden that grieves you, is the cry to God that comes from you."

If it wasn't for the burdens of life, there would be less brokenness before God. If it wasn't for our trials, there would be less travailing. If it wasn't for our sicknesses, there would be less seeking the Savior. Thank God for the fruit of affliction.

A Craving Fulfilled

But I would feed you with the finest of the wheat;
and with honey from the rock I would satisfy you.

PSALM 81:16, NASB

There is something about the winter months, especially around Christmas, which finds many people more aware of their inner cravings than at any other time. Unfortunately, many people are never pointed in the direction that will lead them to fulfillment. In the words of George Swinnock, "We must set God before [them], and allow [them] to begin feeding on Him." He continued:

A man that is hungry finds his stomach still craving something he wants, without which he cannot be well. Give him music, company, pictures, houses, honors...yet there follows no satisfaction (these are not suitable to his appetite). But set before this man some wholesome food, and let him eat, and his craving is over. So it is with a man's soul as with his body.

The soul is full of cravings and longings, spending itself in rushing out after its proper food. Give it the credit, profits, and pleasures of the world, and they cannot abate its desire. It craves still, for these do not answer the soul's necessity. But, set God before him, and allow him to begin feeding on Him, and the soul is satisfied. Its dogged appetite after the world is now cured! He, tasting His manna, tramples on the onions of Egypt. "He that drinketh of this water shall thirst again, but he that drinketh of the water which I shall give him shall never thirst" (John 4:13,14).

There is nothing more pleasing to the Lord than a spiritually hungry soul. Be alert. This time of year there will be many opportunities to point people in the right direction—toward a craving fulfilled.

2 CHRONICLES 19—20; REVELATION 8; ZECHARIAH 4; JOHN 7

A Better Plan

For we have not an high priest which cannot be touched with the feeling of our infirmities; but was in all points tempted like as we are, yet without sin.
HEBREWS 4:15

One night a young man came to me after the sermon. His eyes were hollow and glassy. He pulled up his sleeve, revealing dark track marks up and down his left arm. In a broken voice, he asked, "Can your God help me with my addiction?"

I pulled up my own sleeve, took his hand, and said, "Put your finger right there." He put his fingers on a knot on my arm. It was evidence of my past drug abuse. I had injected some morphine and missed the vein. There was an immediate connection between us. With tears in his eyes, he grabbed me and said, "You've been there! You know what I'm going through!"

Even though I was standing there in church with a suit on, and this young man was in tattered old blue jeans and had dirty, matted hair, the fact that we had both lived a sinful life bonded us together.

I've been there, friend. I've seen more than my share of hell. When I look into the eyes of someone like that young man and I see pain, either from drug addiction, a broken marriage or an abused life, something inside me begins to cry because I know things don't have to be like that.

God had a much better plan when He created us. Regardless of what you're going through this Christmas season, please remember that Jesus Christ came that you might experience an abundant life. He identifies with your suffering. You can say to Him, "You've been there...You know what I'm going through."

Don't Be So Foolish

*He has given food to those who fear Him;
He will remember His covenant forever.*
PSALM 111:5, NASB

There is a plant outside our kitchen window that houses a nest full of baby birds each spring. One day, I pulled back the leaves to take a peek inside and found their mouths wide open, waiting for a worm. I remember thinking, *These little guys don't just* think *they're going to get a worm, they* know *a worm is coming.* There's a lesson to be learned from this, and Jeremy Taylor teaches it well in his writings.

> Does not God provide for all the birds, and beasts and fishes? Do not the sparrows fly from their bush and every morning find meat where they laid it not? Do not the young ravens call to God, and He feeds them? And is it reasonable that the sons of the family should fear that the father would give food to the chickens and the servants, his sheep and his dogs, but give none to them? He would be a very bad father that should do so; or he is a very foolish son that should think so of a good father.
>
> We have lived at God's charges all our life, and thus far He has not failed us; we have no reason to suspect Him for the future.

There is no reason or excuse to be concerned about tomorrow. This year is almost over; has God taken not care of you up to this point? Do you not think He will provide for the future? Don't be so foolish to let the circumstances around you overshadow the promises of God. What He said He will do, He will do.

Today's Appointed Path

Therefore do not be anxious for tomorrow; for tomorrow will care for itself. Each day has enough trouble of its own.

MATTHEW 6:34, NASB

A Lutheran minister once told my mother that worry is something God never intended for her to do. She was completely consumed by fear that I was going to die from a drug overdose or a gunshot wound. She had seen me in a stoned, drunken stupor for many years. This only fueled her fears and intensified her worries. Oh, if she'd only known what God had planned!

Phillips Brooks counseled his flock of believers in the subject of trusting God. Read his words and let them encourage you.

> What a vast proportion of our lives is spent in anxious and useless forebodings concerning the future—either our own or those of our own dear ones. Present joys and blessings slip by and we miss half their flavor, all for lack of faith in Him who provides for the tiniest insect in the sunbeam.
>
> Oh, when shall we learn the sweet trust in God that our little children teach us every day by their confiding faith in us? We who are so faulty, so irritable, so unjust—and He, who is so watchful, so kind, so loving, so forgiving. Why cannot we, slipping our hand into His each day, walk trusting over that day's appointed path, thorny or flowery, crooked or straight, knowing that evening will bring us sleep, peace and home?

My mom's prayers were answered. Her son was saved. God knows what path you are on, and He'll bring you through.

2 CHRONICLES 24; REVELATION 11; ZECHARIAH 7; JOHN 10

DECEMBER 21

In View of the Gallows

For Christ sent me not to baptize, but to preach the gospel: not with wisdom of words, lest the cross of Christ should be made of none effect.

1 CORINTHIANS 1:17

This world is in desperate need of fiery Holy Ghost preachers—ones who will not hesitate to raise their voices in the marketplace and proclaim liberty to those in bondage, salvation to the lost and healing to the sick. This world has had enough of anemic ministers and tainted messages. It's time for the truth to be told.

"I am tormented with the desire of writing better than I can," declared Thomas Watson.

> I am tormented with the desire of preaching better than I can. But I have no wish to make fine, pretty sermons. Prettiness is well enough when prettiness is in its place. I like to see a pretty child, a pretty flower—but in sermons prettiness is out of place.
>
> To my ear, it should be anything but commendation, should it be said to me, "You have given us a pretty sermon." If I were put upon trial for my life, and my lawyer should amuse the jury with jesting or bury his arguments beneath a profusion of flowery rhetoric, I would say to him, "What are you doing? You care more for your vanity than for my hanging! Put yourself in my place—speak in view of the gallows—and you will plead my case plainly and earnestly instead."

Hell awaits all nonbelievers. If we really believed that, our voices would be seasoned with fire. Oh, that God would impart to every serious believer a divine vision of hell! Then they would preach as dying men to dying men.

Active or Passive?

I know thy works, that thou art neither cold nor hot: I would thou wert
cold or hot. So then because thou art lukewarm, and neither cold nor hot,
I will spew thee out of my mouth.
REVELATION 3:15,16

Are you a radical disciple or a passive observer? Is your relationship with God a flame that burns within you or a big wet blanket that extinguishes the fire? Are you cold as ice or molten like lava? Are you following Jesus, or do you follow whoever comes along and says something interesting? Are you willing to take a stand for something, or are you ready to stand for just about anything?

Martin Luther was yet a Roman Catholic when he began reading his Bible more and more seriously, believing what it said and applying it to his life. He never planned on starting the Protestant Reformation, but his ideas—which were based on the truths of Scripture—propelled this powerful movement. For Luther, it was like a fire caught up in his soul. His writings expressed his concern.

> Far from being alarmed, it gives me great joy to see that the gospel is now, as in former times, a cause of trouble and discord. This is the characteristic and the destiny of the Word of God. "I came not to send peace, but a sword" said Jesus Christ (Matthew 10:34).

When God revealed His truth to humanity, He didn't send us a Hallmark card with a smiley face on the front. He sent us a tough message that invades our souls and transforms our lives. In a few days, we will be entering a new year. Make up your mind now. Will you be on fire or lukewarm? Will you be actively radical, or without passion, and passive?

Answering Love

All things have been handed over to Me by My Father; and no one knows the Son, except the Father; nor does anyone know the Father, except the Son, and anyone to whom the Son wills to reveal Him.
MATTHEW 11:27, NASB

There is a heaven-sent fellowship between a child and his father that can only be fully understood through experience. I have noticed, through the rearing of children, that much of our communication takes place in silence. Just a look from Daddy's face can send my little girl's heart to sleep in peace. Just a wave of my hand while my son rides by on his bike is as if I walked over to his side and lavished him with love. This is something God has built into the family unit. And if it's like this with an earthly family, oh, how much richer is it with the heavenly.

One of the most respected preachers of all time, Alexander Maclaren, celebrates this relationship through his writings.

> Fatherhood! What does that word itself teach us? It speaks of the communication of a life and the reciprocity of love. It rests upon a Divine act, and it involves a human emotion. It involves that the Father and the child shall have kindred life—the father bestowing, and the child possessing. And it requires that between the Father's heart and the child's heart there shall pass a correspondence, a love answering, flashing backwards and forwards, like the lightning that touches the earth and rises from it again.

I mentioned earlier of the unspoken language between my children and me. But oh, when we open our mouths and begin to utter words of love and praise! I call it "love answering love" and it lifts our hearts to the heavens.

2 CHRONICLES 27—28; REVELATION 14; ZECHARIAH 10; JOHN 13

The Father Has Plenty

*But of him are ye in Christ Jesus, who of God is made unto us wisdom,
and righteousness, and sanctification, and redemption: that, according as it
is written, He that glorieth, let him glory in the Lord.*
1 CORINTHIANS 1:30,31

There is a weekly ritual in the Hill family every Sunday afternoon on the way home from church. First, we have a vote on which fast-food restaurant to stop at. Once the votes are in, I drive up to the window and begin reciting our order. I find it interesting that my children never question me about cost. They just tell me what they want; Daddy orders it and pays the bill. This is the nature of a child. Hannah Whitall Smith explored this more deeply.

Sometimes I think that the whole secret of the Christian life...is revealed in the child relationship. Nothing more is needed than just to believe that God is as good a Father as the best ideal earthly father, and that the relationship of a Christian to Him is just the same as that of a child to its parent in this world. Children do not need to carry about in their own pockets the money for their support. If the father has plenty, that satisfies them, and is a great deal better than if it were in the child's own possession, since in that case it might get lost. In the same way it is not necessary for Christians to have all their spiritual possessions in their own keeping. It is far better that their riches should be stored up for them in Christ, and that when they want anything they should receive it direct from his hands. He is God, and apart from Him we have nothing.

Next time you're burdened with the concerns of this life, remember your Father. He has plenty and will freely give it to you.

2 CHRONICLES 29; REVELATION 15; ZECHARIAH 11; JOHN 14

Let Us Now Go

And it came to pass, as the angels were gone away from them into heaven, the shepherds said one to another, Let us now go even unto Bethlehem, and see this thing which is come to pass, which the Lord hath made known unto us.

LUKE 2:15

Throughout the years I have met people who have cynically said to me, "If God was really concerned about me, He would come down and help me." When I hear this statement, and I've heard it plenty of times, my response is always the same: "My friend, God is concerned about you, He does love you, and He's already done something about it. He sent His Son, Jesus Christ, to die for your sins and offer you a way to heaven."

Of course, this answer always irritates. That's not what people want to hear. But I find the truth of it in the Christmas story. The angels appeared to the shepherds with an announcement that would change the destiny of mankind. They said, "For unto you is born this day in the city of David a Saviour, which is Christ the Lord" (Luke 2:11). This signified that God had done something for mankind. He saw man's desperation, and sent His Son. Now it was time for man to sense his own desperation and go to Him.

Today's scripture speaks of a decision made by the shepherds that must be made by everyone who chooses to see the Christ Child. They said, "Let us now go even unto Bethlehem...." They realized that Jesus was not going to come to them; they must go to Him.

This is our lesson for Christmas Day. For those who are waiting for God to come, they need not wait any longer. He came 2,000 years ago. Now, like the shepherds, we must individually go to Him.

2 CHRONICLES 30; REVELATION 16; ZECHARIAH 12—13:1; JOHN 15

To Be Continued...

*The LORD will perfect that which concerneth me: thy mercy, O LORD,
endureth for ever: forsake not the works of thine own hands.*

PSALM 138:8

Over the last several years, I've found myself using a phrase that
depicts exactly what's happening through our evangelistic efforts. It's
called "the chain of grace," and it works like this: One person will be
saved on a Wednesday night and bring a friend on Thursday. The
Thursday person will get saved and bring a neighbor on Friday. The
next night, the neighbor's unsaved friends show up and receive Christ
as Savior. The chain gets longer.

Not only is this true in evangelism, but also in our personal, spiritual lives. Charles Spurgeon often spoke of the endless mercies of God.

It is by no means pleasant when reading an interesting article
in your magazine to find yourself pulled up short with the
ominous words, *"to be continued."* Yet, they are words of good
cheer if applied to other matters. What a comfort to remember that the Lord's mercy and lovingkindness is *to be continued!* As much as we have experienced in the long years of our
pilgrimage, we have by no means outlived eternal love.
Providential goodness is an endless chain, a stream which follows the pilgrim, a wheel perpetually revolving, a star forever
shining, and leading us to the place where He is who was once
a babe in Bethlehem. All the volumes which record the doings
of Divine grace are but part of a series *"to be continued."*

There is no end to the chain of grace. You cannot exhaust God's
mercy. It is to be continued.

2 CHRONICLES 31; REVELATION 17; ZECHARIAH 13:2-9; JOHN 16

Absent Without Leave

Wherefore let him that thinketh he standeth take heed lest he fall.
1 CORINTHIANS 10:12

I trust you have lived victoriously through this holiday season. For some, Thanksgiving, Christmas and New Year's serve as a time for celebrating God's blessing and faithfulness. Other people find this time to be one of testing and trials. They entered this season full of anticipation and victory, but are closing the holidays in defeat and disappointment.

One of the reasons for this is the continual bombardment of temptations that surround this time of year. Get-togethers, such as family reunions or office parties, serve as battlefields for those who thought they stood strong. How many thousands of soldiers will fall by placing themselves in harm's way? Countless Christians will join the ranks of the lukewarm, and many will never return to their first love.

The fiery evangelist Dwight L. Moody warned his audience of this impending danger.

> I would that everyone who today is being lulled into a belief that his appetite is gone, could see his danger and understand that the enemy is not gone, but only lurking. The ranks of the backsliding army draws all its recruits from those who *think they stand.*

If you've found yourself AWOL during this holiday season, get out of the devil's trenches, march back to base and surrender yourself to Jesus. He stands ready to forgive.

2 CHRONICLES 32; REVELATION 18; ZECHARIAH 14; JOHN 17

And forgive us our debts, as we forgive our debtors.
MATTHEW 6:12

"But you don't know what he did to me!" says the disgruntled church member. "I'll forgive him if he first comes and apologizes to me."

Just a few feet away another complaint is heard. "I've been in this church for the last 10 years. The choir director knows how much I've wanted to sing a solo. I can't believe *she* was chosen to sing the special in the Christmas cantata." My friend, these are just two imaginary members demonstrating what takes place far too often. It's time to sit down at the table and call a truce to the endless barrage of accusations. With the cup of the Lord in one hand and the bread of His presence in the other, we need to begin demonstrating the love and kindness of our Redeemer.

"It's communion every day," said Henry Ward Beecher. "The body of Christ is wherever human bodies are, and he who has any bitterness against his brother is always committing sacrilege." Reverend Beecher further points out that saying "I can forgive, but I cannot forget" is only another way of saying, "I will not forgive." He states, "A forgiveness ought to be like a cancelled note, torn in two and burned up, so that it never can be shown against the man."

Only a few more days remain in this year. There is no good reason to harbor unforgiveness and carry it into the new year. Whatever it takes, get it out of your system. Think of what Jesus has forgiven you of, and it will be much easier to forgive your brother. Do it now while there is still time.

2 CHRONICLES 33; REVELATION 19; MALACHI 1; JOHN 18

Let your light so shine before men, that they may see your
good works and glorify your Father in heaven.
MATTHEW 5:16, NKJV

Christians are constantly under observation. Upon receiving Christ as Savior, I found myself under daily scrutiny from my family and friends. One close friend was certain that this "Jesus thing" would never last. Another friend tried to tempt me with a bag of marijuana. Each one of these was out to prove that my new Christian life wasn't going to last. But oh, were they wrong! I had chosen to live holy, and it was a sweet fragrance to God and to those around me. Eventually, many of those who criticized were saved. There is nothing like a holy life!

Robert Murray McCheyne was so much like Jesus that his colleagues nicknamed him "Holy McCheyne." No one was more qualified to write about holiness than this great man of God.

Live holier lives: When a holy believer goes through the world filled with the Spirit, the fragrance fills the room. If the world were full of believers, it would be like a bed of spices.

If you lived a holy, consistent life, how many souls might be saved as a result. Wives might thus win their husbands without a word when they see your chaste conversation. Parents might in this way save their children when they see you holy and happy, as children have often thus saved their parents. Let your light shine before men. The poorest can do this as well as the richest, the youngest as well as the oldest. Oh, there is no argument like a holy life!

Call It Down

If my people, which are called by my name, shall humble themselves, and pray, and seek my face, and turn from their wicked ways; then will I hear from heaven, and will forgive their sin, and will heal their land.

2 CHRONICLES 7:14

There have always been pockets of believers sprinkled throughout the land, earnestly seeking God, motivated by a desperate desire for revival. God has always had His remnant. They have a hold on the horns of the altar. The darkness of night was pierced by their agonizing pleas for a visitation from God. Their white-hot prayers lit up the sky, just as lightning displaces utter blackness.

As sin was in full swing, as sinners were in the dance halls two-steppin' with the devil, just a few doors down in a small apartment would be a dear saint of God. She'd be facedown on the pinewood floor, pounding her fists, blasting out fiery arrows of intercession to heaven.

Yes, the corridors of heaven would ring with the consistent, dogmatic, God-demanding, heartfelt, soul-stirring, tear-drenched, insistent, persistent, unceasing, unwavering, crystal-clear cries for mercy.

Before long, the faithfulness of these dear believers would reign supreme. God would answer from heaven and pour out showers of mercy. If it wasn't for these dear saints of God, there would be no revival.

This year is all but gone. Perhaps God will allow us a few more months, maybe a year, maybe more of life here on earth. We can't go on in our present state. We must have a nationwide move of God. The power from on high must fall. This upcoming year, be the one who calls it down!

A Word from the Lord

Draw nigh to God, and he will draw nigh to you. Cleanse your hands, ye sinners; and purify your hearts, ye double minded.

JAMES 4:8

The Lord spoke this word to me and it must be shared with you. These are serious days. He's calling us closer.

Live unsettled. Don't sink too deep into the soil of this earth. Keep your head up and your feet moving. Stay alert. Be sober.

I'm coming. The day of My return is at hand. Loose yourself of any ties that bind. If you don't loose yourself, I'll help loose you. I want no obstacles. I will return for a "pilgrim people." My final work is at hand. My Spirit's wooing is about to cease. No one will grieve Me anymore. No one will quench My Spirit anymore. No one will resist Me anymore. Their days will be over.

My warm season of grace and mercy will soon turn to a chilling winter of judgment and wrath. The warm days of My wooing will be exchanged for the fiery days of My vengeance. My pleading for the souls of man, the passionate cry of My faithful harvesters, the unselfish service of My holy servants, all their labor, all the charity, all the pain, all the suffering, it will be over.

I have heard the groans of nature. I have heard the midnight cries. My Bride has been longing to be with Me. The tree has born forth its fruit. The fertile soil has yielded the harvest. The planting will stop. The laborers will leave. The sickle will rust.

It's almost over. I'm coming back. I will not delay My coming to you, so don't delay your coming to Me.

2 CHRONICLES 36; REVELATION 22; MALACHI 4; JOHN 21

Legacies

It is impossible here to give the appropriate honor due each of the great men and women of God quoted in this book. Many of their lives reflected a fight for freedom and the spreading of the gospel of Christ, the fruits of which we reap today. Some left legacies that stand as monuments, while others led obscure lives. All heralded the benefits of following Jesus. In this brief space we have done our best to compile information about each person's life, ministry and death. You may notice that some descriptions are more brief than others. This is by no means a show of favoritism. It is simply due to a shortage of information.

In some descriptions you will see the term "nonconformist." This label was given to those who refused to conform to the laws of England over the Church of Christ. To these men "conforming" often meant compromising the gospel and all they believed in.

ALLIENE, JOSEPH 1633-1668
Joseph Alliene was imprisoned on two occasions for nonconformity to the established Church of England. He died at only 35 years of age, due to an illness worsened by his confinement. His book, *Alarm to the Unconverted* is one of the most useful and widely circulated books of practical Christianity ever published.

ARTHUR, WILLIAM 1819-1901
Born in Scotland, Arthur began preaching by the age of 16. Having served as a missionary himself, he was passionate about their support and elevated the importance of mission work among several denominations.

BANKS, LOUIS ALBERT, D.D. 1855-1933
An American Methodist Episcopalian pastor, writer and supporter of the temperance movement. Reverend Banks was the author of books on many subjects, including *Great Sinners of the Bible*, published in 1899.

BAXTER, RICHARD 1615-1691

Baxter's industrious nature and natural talent helped him become a widely learned man. By 1640 he had become a pastor devoted to his flock. Not satisfied with merely correcting sin from the pulpit, he made a practice of visiting his parishioners in their homes and teaching them in private as well. He became their friend as well as their pastor.

BEECHER, HENRY WARD 1813-1877

An imaginative, witty American preacher, Beecher was pastor of a Plymouth Congregational Church in New York for many years. He was known as one of the leaders of the antislavery movement, even taking the message to England. He was always drawn to the oppressed.

BOGATZKY, CARL HEINRICH VON 1690-1774

Author of *A Golden Treasury for the Children of God*, published in the 1800s. It is a daily devotional collection focusing on making a distinction between basic morality and true Christianity.

BONAR, ANDREW 1810-1892

The youngest of the three well-known Bonar brothers, Andrew was also an earnest and gifted evangelical preacher. He was greatly concerned about souls, and his preaching was full of urgency. He was also a noted author, compiling books on his friend Robert Murray McCheyne, on Samuel Rutherford and others.

BONAR, HORATIUS 1808-1889

Well known throughout Scotland as a fiery evangelical preacher, Horatius Bonar is remembered in this century as a hymn writer. His famous hymn "What a Friend We Have in Jesus" has been sung in many churches around the world. His first attention, however, was given to the salvation of souls. When he preached he had a particular knack for holding the attention of the young. One of the most prominent of his written works is *The Night of Weeping*.

BOOTH, GEN. WILLIAM 1829-1912

A revivalist, author, songwriter and founder of the Salvation Army, Booth grew up in poverty. He came to know Jesus as his Savior in 1844. He became known for his personal holiness and profound compassion for mankind. His book *In Darkest England and the Way Out* tells of his motivation and philosophy. One of his most famous hymns is "Send the Fire." At his funeral, 150,000 people from all classes were in attendance.

BOOTH, WILLIAM BRAMWELL 1856-1929
The son of General William Booth, Bramwell carried high the torch of the Lord after the death of his father. His many writings include *Echoes and Memories* and *Our Master*.

BOSTON, THOMAS 1676-1732
A Scottish Presbyterian divine and writer, his exceptional writings were widely popular in Scotland and among English Presbyterians.

BOUNDS, E. M. 1835-1913
Born in northeastern Missouri, Bounds studied law and received his law degree in 1854. Only five years later, he responded to a call to the ministry. He preached in churches and on battlegrounds (during the Civil War), and retired from the pulpit in 1894. He spent the next nineteen years of his life devoted to intercessory prayer, writing and itinerant revival preaching.

BRAINERD, DAVID 1718-1747
A celebrated missionary to the American Indians, Brainerd was born at Haddam, Connecticut. He was appointed by the Scotch Society for Promoting Christian Knowledge as their missionary to the Indians in 1743. His ministry was well received by the Kaunameek and the Delaware tribes. In one year, no less than 100 Indians were baptized, nearly half of them adults who continued in the faith. In 1746 he went to minister among the Susquehanna tribe, but his health had been spent in the three years prior. He retired to the home of Jonathan Edwards in 1747, where he died in October of that year. The love of Christ and a benevolent desire for the salvation of men burned in his breast with the ardor of an unquenchable flame. Obstacles that would have cooled the zeal of many proved no discouragement to him. There are few who equal Brainerd's great labors, for which he endured severe hardship and self-denial.

BRIDGE, WILLIAM 1600-1670
There is little recorded about this man other than that he was noted as a nonconformist minister.

BROOKS, PHILLIPS 1835-1893
Born in Boston, Brooks was noted as an Episcopalian clergyman of striking oratorical power. Among other positions, he was the rector of Holy Trinity Church in Philadelphia for 10 years.

BROOKS, THOMAS 1608-1680
An English preacher and writer, Brooks's works were often quoted by Charles Spurgeon in his writings (*Treasury of David*). Statements like, "Men of greatest holiness have been men of greatest boldness," frame a picture of a man devoted to God, ready to be used by the Master.

BUNYAN, JOHN 1628-1688
Bunyan was born near Bedford, England, and was converted in 1653. He was thrown into prison for preaching to the Baptist congregation at Bedford and tagged shoelaces for twelve and a half years while in confinement. In the midst of that imprisonment, he composed the book *Pilgrim's Progress*. At the end of his sentence, he was made pastor of the Baptist church in Bedford, and his preaching drew large audiences. His death resulted from catching a fever while riding home in heavy rain after reconciling a father to his son.

CARYL, JOSEPH 1602-1673
Born in London, Caryl is noted as a minister of good abilities, learning and industry. His known literary work is *Exposition with Practical Observations on the Book of Job*.

CHADWICK, SAMUEL 1860-1932
President of Cliff College in Sheffield, England, and early mentor of Leonard Ravenhill, this holy man was used of God to ignite the fire of God in his listeners. Statements like, "Brethren, the crying sin of the Church is her laziness after God," are typical of the contents found in his lectures, sermons and many books.

CHALMERS, THOMAS 1780-1847
Born in Fifeshire, Scotland, Chalmers was given first to the study of physical science. After his conversion around 1809, he devoted his time to the promotion of the gospel. In 1843, he and several other key ministers led the break from the established Church of Scotland to

form the Free Church of Scotland. It is recorded that he "traveled over the length and breadth of Scotland, breathing his own burning spirit into every class."

CHARNOCK, STEPHEN 1628-1680
Born in London, Charnock became known as an eminent English nonconformist. Of his preaching it is said that he was "grave without being dull, and explicit without being wearisome."

COWPER, WILLIAM 1566-1619
A distinguished Scotch divine, William Cowper was born in Edinburgh. A collection of His works were published after his death, including the book *Heaven Opened*.

CUYLER, CORNELIUS, C.D.D. 1783-1850
Born at Albany, New York, Cuyler was pastor of the Second Presbyterian Church, Philadelphia, for over 20 years. It is said that "his ministry was characterized by several powerful revivals of religion, in which his wisdom, zeal and success were notable."

DAVIES, SAMUEL 1723-1761
Born near Summit Ridge in Delaware, Davies was ordained an evangelist in 1747, at which time he undertook a mission to Hanover County, Virginia. Not long after, he was chiefly responsible for founding the Presbytery of Hanover in 1755.

DICKSON, ALEXANDER (N.D.)
An esteemed preacher and writer, Dickson's book *Beauty for Ashes*, published in 1878, has touched many lives.

DODDRIDGE, PHILIP, D.D. 1702-1751
Born in London, Doddridge was raised by parents who took great pains to teach their children in the things of Christ. In the sitting room of their home were Dutch tiles painted with scenes from the Old and New Testaments, which his mother used to introduce him to the Bible. Among his efforts, he became dean of the academy he and others established for preparing young men for the work of the ministry. Many of his students rose to distinction in England, Scotland, America and Holland.

DRUMMOND, HENRY 1851-1897

Perhaps the original "campus crusader," this Scottish evangelist was known on college and university campuses throughout the world, beginning the Student Movement. Under the guidance of Moody and Sankey, his meetings attracted thousands. In an age where science and Christianity seemed to contradict each other, he was noted for an unusual ability to reconcile the two while drawing his listeners to Jesus.

DWIGHT, TIMOTHY, D.D., LL.D. 1752-1817

The grandson of Jonathan Edwards the elder, and nephew of Jonathan Edwards, Timothy was born at Northampton, Massachusetts. He tutored at Yale for six years after his graduation in 1769, and was later licensed to preach. At the death of his father, he took over the family affairs. Nearly 20 years later, his reputation earned him the presidency of Yale College in 1795.

EDWARDS, JONATHAN 1703-1758

Born in Connecticut, Edwards caused a turn in American preaching. It is said that since his day no one merely possessing an eloquent tongue and skilled mind could make such an impression from the pulpit. Edwards spent more time with the Lord and his books than in the social gatherings of his congregation. Though offensive to some, it was perhaps this devotion that brought such an anointing to the pulpit. His sermon, "Sinners in the Hands of An Angry God" is widely recognized and as effective today as when it was preached over two hundred years ago.

FINNEY, CHARLES 1792-1875

After practicing law for a season, Finney was deeply stirred in his spirit through reading the Bible. After his ordination in 1824, he began to evangelize, drawing attention from many places. His law background enabled him to make such a "case" for salvation that few if any of his hearers could resist. He stressed the deity of Jesus Christ, His atonement, justification by grace through faith, and the power of the Holy Ghost to transform man.

FLAVEL, JOHN 1627-1691

Flavel was born in Worcestershire, England. Having devoted himself to preaching the gospel, he became a pastor by age 23. He was ejected from his position in 1662 for nonconformity, yet, he did not forsake his flock. Moving far enough out of town to be out of the reach of legal disturbance, he commenced preaching again, and many of his flock would travel far to come and hear him. When James II dispensed with the laws which had once forbade his preaching, Flavel fervently resumed his self-sacrificing labors.

FLETCHER, JOHN 1729-1785
An eloquent English preacher, Fletcher ruffled the feathers of the "gentlemen," and many of the clergy, for he brought conviction of the barbarous practices of the one and disrupted the quiet of the lifeless routine of the other. Overall, he was loved by those he ministered to. He poured his heart into preaching and even opened a schoolroom for the poorer children of his area.

FULLER, THOMAS, D.D. 1608-1661
Born in Northamptonshire, England, Fuller became respected not only as a divine but as an historian. It is said that he possessed a remarkably tenacious memory, as well a large share of wit and quaint humor that he sometimes allowed to run riot in his writings.

GILL, JOHN, D.D. 1697-1771
An eminent biblical scholar, Gill was born in Kettering, England. Though he was a devoted scholar, he left school and began preaching by the age of nineteen. He pastored for 54 years before his death.

GOFORTH, JONATHAN, D.D. 1859-1936
Born in Canada, Goforth was a Presbyterian missionary to the people of China. In his book *By My Spirit*, he takes the reader through the trials and triumphs of true revival. Goforth was wonderfully used of God to spread revival fires among those to whom he ministered.

GORE, BISHOP CHARLES 1853-1932
Born in Wimbledon, Surrey, Gore is known as an Anglican bishop and author of many books, including *The Incarnation of the Son of God* and *The Creed of the Christian*.

GREY, LADY JANE 1536-1553
Lady Grey was merely 17 years old in 1553 when she was reluctantly placed on the throne of England after the death of Edward VI. It is said

that she would have made an excellent queen, though her reign lasted only nine days. Her cousin, Mary Tudor, rallied an army and marched on London. Grey was imprisoned for treason and beheaded.

GURNALL, WILLIAM 1617-1679
An English divine, Gurnall was known as a "man of great excellence of character." He wrote *The Christian in Complete Armor*, a work still highly respected today.

GUTHRIE, WILLIAM 1620-1655
Guthrie is respected as an eminent clergyman of the Presbyterian Church of Scotland. His principal work is *The Christian's Great Interest*, which has been translated into many languages.

HALL, JOSEPH, D.D. 1574-1656
Joseph Hall is most commonly remembered as the Bishop of Norwich. He was a "man of very devotional habits." His writings include *A Century of Meditations; Heaven Upon Earth;* and *Paraphrase of Hard Times*, an autobiographical account of his persecution under Parliament.

HALL, NEWMAN 1816-1834
An English dissenting minister, pulpit orator and author. One of the most popular preachers of his time, Hall's devotional writings were widely read.

HALL, ROBERT 1764-1831
Hall began showing great talent for the ministry under the instruction of his father, a distinguished Baptist pastor. It is said that one of his favorite books was Edwards's *On the Will*, which he had studied many times before he was nine years old. He excelled in every way, becoming an esteemed Baptist minister. During the 20 years before his death, he also made his mark as an established writer.

HENRY, MATTHEW 1662-1714
It is recorded that while much of Matthew Henry's celebrated commentary came from his own lectures, many of the quaint sayings and concise remarks within its pages came from notes Henry made in childhood during family worship times led by his father. After being stricken with paralysis in May of 1714, he said to a friend, "You have

been used to take notice of the sayings of dying men; this is mine: That a life spent in the service of God, and communion with Him, is the most pleasant life that anyone can live in this world." Henry's *Exposition of the Old and New Testament* remains a timeless classic today.

HILL, ROWLAND 1744-1833
Hill began his ministry as an itinerant preacher. It is said that "his vigor of thought, earnestness, eccentricity and wit drew thousands to listen to him." The death of his father in 1780 left him quite wealthy. With the help of his numerous friends, he built Surrey Chapel, London, in 1782. There he preached to vast congregations for many years.

HOPKINS, EZEKIEL, D.D. 1633-1690
Born in Sanford, Devonshire, Bishop Hopkins is remembered as an English prelate and author. Among his works are *Exposition of the Lord's Prayer* published in 1691 and *The Doctrine of the Two Covenants*, published in 1712.

HOWE, JOHN 1630-1705
Howe became known as one of the greatest of English theologians, often referred to as the "Platonic Puritan." His writings are still highly esteemed and a challenge to the reader.

JAY, WILLIAM 1769-1853
The son of a poor stonecutter, Jay obtained his education through the influence and charity of friends. When not quite 16 years of age, he began preaching. Before he turned 21, he is said to have delivered no less than 1,000 sermons. A very distinguished English Independent minister, he was "beloved and trusted by religious professors of all sects."

JOWETT, JOHN HENRY 1864-1923
One of the greatest preachers in the English speaking world, Jowett was well known for his illustrations, images and metaphors. He pastored both in England and the United States. Jowett's sermons and devotional articles were published in large numbers and are still in circulation.

KEMPIS, THOMAS À 1380-1471

Born to the Hemerken family (Hemerken means "little hammer"), he is known as Kempis due to his native home of Kempen, a village of the diocese of Cologne. His book *The Imitation of Christ* has been translated and reprinted nearly as many times as the Bible and has influenced countless lives.

KNOX, JOHN 1505-1572

John Knox was born in East Lothian and known historically as the Reformer of Scotland. He was well educated and always endeavored to increase his knowledge, even seizing his first opportunity to learn Hebrew around the age of fifty. He had become Protestant, and by 1542 his life was in jeopardy at every turn, though he was not afraid to die for his beliefs. It is said of him that he "had learned plainly and boldly to call wickedness by its own terms, a fig a fig, a spade a spade." He died peacefully in his sleep. The day he was laid in his grave it was said of him, "There lies he who never feared the face of man."

KRUMMACHER, FRIEDRICH WILHELM 1796-1868

Krummacher was hailed as one of Germany's most eloquent preachers of his day. Dissatisfied with the limits of spiritual teaching, he searched and read on his own for deeper insight into the things of God. It was an effort well rewarded, for his preaching touched the lives of many.

LATIMER, HUGH 1490-1555

Latimer is often referred to as the "John Knox of England," holding a place in history as the Reformer of England. His character has been described many ways: "An earnest, hopeful, happy man, fearless, open-hearted, hating nothing but baseness and fearing none but God. Not throwing away his life, yet not counting it dear when the great crisis came—calmly yielding it up as the crown of his long sacrifice and struggle." Latimer was martyred under the reign of "Bloody Mary" on October 16, 1555. As he and his companion Ridley were about to be burned at the stake, Latimer said to his friend, "Be of good comfort, master Ridley, and play the man: we shall this day light such a candle, by God's grace, in England, as I trust shall never be put out."

LEIGHTON, ROBERT 1611-1684

A Scottish prelate, Leighton was one of the most distinguished preachers and theologians of the seventeenth century. Though Leighton published nothing during his lifetime, many of his works have been published since. All of his writings received the highest commendations because of the great evangelical spirit that pervades them.

LUTHER, MARTIN 1483-1546

Luther's name marks the new era in the history of Europe. His first movements as a reformer began in October 1517, upon his presentation of 95 theses to be argued. Among them was the argument that "the command of Jesus to *repent* implies that the *whole life* is to be a repentance, not to be confounded with the confession and satisfaction made to a priest." He is described as so ingenious that if all the world had conspired to cover up his faults, his own hand would have uncovered them. This man, who became the father of the Lutheran Church, was also father to six children. He died in full peace and assurance of the truth of the doctrine he had taught.

MACLAREN, ALEXANDER 1826-1910

Born in Glasgow, Maclaren became known as a brilliant expository preacher. Every day, for more than 68 years, he made it his practice to read one chapter of the Bible in original Hebrew and one chapter in original Greek. One of his best known works is *Expositions of the Holy Scriptures*.

MASON, WILLIAM 1725-1797

Mason became known as an English poet who also ministered in various churches in England.

MCCHEYNE, ROBERT MURRAY 1813-1843

In his short life, Scottish pastor R. M. McCheyne was used of God to influence thousands toward holiness. His memoirs, first published in 1844, speak to everyone hungry for personal sanctification in revival Of the thousands of books in my library, I cherish McCheyne's writings most of all.

MEYER, F. B. 1847-1929

Showing his excellence as a preacher, it is recorded that Melbourne Hall was built in 1878 specifically for him. His evangelistic sermons became his strong suit, especially due to his direct appeals to forsake all things that stood in the way of complete acceptance of Jesus not only as Savior but also as Lord.

MILLER, J. R. 1840-1912
The Reverend J. R. Miller was a turn-of-the-century American preacher and the author of the books *Making the Most of Life*, *Building of Character*, *Things to Live For* and *Silent Times*, a book to help bring the Bible into daily life.

MOODY, D. L. 1837-1899
The story of D. L. Moody is one that deserves further study in order to truly appreciate this great man of God. Beginning with his evangelistic work with street children to his powerfully effective preaching as he traveled with hymn writer Ira Sankey, his life was fully devoted to the service of the Lord.

MÜLLER, GEORGE 1805-1898
Müller was a great man of faith who dedicated his life to helping orphan children. He was well known for his adamant belief that God would provide everything needed for his orphanage. He never asked man for a thing, and God miraculously met his every need. His book *Counsel to Christians* has encouraged many in their walk with the Lord.

MURRAY, ANDREW 1828-1917
Murray is one of the most widely read authors of Christian devotional literature in the nineteenth and twentieth centuries. His sermons had a profound effect on all who heard him preach. Among his most known works are *The Holiest of All*, a commentary on the book of Hebrews; *Have Mercy Upon Me*, meditations on Psalm 51; and *The Prayer Life*.

NEWTON, JOHN 1725-1807
From the time of his birth in London, John Newton's mother had set him apart for the ministry. After her death, however, when he was eight, he soon fell into a life of sin. At seventeen he went to sea with his father and his life took an even darker turn. But after his conversion he gave himself to careful study of the Bible and once again pursued a

life in ministry. It was from that converted life that we have the beloved hymn *Amazing Grace*—Newton's testimony in song.

OWEN, JOHN 1616-1683
Owen was a noted Puritan minister born near Oxford, England. Many of his works have been reprinted and remain among the classics of English Christian literature.

PARKER, JOSEPH 1830-1902
One of the greatest preachers of the nineteenth century, Parker preached his first sermon at eighteen years of age. He fervently pursued his calling and became the pastor of City Temple in London, where he preached for thirty-three years. His was the second largest congregation in that city, after that of Charles Spurgeon's Metropolitan Tabernacle. One of his best known works is *The People's Bible*, which came from notes taken as he preached through the entire Bible.

PIKE, J. G. 1784-1854
Celebrated minister and author of several books including, *Religion and Eternal Life or Irreligion and Perpetual Ruin*; *Persuasives to Early Piety*; and *A Guide for Young Disciples of the Holy Saviour, in Their Way to Immortality*.

PLUMER, WILLIAM 1802-1880
Born in Philadelphia, Plumer became an eminent American Presbyterian divine, pulpit orator and author. One of his books, *Short Sermons for the People*, was quoted in this devotional.

RAVENHILL, LEONARD 1907-1994
One of the greatest revivalists of this century, Leonard Ravenhill was best known for his uncompromising stand against sin and his unflinching zeal for revival. I was privileged to have Brother Ravenhill as my mentor for several years. His best-selling book, *Why Revival Tarries*, is a must-read for anyone hungry for a genuine move of God.

ROGERS, TIMOTHY 1660-1729
Born at Barnard Castle, Durham, England, Rogers was a celebrated minister of the gospel. His writings have been often quoted by C. H. Spurgeon in *The Treasury of David*.

RUTHERFORD, SAMUEL 1600-1661

Born in Roxburghshire, Rutherford was an eminent Scottish minister. Few men have preached Jesus Christ as he did. Some of his best preaching was delivered on the subject of the names of our Lord. Yet, Rutherford had a harsh side, heaping scorn upon men he believed to be false teachers.

SCOTT, THOMAS, D.D. 1747-1821

Beginning his ministerial life as a rationalist, Scott was soon converted, a tale which could be one of the most touching autobiographies ever written. His most noted work however, is a five-volume commentary called *The Holy Bible with Notes,* which is considered more devotional than technical.

SIBBES, RICHARD, D.D. 1577-1635

A learned English Puritan divine, he was born at Sudbury, Suffolk. His works were numerous, including *The Bruised Reed and Smoking Flax.* Reverend Richard Baxter stated that he, in great measure, owed his own conversion to the *Bruised Reed.*

SMITH, HANNAH WHITALL 1832-1911

American Quaker esteemed as an evangelist, reformer and author, Smith is also noted as having cofounded the Women's Christian Temperance Union. Her most famous work, *The Christian's Secret of a Happy Life,* is still in print today.

SOUTH, ROBERT, D.D. 1633-1716

Born in Hackney, Middlesex, South became a King's Scholar at Westminster at the age of fourteen. Dr. South was a man of uncommon abilities and attainments, of judgment, wit and learning.

SPURGEON, CHARLES HADDEN 1834-1892

Though Spurgeon was not a theologian in the usual sense of the word, he had a great ability to stress the teachings of the Bible. Fondly referred to as the "Prince of Preachers," he always tried to preach in such a way as would be understood by all, using a free, conversational style. His many and varied writings are still blessing thousands today, notably *The Treasury of David,* an exposition of the psalms, and *The Metropolitan Tabernacle Pulpit,* a series of sermons delivered at the church Spurgeon pastored for years.

SWINNOCK, GEORGE 1627-1673
Born in Maidstone, Kent, Swinnock ministered for many years to a large congregation in Maidstone. *The Works of George Swinnock*, a five-volume set of sermons and writings, were originally published in 1868 and again in 1992 by Banner of Truth.

TAYLOR, JEREMY, D.D. 1613-1667
A distinguished Anglican divine, Taylor has been esteemed as the "Homer of divines," the "Shakespeare of the Church," and the "Spenser of English theological literature."

TORREY, JOSEPH, D.D. 1798-1867
Born at Rowley, Massachusetts, Torrey graduated Dartmouth College at the age of 19. While working at the University of Vermont, he was chosen as the university's professor of intellectual and moral philosophy. He served there until his death.

VENN, HENRY 1724-1797
Born in Barnes, Surrey, Venn is noted as a pious clergyman of the Church of England after a long line of ancestry who had served in the same manner. He is most noted for his book *The Complete Duty of Man*.

WATSON, GEORGE, D.D. 1845-1923
Respected turn-of-the-century minister and author of many books, such as *Soul Food*; *White Robes*; and *Holiness Manual*.

WATTS, ISAAC, D.D. 1674-1748
Known as a celebrated divine, poet, and author of many hymns, Watts was born at Southampton, England. He wrote for all classes of readers and students of all ages, in the areas of science, literature, poetry and divinity. He pastored and wrote for the last 36 years of his life.

WELCH, JOHN 1576-1622
Another in the line of reformed Church of Scotland, Welch was a man devoted to prayer and the ministry. He married the daughter of John Knox, and together they raised three sons. Of all the duties of which he was excellent, the most excellent was prayer. He often woke during the hours of the night and wailed in prayer about the condition of his flock. He left quite a distinguished mark on the history of Scotland and upon Christianity in general.

WESLEY, JOHN 1703-1791

Known as the founder of Methodism, John Wesley was born at Epworth, Lincolnshire, England. Wesley was governed in all he thought, felt and did by that single purpose which he avowed at the beginning of his evangelical career when he affirmed his belief that God had called him "to declare to all that were willing to hear the glad tidings of salvation." This conviction shaped his life. It dwelt in his conscience; it absorbed his affections; it governed his will. Age did not quench his zeal. He pursued this end until his death at eighty-eight.

WESLEY, SUSANNAH 1669-1742

Susannah became the wife of Samuel Wesley in 1689 and bore nineteen children in twenty-one years. Nine of the children died at various stages of infancy. The ten children she raised to adulthood became the fruit of a woman who gave herself to their teaching and counsel. She was a model mother, and her sons, (the best known are John and Charles Wesley) owed a great deal of their success to her prudent counsel.

WHITEFIELD, GEORGE 1714-1770

Born in Gloucester, England, George's father, a tavern keeper, died while George was just a child. It was his mother's pious example and Christian training that greatly influenced him. His preaching in America and London blew the fires of revival across both nations. One commentary states that "Whitefield was not a learned man, like his contemporary Wesley; but he possessed an unusual share of good sense, general information, knowledge of the Holy Scriptures, and an accurate acquaintance with the human heart. Few ministers have been equally useful since the days of the Apostles."

WILBERFORCE, SAMUEL, D.D. 1805-1873

As an English prelate, most of his preaching was to the upper class and royalty of England. He was killed by a fall from his horse while riding near Dorking on July 19, 1873.

KNOCKIN' AT HEAVEN'S DOOR

STEPHEN HILL

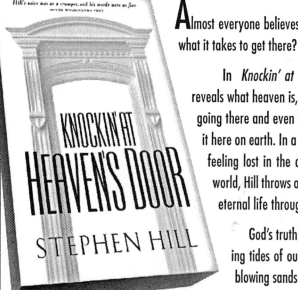

Almost everyone believes in heaven, but do we know what it takes to get there?

In *Knockin' at Heaven's Door*, Stephen Hill reveals what heaven is, how you can be sure you're going there and even how to experience a taste of it here on earth. In a day where we find ourselves feeling lost in the depths of a dark and lonely world, Hill throws out a lifeline – the promise of eternal life through Jesus Christ.

God's truth stands as a rock in the shifting tides of our time, a tall pillar amid the blowing sands of chaos and change. We do not need to change God's truth; rather, we need to let God's truth transform us. When Hill spoke at the Brownsville Assembly of God in Pensacola, Florida one Sunday several years ago, heaven opened up and God poured out an incredible blessing on the people who were there. Since then, millions of people have visited the church to receive a touch from God. From Steve Hill, they hear the simple, yet riveting message of truth...now it's your turn.